# SHAPING FOREIGN POLICY IN TIMES OF CRISIS

*Shaping Foreign Policy in Times of Crisis* grew out of a series of meetings that the authors convened with all ten of the living former U.S. State Department Legal Advisers (from the Carter Administration to that of George W. Bush). Based on their insider accounts of the role that international law actually played during the major crises on their watch, the book explores whether international law is real law or just a form of politics that policymakers are free to ignore whenever they perceive it to be in their interest to do so.

Written in a style that will appeal to the casual reader and serious scholar alike, this book includes a foreword by the Obama Administration's State Department Legal Adviser, Harold Koh; background on the theoretical underpinnings of the compliance debate; roundtable discussions with the U.S. State Department Legal Advisers and with Foreign Ministry Legal Advisers; an in-depth case study of the treatment of detainees in the war on terror; and a comprehensive glossary of the terms, names, places, and events that are addressed in the book.

Michael P. Scharf is the John Deaver Drinko–Baker & Hostetler Professor of Law and Director of the Frederick K. Cox International Law Center at Case Western Reserve University School of Law.

Dr. Paul R. Williams holds the Rebecca Grazier Professorship in Law and International Relations at American University, where he teaches in the School of International Service and the Washington College of Law.

Scharf and Williams both served in the Office of the Legal Adviser during the elder Bush and Clinton Administrations. In February 2005, Scharf, Williams, and the Public International Law and Policy Group, a nongovernmental organization they cofounded and direct, were nominated for the Nobel Peace Prize by six governments and the Chief Prosecutor of the Special Court for Sierra Leone for their work in helping with peace negotiations and war crimes prosecutions.

# Shaping Foreign Policy in Times of Crisis

## THE ROLE OF INTERNATIONAL LAW AND THE STATE DEPARTMENT LEGAL ADVISER

**Michael P. Scharf**

Case Western Reserve University School of Law

**Paul R. Williams**

American University Washington College of Law

CAMBRIDGE
UNIVERSITY PRESS

CAMBRIDGE UNIVERSITY PRESS

Cambridge, New York, Melbourne, Madrid, Cape Town, Singapore,
São Paulo, Delhi, Dubai, Tokyo

Cambridge University Press
32 Avenue of the Americas, New York, NY 10013-2473, USA

www.cambridge.org
Information on this title: www.cambridge.org/9780521167703

First published 2010

Printed in the United States of America

*A catalog record for this publication is available from the British Library.*

*Library of Congress Cataloging in Publication data*

Scharf, Michael P., 1963–
Shaping foreign policy in times of crisis : the role of international law and the state
department legal adviser / Michael P. Scharf, Paul R. Williams.
  p.  cm.
Includes bibliographical references and index.
ISBN 978-0-521-76680-7 (hardback)
1. International law – United States.   2. United States – Foreign relations – Law and
legislation.   I. Williams, Paul R.   II. Title
KF4581.S33   2010
342.73′0412 – dc22        2009036861

ISBN 978-0-521-76680-7 Hardback
ISBN 978-0-521-16770-3 Paperback

*Dedicated to the memory of Henry T. King, 1919–2009*

*Henry King was the youngest prosecutor at the Nuremberg trial; he subsequently served as General Counsel of the Agency for International Development during the Eisenhower Administration; worked as chief corporate international counsel for TRW Inc. and as counsel for Squire, Sanders & Dempsey LLP; headed the ABA's International Law Section; founded the Greater Cleveland International Lawyers Group; was appointed Honorary Consul of Canada to Cleveland and Northeast Ohio; and served for twenty-eight years as a Case Western Reserve University School of Law Professor and Director of Case's Canada–United States Law Institute.*

*He was an extraordinary colleague, mentor, and friend.*

# Contents

# Acknowledgments

Several people and entities deserve special recognition for the assistance they have furnished us during this project. Foremost among those are the ten former State Department Legal Advisers, who provided their candid accounts of the role of international law during the crises that occurred on their watch: Herbert Hansell, Roberts Owen, Davis Robinson, Abraham Sofaer, Edwin Williamson, Michael Matheson, Conrad Harper, David Andrews, William Taft IV, and John Bellinger III. Special thanks also to Harold Hongju Koh, the current occupant of that position, who provided such an insightful foreword to the book.

In addition, we would like to thank Professor Carol Fox for editing the transcripts of the sessions with the Legal Advisers; attorneys Lauren Baillie and Bridget Rutherford from the Public International Law & Policy Group for their research assistance; Jennifer Hines for preparing the index; and the following Case Western Reserve University School of Law and American University Washington College of Law students, who helped with the footnotes: Sarah Antonucci, Andrew Bramante, Brant Dichiera, Corey Fredericks, Kavitha Gridhar, Jennifer Hoover, Brian Klesh, Allison Kretz, Jared Livingston, Jennifer Mesko, Obiahjulu Okuh, Tom Renz, Mathew Shupe, and Nadeah Vali.

Moreover, we would like to express our gratitude to the following academic colleagues, who provided comments on an early draft of the book manuscript: Laura Dickinson of Arizona State Law School, Charles Garraway of Chatham House, Larry Helfer of Duke Law School,

Linda Malone of William and Mary Law School, Greg McNeal of Penn State Law School, Michael Newton of Vanderbilt Law School, Mark Osiel of the T.M.C. Asser Institute, Elies van Sliedregt of Free University in Amsterdam, and Ingrid Wuerth of Vanderbilt Law School.

We are also deeply appreciative of the financial and institutional support provided by the Carnegie Corporation of New York, the Public International Law and Policy Group, Case Western Reserve University School of Law, and American University, without which this project would not have been possible. In addition, we thank the American Society of International Law (ASIL) for hosting our U.S. and foreign Legal Adviser roundtables, and then ASIL President Anne Marie Slaughter for moderating the session with the U.S. Legal Advisers.

We are also indebted to John Berger, who had faith in this project from the beginning, and his team at Cambridge University Press, who improved our text in innumerable ways. Many thanks to freelance copy editor, Ellen Tirpak.

We also thank the editors of the Cardozo Law Review, noting that portions of this work were originally published in Michael P. Scharf, *International Law in Crisis: A Qualitative Empirical Contribution to the Compliance Debate*, 31 CARDOZO L. REV. 45 (2009).

Finally, and most importantly, we would like to thank our wives, Trina Scharf and Kathy Williams, and our families, who permit us to live, work, and write in ways that often complicate their lives.

# Foreword: America's Conscience on International Law

## Harold Hongju Koh*

What role does international law play in foreign policy crises? That is a question regularly discussed in the academy, but all too often without the reality check of experience in the arena.

In the United States of America, law and tradition have assigned the role of "conscience of the government" regarding compliance with international law to the little-known Office of the Legal Adviser of the Department of State.[1] Created by statute in 1931, and resting on a tradition of legal advice within the Department that dates back to 1848, the Office of the Legal Adviser is charged with advising the Secretary of State on all legal issues, domestic and international, and with advising all branches of the U.S. Government on how to formulate and implement the foreign policies of the United States in accordance with international law and the responsible development of international institutions.[2] Although the Legal Adviser is appointed by the President, by and with the advice and consent of the Senate, and heads an office of nearly two hundred government attorneys, until now, the history and function of that office have been far less well chronicled than those of smaller

* The Legal Adviser, United States Department of State (2009–); U.S. Assistant Secretary of State for Democracy, Human Rights, and Labor (1998–2001); Martin R. Flug Professor of International Law (on leave) and former Dean (2004–2009), Yale Law School. This foreword draws heavily on testimony delivered at my April 28, 2009, confirmation hearing to be Legal Adviser and a previously published tribute to former Legal Adviser Abram Chayes, *see* Harold Hongju Koh, *An Uncommon Lawyer*, 42 HARV. INT'L L.J. 7 (2001).

elite U.S. Government legal offices, such as the Office of the Solicitor General and the Office of Legal Counsel at the Department of Justice.[3]

This book fills that gap by using the lens of oral history. Supported by a grant from the Carnegie Corporation of New York, Professors Michael Scharf and Paul Williams solicited all living former State Department Legal Advisers to discuss the influence of international law during the foreign policy crises that transpired on their watch. This volume begins by reviewing the scholarly debate about the nature of international legal obligation, presents a brief history of the Office of the Legal Adviser, and provides first-person descriptions of the paths that led each of the former Legal Advisers to their posts. The heart of the book rests in first-person accounts by ten different Legal Advisers, covering the administrations of Presidents Jimmy Carter (Herbert Hansell and Roberts Owen), Ronald Reagan (Davis Robinson and Abraham Sofaer), George H. W. Bush (Edwin Williamson and Michael Matheson), Bill Clinton (Conrad Harper and David Andrews), and George W. Bush (William Taft IV and John Bellinger III). The closing chapters illuminate the competing and shared perceptions of the role of the office and its impact on national compliance with international law, through roundtable discussions among the former U.S. Legal Advisers, as well as among former foreign ministry Legal Advisers from the United Kingdom, Russia, China, India, and Ethiopia.

I read this illuminating book in draft, while preparing for my own confirmation hearing as Legal Adviser of the State Department in the Obama Administration. I was asked by Secretary of State–designate Hillary Rodham Clinton to take that post shortly before President Barack Obama's January 2009 inauguration, was nominated by the President in late March, and had my confirmation hearing in late April. The Legal Adviser's role had fascinated me throughout my legal career. My late father, Dr. Kwang Lim Koh, studied international law in South Korea and came to Harvard Law School in the 1950s to study the law of the sea under the tutelage of Professors Manley O. Hudson and Louis B. Sohn. After studying government and international relations in college and graduate school, I took a class at Harvard Law School taught by former Legal Adviser Abe Chayes, whose book about the Cuban Missile Crisis helped me see how and why legal arguments matter in the shaping of U.S. foreign policy.[4] I worked on transnational and international law cases as a law clerk to Judge Malcolm Richard Wilkey of the D.C. Circuit Court and Justice Harry A. Blackmun of the U.S. Supreme Court and partnered with lawyers from the Legal Adviser's office while serving both Republican and Democratic administrations as an Attorney-Adviser at the Office of Legal Counsel at the Department of Justice from 1983 to 1985, and later as Assistant Secretary of State for Democracy, Human Rights, and Labor from 1998 to 2001. As a young lawyer, I interviewed to work at the Office of the Legal Adviser. Since the early 1980s, I collaborated frequently with the talented attorneys from that office, encounters that confirmed my view that that office ranks with the finest legal offices in the U.S. Government and as the most outstanding international law firm in the world. When I came to teach at Yale Law School in 1985, I frequently used examples from the Legal Advisers' work to teach and write on national security and foreign relations law, international human rights law, the law of international organizations, and international business and trade law. I worked both with and against State Department lawyers while pursuing numerous human rights lawsuits, along with my students, on behalf of Yale's Lowenstein International Human Rights Clinic. Finally, while serving as a Yale Law School professor, and later as Dean from 2004 to 2009, I sent many students to "L" as part of my decanal effort to support the rule of law in an age of globalization.

These years of exposure have given me the strong sense that the Legal Adviser's key role is to promote the rule of law based on principle, not politics. As Abe Chayes once put it, whether inside or outside the government, there is "nothing wrong" with a lawyer "holding the United States to its own best standards and best principles."[5] The Legal Adviser must provide the President and the Secretary of State with the very best legal advice possible and urge both our country and others to uphold the rule of international law, to the extent consistent with our own law. Ideally, the Legal Adviser should act not just as a counselor but also as a conscience to the U.S. Government with respect to international law. As counselor, the Legal Adviser should always accurately advise his client as to what domestic and international law says.[6] But as the government's conscience on international law, wherever possible, the Legal Adviser should search for options that promote the sound development of international law and warn his clients not to follow an option that is awful, even if it may be lawful.[7]

The dawn of the Obama presidency represents a pivotal moment for the United States' relationship with international law, which may well require a revised role for the Legal Adviser. After the traumas of Abu Ghraib, the torture opinions (recounted in Chapter 16 of this book), Guantánamo, unsigning the International Criminal Court treaty, and withdrawing from the Kyoto climate talks, displaying renewed American respect for international law and institutions will be critical as the United States seeks to resume American leadership in a new global century. As President Obama recognized in his first joint address to Congress, "a new era of engagement has begun." In that era, "living our values doesn't make us weaker, it makes us safer and it makes us stronger."[8] At her confirmation hearing as Secretary of State, Hillary Clinton similarly argued that American foreign policy should "use what has been called 'smart power,' the full range of tools at our disposal," including the legal tool, to place "diplomacy [at] the vanguard of foreign policy."[9] To strengthen America's position of global leadership, she suggested, respect for law is an essential element of American "smart power," and intense creative diplomacy must be accompanied by equally intense lawyering.

The defining image of the Obama era will not be of a world divided by the Berlin Wall, but of a world interconnected by a World Wide Web. That web and the social networks that run through it geometrically multiply the links between domestic and international law and make the role of the Legal Adviser even more vital. What all of this suggests is that, in the twenty-first century, the Legal Adviser must function not simply as a counselor and a conscience but also as a public diplomat and educator, explaining both inside and outside of the government why obeying the law is both right and smart, for nations as well as individuals; why respecting constitutional checks and balances in foreign affairs is both constitutionally required and wise policy; and why making and keeping our international promises promotes our sovereignty and makes us safer. Believing those things does not undermine the notion that the U.S. Constitution is controlling law in the United States or that the Constitution ultimately directs whether and to what extent international law should guide courts and policymakers.

As I came to see during my confirmation process, many Americans continue to give too much weight to three enduring myths about international law, which this book does much to debunk. The first myth is that somehow "international law is not really law," so Americans have no reason to follow it. But respecting international law was one of the founding credos of our country. In the framing act of our nation's birth, the authors of the Declaration of Independence chose to pay "decent respect to the opinions of mankind." Yet Americans who would never dream of disobeying the law at home still argue that obeying international law should be done only when convenient and in America's interest. But in most cases, following international law *is* in America's interest. Like individuals who obey domestic law, nations who obey international law find that it is both the right and the smart thing to do. No law is a straitjacket, but as Americans have learned since 9/11, if we don't obey international law, we squander our moral authority and shrink our capacity to lead. When we break international law, we weaken its power to protect our own citizens – how can the Geneva Conventions protect our own soldiers abroad, if we violate them at home? And how can we protest other countries' torturing of our citizens if our own public officials – past and present – condone or publicly defend the use of torture?

A second myth: some believe that our foreign policy should be left to the president alone, operating in secret. But as we learned during Vietnam, Watergate, and Iran-Contra, checks and balances don't stop at the water's edge. Our constitutional system was designed – and indeed works better – when the President and his subordinates must answer to people who don't work for them, particularly those in Congress and in the courts.

A third and final myth is that the United States cannot take part in the international system without surrendering our sovereignty. But today, protecting sovereignty means engaging with the world, not retreating into our shell.[10] Laws are sometimes called the "wise restraints that make us free." Far from constricting us, international law *frees* us to pursue our global engagements. We are free to travel abroad; to take money out of foreign ATMs; and to speak with, buy from, sell to, and borrow from foreigners precisely because international law gives us the orderly frameworks to do so. As each day's headlines show, globalization is inevitable, is accelerating, and must be managed. Each emerging challenge – whether financial meltdown, energy crisis, climate change, swine flu, nuclear proliferation, piracy, or even terrorism – is not local but global. We live in an interdependent world, and in tackling our challenges, international law is not the problem, it's more often a solution. And if we don't work on building a framework of international law, too often we will have no good solution.

The most powerful lesson that emerges from reading this book is that, even during crisis situations, international lawyers should not be just potted plants. Properly deployed, they can identify otherwise invisible legal constraints and fathom available legal channels through which policy decisions can flow. By so doing, they help shape policy decisions, which in turn shape legal instruments, which in time become internalized into bureaucratic decision-making processes. And through this process, the word can become flesh. Law influences policy, which in turn makes law; this is a thumbnail description of "transnational legal process," which I have argued is the key to understanding why nations obey international law.[11]

In the end, this book, full of lessons learned in the crucible, casts important light on what it means to be a lawyer committed to the rule of law in international affairs. For if international relations are to be more than just power politics, international lawyers must be moral actors who see their job as more than simply doing as they are told. True international lawyers fuse their training and skill with moral courage and guide the evolution of legal process with the application of fundamental constitutional and international norms. "If we seek to strengthen the role of law in the relations among states," Abe Chayes wrote shortly after he left the Legal Adviser's Office, "it follows that we should devote our energies to disclosing and articulating the common values and interests among them, of which law is an expression."[12]

In the end, this book teaches that foreign policy decisions most fully conform with international law when the international lawyers are at the table while important decisions are being made.[13] By having the courage to argue with their clients, to invoke illegality, to bring lawsuits and to negotiate treaties, international lawyers guide difficult policy choices into lawful channels and stand up for the rule of law.[14] Or, as former Legal Adviser Herman Phleger reportedly said, the job of the Legal Adviser is, quite simply, to "speak law to power."

# Introduction

"L" – that is the enigmatic name by which the State Department Legal Adviser is known throughout the U.S. Government. It is also the name of his office, which includes more than 170 Attorney-Advisers stationed in Washington, DC, and abroad. While L may be little known outside government circles, the importance of the office is considerable: virtually no foreign policy decision can be made without first receiving clearance from L, and no delegation can be sent to an international negotiation or international organization without a representative of L. Just as the Solicitor General is the government's point man for constitutional questions, the Legal Adviser is the government's principal expert in international legal affairs. And just as the Solicitor General argues cases for the government before the U.S. Supreme Court, L argues on behalf of the United States at the International Court of Justice and other international tribunals.

Through the years, numerous scholars and practitioners have grappled with the question of the role of international law in shaping foreign policy. Unfortunately, what John Chipman Gray wrote in 1927 remains true today: "On no subject of human interest, except theology, has there been so much loose writing and nebulous speculation as on International Law."[1] In an age in which a growing number of academicians and even high-level government officials have opined that international law "is just politics," an understanding of the role that L and international law have played in shaping contemporary American foreign policy is more important now than ever before.

The inability of scholars and practitioners to precisely articulate the role of international law stems from four factors. First, many authors approach the question as an argument, asserting from the early pages of their work that international law matters, does not matter, should matter, or should not matter. Second, many of the best international legal scholars are positivists and thus are simply concerned not with the "role" of law but rather with the content of international law. Third, few members of the legal profession actually practice public international law. For instance, although the U.S. State Department employs more than 11,500 foreign service officers and specialists, they employ only 170 lawyers. In many small states, there is a single Foreign Ministry Legal Adviser who may hold the position for decades. The lawyers who practice regularly before the International Court of Justice number, at most, a few dozen. Fourth, the application of international law to the formulation of foreign policy nearly always occurs within the closed – and classified – confines of foreign ministries and other government agencies. This so-called black box is difficult for legal scholars and social scientists to penetrate to the degree necessary for sound analysis.[2]

In order to contribute to the development of an understanding of the role played by international law in shaping foreign policy, we determined that, given our background as former Attorney-Advisers in the U.S. Department of State, our best value added would be to penetrate the black box by bringing together former Legal Advisers and querying them about their experiences with the relationship between international law and the formulation of foreign policy.[3] Although this is a modest contribution, it is unique in that never before have all the living U.S. Department of State Legal Advisers been brought together in a structured conversation about the role of international law in shaping foreign policy. Admittedly, the approach is United States–focused because that is the black box to which we have access. We have sought to set the platform for a wider discussion by those with access to other foreign ministries by including a colloquy among former British, Russian, Chinese, Indian, and Ethiopian Legal Advisers, which we arranged in cooperation with the American Society of International Law (ASIL).

To contribute to the illumination of the role played by international law in shaping foreign policy, we undertook six major activities. These six activities sought to explore the contours of the relationship between international law and foreign policy, as well as the unique and challenging role of the Legal Adviser in maintaining the balance between the proper application of international law and protection of his government's national interest.

First, we met with a small number of former Department of State and Foreign Ministry Legal Advisers to identify the themes to be addressed throughout the structured conversation. Together with these Legal Advisers, we developed five questions to guide the conversation:

> Whether the Legal Advisers perceived international law to be binding law, such that it should be able to constrain the options available to the U.S. Government when dealing with a crisis central to its national security?

> Whether the international legal rules relevant to a particular situation or crisis were clear enough to significantly shape the policy options available to the U.S. government?

> Whether the Legal Adviser believed he had a duty to oppose policies or proposed actions that conflicted with international law, in those situations in which such conflict was objectively manifest?

> Whether the position taken by the Legal Adviser was seen as influential in cases in which he advised against a course of action on the grounds that it violated international law?

> And, whether the Legal Advisers perceived international law to hinder or promote their government's interests in times of crisis?

It was also agreed that it would be useful to use the unique opportunity created by this project to elicit answers to questions such as how the Legal Advisers acceded to their positions, how international law played a role in resolving the foreign policy crises that occurred during their tenure, and how the legal interpretations of these policy crises and issues have evolved since their time in office.

Second, we convened a closed-door historic meeting of all the living former State Department Legal Advisers at the Carnegie Endowment for International Peace in Washington, DC. The conversation centered on the five primary questions. Fortunately, the group has enjoyed exceptionally good health and longevity, and we were able to assemble contributions from ten former Legal Advisers covering the administrations of Jimmy Carter (Herbert Hansell and Roberts Owen), Ronald Reagan (Davis Robinson and Abraham Sofaer), George H. W. Bush (Edwin Williamson and Michael Matheson), Bill Clinton (Conrad Harper and David Andrews), and George W. Bush (William Taft IV and John Bellinger III).

Over the course of the gathering and subsequent exchanges, each Legal Adviser was asked to recount the role that his office and international law played in responding to the three most important international crises occurring during his tenure. Each presentation was followed by a series of questions and comments posed by the other Legal Advisers, as well as ourselves (who have served as Attorney-Advisers in L).

Third, we arranged with the ASIL to convene the Legal Advisers for an open roundtable discussion at the ASIL annual meeting. The topics for this roundtable were identified as the impact of each Legal Adviser's previous legal and political background on how he approaches the role of international law; who the Legal Advisers see as their primary client (the President, the Secretary of State, the American people, international law writ large, or their own conscience?); instances in which international law constrained U.S. policy directives, and areas in which it failed to do so; the role of other agencies with a legal mandate in the formulation of foreign policy; and a detailed examination of the case of humanitarian intervention.

Fourth, we again arranged with the ASIL to convene a panel of former Foreign Ministry Legal Advisers from the United Kingdom

(Frank Berman), Russia (Leonid Skotnikov), China (Xue Hanqin), India (P. S. Rao), and Ethiopia (Seifeselassie Lemma). The panel was structured around the same five questions presented to the former U.S. Legal Advisers.

Fifth, we examined the efforts of the U.S. Government to develop a response to the terrorist attacks of 9/11 and to conduct the war on terror within the parameters of international law. In particular, the legal to-and-fro between the Department of State, Department of Justice, and the White House over the legality of certain coercive measures applied to detainees and the operation of the Guantánamo Bay detention center provides a rich text for further illuminating the role of international law and U.S. Legal Advisers in shaping the U.S. Government's approach. The release of the so-called Torture Memos, the publication of memoires written by their authors, and the findings of a bipartisan investigation have provided a rare glimpse into the black box, which so often obfuscates the understanding of the role of international law, and we have tried to synthesize the information into an accessible and brief case study.

Sixth, to ensure this work is accessible to a wide range of audiences, we prepared a succinct introductory review of the scholarly debate regarding compliance with international law. Although the question of the role of international law in shaping foreign policy is much broader than the question of compliance, there is no doubt that compliance is a key component, and thus we thought it necessary to include this brief review of both the historical and contemporary compliance debate. To promote accessibility, we have also included a comprehensive glossary, which provides historic background to the events, treaties, institutions, cases, concepts, and terms mentioned in the book.

Throughout this book, we have chosen to keep the material as close as possible to the format of the original narratives for three reasons: First, we wanted the Legal Advisers to speak directly to the reader, without the filter of editors whose own preconceptions or agendas might unconsciously alter the meaning. Second, we wanted the Legal Adviser's views to be presented in context, so that the reader might fully grasp the nuances of their positions. Third, we wanted this book to be accessible to as wide a readership as possible, rather than being of interest and use only to scholars versed in the sometimes arcane language of the law or international relations theory.

Although the narratives contained within this book provide a unique perspective into the question of how international law, as interpreted and applied by the Legal Adviser, shapes the development of foreign policy in times of crises, certain limits must be recognized regarding the value of our approach. For example, because the accounts of the Legal Advisers are not contemporaneous with the events that they describe, there is the potential for memory lapses and revisionism. In addition, due to reasonable time constraints, the narrative of each Legal Adviser is limited to highlights, providing a somewhat perfunctory account of the internal interplay of normative and institutional factors. Moreover, although L plays a uniquely important role with respect to the U.S. Government's interpretation and application of international law, there are other legal officers within the bureaucracy (such as at the White House, the National Security Council, the Department of Defense, the Department of Justice, and the Commerce Department) whose influence relative to L's rises and falls depending on the type of international issue or political factors. Thus, the focus on L tells only part of the story within a disaggregated government. As discussed in Chapter 15, this is often not, in fact, the case with the formulation of foreign policy in other states.

The project was designed and implemented under the auspices of the nonprofit Public International Law and Policy Group (a global *pro bono* law firm) and financially supported by the Carnegie Corporation of New York.

# SHAPING FOREIGN POLICY IN TIMES OF CRISIS

# 1   The Compliance Debate

I**N THE FOLLOWING CHAPTERS, FORMER U.S. STATE DEPART-**
ment Legal Advisers discuss a number of crises during which
they were called on to provide legal assistance as the government sought to craft an appropriate and effective response. The question
of the degree to which States believe they are obligated to follow international law is a key, but not exclusive, element of the role international
law will play in shaping foreign policy. As such, the so-called compliance
debate factors significantly into a Legal Adviser's approach and is heavily
reflected in the structured conversations with the Legal Advisers in the
subsequent chapters. Although each of the Legal Advisers, regardless of
their nationality or political party, subscribes to the view that law does
matter and there is an obligation by States to comply with international
legal obligations, their views are quite varied when it comes to which
norms and principles constitute binding law, the interpretation of those
binding rules, and the Legal Advisers' obligations when they believe that
their government is violating international law. Most importantly, and
possibly most interesting, is that the Legal Advisers hold a diverse array
of perspectives and have differing opinions as to their role in ensuring
proper adherence to international law and their individual approaches
to fulfilling that role.

To ensure that the reader is able to follow and appreciate the nuanced
approaches of the different Legal Advisers, this chapter briefly reviews
the scholarly debate regarding State compliance with international law.

Since the decline of the Roman Empire and the attendant weakening of the Roman Legion at the end of the fourth century AD, no sort of constabulary has existed to implement rules of international law. Subsequently, international rules have been subject to sporadic enforcement through protest and condemnation, reciprocal suspension of rights and benefits, unilateral or multilateral economic and political sanctions, and sometimes through individual or collective use of armed force.

Given the lack of a pervasive mechanism to ensure compliance, scholars and policymakers have pondered whether international law is really binding law. The question has been debated since ancient times and remains one of the most contested questions in international relations. As described below, major historic developments, such as the Peace of Westphalia, the conclusion of World War II, the onset of the Cold War, the proliferation of international institutions in the 1970s and 1980s, the collapse of the Soviet Union in 1989, and the terrorist attacks of September 11, 2001, have each rekindled and reshaped this debate.

This chapter begins by examining the development of the major schools of compliance theory in the context of their historic settings and with reference to the relevant interpretive communities. Although scholars writing on this subject often perceive or present themselves as pure scientists examining the question solely in the abstract, the field is more akin to applied science and the conscious or subconscious agendas of those writing in it are comprehensible only in light of the background events and developments at the time of their publications and an understanding of the audience they are seeking to influence. With this in mind, the second part of this chapter focuses on the contemporary debate, while examining the underlying motivations of the major participants and their perceptions of the community that they are trying to influence with their arguments.

## Compliance Theory in Historical Context

The modern age of international law is said to have been inaugurated with the 1648 Peace of Westphalia, which ended the Thirty Years

War by acknowledging the sovereign authority of various European Princes.[1] During the next three hundred years, up until World War II, there were four major schools of thought regarding the obligation to comply with international law.[2] The first was "an Austinian positivistic realist strand," which held that nations never obey international law because it is not really law.[3] The second was a "Hobbesian utilitarian, rationalistic strand," which held that nations sometimes follow international law, but only when it serves their self-interest to do so.[4] The third was a "Kantian liberal strand," which held that nations generally obey international law out of a sense of moral and ethical obligation derived from considerations of natural law and justice.[5] The fourth was a Bentham "processed-based strand," which held that nations are induced to obey from the encouragement and prodding of other nations through a discursive legal process.[6] The modern debate has its roots in these four theoretical approaches.

In the aftermath of World War II, the victorious Allies sought to establish a "new world order," replacing the "loose customary web of state-centric rules" with a rules-based system, built on international conventions and international institutions, such as the United Nations Charter, which created the Security Council, the General Assembly, and the International Court of Justice; the Bretton Woods Agreement, which established the World Bank and International Monetary Fund; and the General Agreement on Tariffs and Trade, which ultimately led to the creation of the World Trade Organization (WTO).[7] The new system reflected a view that international rules would promote Western interests, serve as a bulwark against the Soviet Union, and emphasize values to be marshaled against fascist threats.[8]

Yet, the effectiveness of the new system was immediately undercut by the intense bipolarity of the Cold War. In the 1940s, political science departments at U.S. universities received from the German refugee scholars (such as Hans Morgenthau who is credited with founding the field of international relations in the United States), "an image of international law as Weimar law writ large: formalistic, moralistic, and unable to influence the realities of international life."[9] With fear of communist expansion pervading the debate, the positivistic, realist strand came to dominate Western scholarly discourse on the nature of international obligation. Thus, one of America's leading postwar international relations theorists, George F. Kennan, attacked the Kantian approach as anathema to American foreign policy interests, saying, "the belief that it should be possible to suppress the chaotic and dangerous aspirations of governments in the international field by the acceptance of some system of legal rules and restraints" is an approach that "runs like a red skein through our foreign policy of the last fifty years."[10]

Even during the height of the Cold War, however, international law had its defenders, and within the community of American legal scholars, a new school of thought arose with roots in the Bentham strand, based on notions of legal process. Thus, the writings of Harvard Law professors Abram Chayes, Thomas Ehrlich, and Andreas Lowenfeld, and Yale Law professors Myres McDougal and Harold Lasswell, hypothesized that compliance with international law could be explained by reference to the process by which these actors interact in a variety of public and private fora.[11] As Abram Chayes, who had himself once served as State Department Legal Adviser, put it, international law may not be determinative in international affairs, but it is relevant and influences foreign policy "first, as a constraint on action; second, as the basis of justification or legitimization for action; and third, as providing organizational structures, procedures, and forums" within which political decisions may be reached.[12] The process approach was later refined by Harvard Law professors Henry Steiner and Detlev Vagts and Yale Law professor Harold Koh, who was appointed State Department Legal Adviser in the Obama Administration in 2009, to include, in addition to States and international organizations, multinational enterprises, nongovernmental organizations (NGOs), and private individuals, which all interact in a variety of domestic and international fora to make, interpret, internalize, and enforce rules of international law.[13]

During the 1970s and 1980s, the legal landscape underwent another major transformation, with the proliferation, growth, and strengthening of countless international regimes and institutions. Despite the bipolarity of the Cold War, international cooperation had persisted and was facilitated by treaties and organizations providing channels for dispute settlement, requiring States to furnish information regarding compliance, and authorizing retaliatory actions in cases of noncompliance. During this period, international relations scholars developed "regime theory," the study of principles, norms, rules, and decision-making procedures that govern such areas as international peacekeeping and debt management.[14] At heart, the regime theorists were rationalists, viewing compliance with international law as a function of the benefits such compliance provides.

This same period saw a revival of the Kantian philosophical tradition. New York University (NYU) Law professor Thomas Frank sought to answer the question "Why do powerful nations obey powerless rules?" in his path-breaking THE POWER OF LEGITIMACY AMONG NATIONS.[15] Frank's answer: "Because they perceive the rule and its institutional penumbra to have a high degree of legitimacy." According to Frank, it is the legitimacy of the process that "exerts a pull to compliance."

The end of the Cold War and the collapse of the Soviet Union in 1989 had a significant affect on compliance scholarship. With the dismantling of the Berlin Wall, the end of Apartheid in South Africa, the United Nation's defeat of Saddam Hussein in Operation Desert Storm, the 1990s were a period of unparalleled optimism about the prospects of international law and international institutions. At the same time, conflict in failed States, such as Somalia and Haiti, the violent break-up of the former Yugoslavia, and the tribal carnage in Rwanda presented new challenges that severely tested the efficacy of international rules and institutions. Meanwhile, the status of the United States as the "sole remaining superpower" encouraged triumphalism, exceptionalism, and an upsurge of U.S. provincialism and isolationism, as well as a preference to act unilaterally rather than multilaterally.[16] During this decade, scholarly writing about compliance with international law featured four prevailing views.

The first was an "instrumentalist" strand, which, like its predecessors, applied rational choice theory to argue that States only comply with international law when it serves their self-interest to do so. What differentiated modern rationalists such as Robert Keohane,[17] Duncan Snidal,[18] Kenneth Abbott,[19] and John Setear[20] from their realist forerunners was the sophistication of their version of the prisoner's dilemma game, introducing international institutions and transnational actors, disaggregating the State into its component parts, and incorporating notions of long-term interests as well as short-term interests.

The second was a "liberal internationalist" strand, led by the former Dean of Princeton's Woodrow Wilson School, Anne-Marie Slaughter, who posited that compliance depends on whether or not the State can be characterized as "liberal" in identity (e.g., marked by a democratic representative government, guarantees of civil and political rights, and an independent judicial system).[21] Slaughter and other liberal theorists argued that liberal democracies are more likely to comply with international law in their relations with one another, while relations between liberal and "illiberal" States will more likely be conducted without serious deference to international law. Professor Slaughter was appointed Director of Policy Planning at the State Department in 2009.

The third, an outgrowth of Kantian theory, was a "constructivist" strand, which argued that the norms of international law, the values of the international community, and the structure of international society have the power to reshape national interests.[22] According to the constructivists, States obey international rules because a repeated habit of obedience transforms their interests so that they come to value rule compliance. The colloquy with the Legal Advisers that appears in the following chapters provides evidence of a constructivist effect, at least with respect to the State Department Office of the Legal Adviser, which represents an important player within a disaggregated government. As a bureaucratic entity with a long institutional memory that is dominated by civil service lawyers, some of whom worked in the office for decades, "L" and other Foreign Ministry legal offices have internalized international law and made its compliance part of their bureaucratic identity.

The fourth post–Cold War approach was a refurbishment of the Harvard/Yale "institutionalist approach," as embodied in works by Abram and Antonia Chayes and Harold Koh. In THE NEW SOVEREIGNTY, the Chayeses dismiss the importance of coercive enforcement, pointing out that "sanctioning authority is rarely granted by treaty, rarely used when granted, and likely to be ineffective when used."[23] Instead, they offer a "management model" in which compliance is induced through interactive processes of justification, discourse, and persuasion. According to the Chayeses, the impetus for compliance is not so much a nation's fear of sanction as it is fear of diminution of status through loss of reputation. To improve compliance, the Chayeses propose a range of "instruments of active management," such as transparency, reporting and data collection, verification and monitoring, dispute settlement, capacity building, and strategic review and assessment. Harold Koh seeks to add an additional level of sophistication to process theory by explaining how and why States internalize the constraining norms through judicial incorporation, legislative embodiment, and executive acceptance.[24] According to Koh, when a State fails to comply with international law, frictions are created that can negatively affect the conduct of a State's foreign relations and frustrate its foreign policy goals. To avoid such frictions in its continuing interactions, the State will shift over time from a policy of violation to one of grudging compliance to eventual habitual internalized obedience.[25]

## The Contemporary Debate

The terrorist attacks of September 11, 2001 and the invasion of Iraq inaugurated the current period of the compliance debate. In the aftermath of 9/11, the United States launched a "preventive war" against Iraq that was widely viewed outside the United States as unjustifiable under international law and then implemented policies regarding the detention and treatment of suspected terrorists that were criticized as inconsistent with the requirements of international law. Seeking to minimize the impact of international law on the Bush Administration's foreign policy agenda, then Ambassador to the United Nations, John Bolton, said: "It is a big mistake for us to grant any validity to international law even when it may seem in our short-term interest to do so – because over the long term, the goal of those who think that international law really means anything are those who want to constrict the United States."[26]

The Bush Administration coined the term "law-fare," and the official National Defense Strategy argued that "our strength as a nation state will continue to be challenged by those who employ a strategy of the weak using international fora, judicial processes, and terrorism."[27] The Administration also persuaded Congress to enact legislation that prohibited U.S. courts from considering international law or jurisprudence in determining the validity of detentions of suspected terrorists at Guantanamo Bay.[28]

It was in this context that Harvard Law Professor Jack Goldsmith, who had served as Assistant Attorney General and head of the Department of Justice's Office of Legal Counsel from October 2003 to June 2004, along with Chicago University Law Professor Eric Posner, published THE LIMITS OF INTERNATIONAL LAW, a potentially revolutionary work[29] that seeks to prove that international law is really just "politics" and that it is no more unlawful to contravene a treaty or a rule of customary international law than it would be to disregard a nonbinding letter of intent.[30] In his subsequent 2007 memoir, THE TERROR PRESIDENCY, Goldsmith identifies himself and Posner as "part of a group of conservative intellectuals – dubbed 'new sovereigntists' in *Foreign Affairs* magazine – who were skeptical about the creeping influence of international law on American law."[31]

THE LIMITS OF INTERNATIONAL LAW, which is an expanded and more developed version of Posner's 2003 article, *Do States Have a Moral Obligation to Obey International Law?*[32] utilizes economics-based rational choice theory and modeling techniques derived from game theory, to advance the thesis that neither customary international law nor treaty-based international law have any "exogenous influence on State behavior."[33] In other words, according to Goldsmith and Posner, when States comply with international law it is not because of its moral pull or a preference for abiding with law, but rather solely due to self-interest.[34]

Using a variety of illustrative historical case studies involving international Agreements (e.g., human rights treaties and trade treaties) as well as customary international law (e.g., ambassadorial immunity and free passage of neutral ships), Goldsmith and Posner propound four models that seek to explain away the behavior that legal scholars have termed "compliance" with international law. The first model, "coincidence," proposes that States may act in accordance with international law simply by acting in their own self-interest, with no regard to international rules or the interests of other States. The second model, "coordination," describes instances in which two or more States create and abide by a rule not out of a sense of obligation, but simply because it is convenient. The third model, "cooperation," applies to situations in which States reciprocally refrain from activities that would otherwise be in their short-term self-interest in order to reap larger long-term benefits. The fourth model, "coercion," results when a State with greater power forces a weaker State to engage in acts that benefit the more powerful State.[35]

Based on their rational choice analysis, Goldsmith and Posner conclude that States have no preference for compliance with international law; they are unaffected by the "legitimacy" of a rule of law; past consent to a rule does not generate compliance; and decision makers do not internalize a norm of compliance with international law. States therefore employ international law when it is convenient, are free to ignore it when it is not, and have every right to place their sovereign interests first – indeed democratic States have an obligation to do so when international law threatens to undermine federalism, separation of powers, and domestic sovereignty.[36]

In THE TERROR PRESIDENCY, Goldsmith candidly reveals the underlying normative purpose behind THE LIMITS OF INTERNATIONAL LAW. Goldsmith writes: "Many people think the Bush administration has been indifferent to wartime legal constraints. But the opposite is true: the administration has been strangled by law, and since September 11, 2001, this war has been lawyered to death. The administration has paid attention to law not necessarily because it wanted to, but rather because it [believed that it] had no choice."[37]

While Special Counsel to Secretary of Defense Donald Rumsfeld, and later as Assistant Attorney General in charge of the Office of Legal Counsel, Goldsmith saw it as his mission to convince those inside the government that international rules that constrain U.S. power and thus compromise national security are not really binding. Particularly telling in this regard was a 2003 interagency memorandum prepared by Goldsmith, titled "The Judicialization of International Politics," which warns: "In the past quarter century, various nations, NGOs, academics, international organizations, and others in the 'international community' have been busily weaving a web of international laws and judicial institutions that today threatens U.S. Government interests." The memorandum continues: "The U.S. Government has seriously underestimated this threat, and has mistakenly assumed that confronting the threat will worsen it. Unless we tackle the problem head-on, it will continue to grow. The issue is especially urgent because of the unusual challenges we face in the war on terrorism."[38] Subsequently, Goldsmith advised White House Chief Counsel Alberto Gonzales that "[t]he President can also ignore the law, and act extralegally," citing "honorable precedents, going back to the founding of the nation, of defying legal restrictions in time of crisis."[39]

THE LIMITS OF INTERNATIONAL LAW can therefore be understood as Goldsmith's effort to bring this argument to a wider audience, and as such, its core assertions have been criticized as allowing Goldsmith and Posner's policy objectives to taint their methodological approach.[40]

Although many realists and rationalists embrace Goldsmith and Posner's approach and conclusions,[41] their book was met with criticism by institutionalists and constructivists, who sought to disprove their thesis in several ways. Professor Peter Spiro of Temple University, a former Attorney-Adviser in L, argues that many of Goldsmith and Posner's reasons for dismissing international law as something less than real law would apply to domestic law as well. According to Professor Spiro, their assertion that "domestic law is enforced in well-ordered societies," whereas "international law is not reliably enforced,"[42] is inconsistent with empirical data on the enforcement of domestic law, including 2005 statistics indicating that a suspect was brought to trial in only 65 percent of homicide cases in the United States.[43]

Professor Spiro thus argues that although international law has traditionally employed horizontal rather than vertical mechanisms of enforcement (such as protests, reciprocal suspension of compliance, and breaking of diplomatic relations) and such compliance has rarely been bolstered by the use of force, this "does not necessarily detract from its salience as a regulator of behavior."[44] It just means international law is more like domestic contract law than domestic tort or criminal law. And while some States violate the Torture Convention's prohibitions on inhumane treatment, the Geneva Convention's prohibition on war crimes, and the UN Charter's prohibition on the use of force, this does not mean that these international rules have no consequence. As with the 65 mph speed limit, international law may not exert a moral pull nor enjoy perfect compliance, but it does deter and constrain unlawful behavior at the margins. According to Spiro, while nearly all international law scholars will acknowledge that if State interests are powerful enough, they may trump contrary international law norms, the same is true with respect to contracts in domestic law. That a business or individual may chose to break a legally binding contract (and suffer the consequences thereof) does not mean that contract law does not exert a compliance pull.

Professor Kenneth Anderson of American University differs with the Goldsmith/Posner paradigm by objecting to their underlying assumption that the only possible basis of legal obligation is morality. Anderson argues that a sense of legal obligation can be based on instrumentalist concerns about reputation as a law-abiding State, long-term self-interest in the maintenance of order, or long-term self-interest in a functioning legal system. Anderson asserts that in seeking to preempt and circumvent this objection, Goldsmith and Posner never explain what they believe constitutes the self-interests of States, but rather they embark upon a circular approach that undermines the utility of their analysis.[45]

A further concern expressed with the Goldsmith/Posner approach is that in order to fit within their simplified prisoner dilemma game theory, they begin with the assumption that the relevant actor is the "State" as a unitary player, represented by its political leaders. The State as they conceive it does not reflect multiple power bases and multiple agendas. To better mirror reality, Professor Spiro suggests that the State should be disaggregated and understood as a nexus of competing and contradictory actors that influence its behavior, including bureaucratic subsets within the Executive Branch, political subsets within the Congress, Supreme Court and lower court judges, as well as nongovernmental organizations outside of the government.[46] As we will see in Chapter 16 on lawyering the response to 9/11, many of these additional actors played key roles in determining the legal framework within which the United States carried out the war on terror.

Other international legal scholars have raised objections to Goldsmith/Posner's methodological approach, arguing that their theory is nonfalsifiable,[47] that it relies on a single-issue game approach,[48] and that their selective use of anecdotal case studies is misleading.[49] In particular, they observe that where a case study reveals a State's compliance with an accepted rule, it is difficult to determine without qualitative empirical data whether the State complied out of self-interest, out of a sense of duty to uphold the law, or a mix of both. As Professor Oona Hathaway points out, with respect to international law, which is primarily consent-based, "utility-seeking and law-abiding behavior is often identical."[50] Professor Golove observes that "Goldsmith and Posner make little effort to investigate direct historical evidence ... of the actual motivations of the individuals who made the decisions on which they focus. Instead they focus on the events themselves and draw speculative inferences about why States acted as they did."[51]

In the interest of contributing to this ongoing debate over compliance theory, the following chapters are intended in part to shed some light into this black box of decision making and help to illuminate why States have chosen to follow or not to follow principles of international law in times of crises.

# 2   A Brief History of L

**A**LTHOUGH THE DEPARTMENT OF STATE WAS ESTABLISHED in 1789 – the same year the U.S. Constitution was adopted – the Office of the Legal Adviser has a much briefer history. In the early years of the nation, the legal work of the Department of State was handled personally by such Secretaries of State as Thomas Jefferson, James Monroe, and James Madison, who were each extremely capable lawyers in their own right.[1] The precursor to the Legal Adviser was the so-called Examiner of Claim, a position established by Congress in 1848 to handle the proliferation of international claims against the United States. In 1906, Congress created the high-level position of Counselor of the Department, whose functions included advising the Secretary of State on questions of international law. But it was not until 1931 that Congress enacted a statute establishing the position of "The Legal Adviser." Since that time, more than twenty distinguished lawyers have filled the position,[2] which, for obscure historical reasons, is spelled as the British do with "e" rather than the common American spelling with an "o."

The Legal Adviser is appointed by the President with the advice and consent of the Senate. His rank within the Department is equivalent to that of an Assistant Secretary of State, and he answers directly to the Secretary of State. He heads an office known as "L," staffed by more than 170 Attorney Advisers, which is responsible for furnishing legal advice on all problems, domestic and international, that arise in the course of

the work of the Department of State. The Attorney Advisers are part
of the civil service rather than the Foreign Service, and are hired directly
by the Office of the Legal Adviser through a recruitment process that
is as competitive for young lawyers as obtaining a U.S. Supreme Court
clerkship (the Office receives about 3,000 applications for four or five
openings a year). The Attorney Advisers are assigned to geographic and
functional offices within L, each under the supervision of an Assistant
Legal Adviser, and each corresponding to one of the geographic and
functional bureaus of the Department of State. These assignments typically last for three years before rotation, giving the Attorney Advisers
sufficient time to develop expertise in the designated area of international law.

The Office of the Legal Adviser has taken on a variety of roles and
characteristics since the office was officially established in 1931. Each
Adviser's function in policymaking depends on the Adviser's personality
and relationship with the Secretary of State and other top-level administration officials. Historically, Legal Advisers worked primarily on the
legal implications of the most important policy questions, leaving general
matters and office management to Deputy and Assistant Legal Advisers.
By the early 1960s and the Kennedy Administration, the Office of the
Legal Adviser was already made up of more than forty attorneys, twenty
treaty specialists, and numerous assistants. However, despite the Office's
authority to become involved in a wide range of legal and policy issues,
office attorneys remained focused on relatively few issues such as sovereign
immunity and NATO. This changed with the appointment of President
Kennedy's Department of State Legal Adviser Abram Chayes.[3]

Chayes began transforming the Office into a proactive and involved
section of the Department of State. By instituting new hiring practices
that rivaled major national law firms, Chayes recruited top-level attorneys and law graduates. Chayes also refocused the Legal Adviser's role
to include policy issues dealing with human rights, trade, and the environment. Throughout his appointment, Chayes and his office became

influential advisors to the Secretary of State and laid the foundation for the modern Office of Legal Adviser.[4]

Today L's legal staff members are involved in treaty negotiations, international claims resolution, representation in international organizations, litigation before international tribunals, and the complex statutory and regulatory framework of the conduct of American foreign affairs. In recent years, the Office has played a particularly prominent role in the creation of new international institutions, such as the Iran–United States Claims Tribunal (which has been described as the "most significant arbitral body in history"),[5] the United Nations Compensation Commission, and the international criminal tribunals for the former Yugoslavia, Rwanda, Sierra Leone, and Cambodia.

The Office is also frequently called on to help craft solutions to disputes between the United States and foreign countries, as well as responses to unlawful behavior of other States. In performing its function of giving opinions concerning international law, the Legal Adviser inevitably acts as both judge and advisor – interpreting international law as applied to a particular set of circumstances and advising on whether proposed actions would be consistent with the law. Due to the open-textured character of many international legal norms and a dearth of precedent, international law questions do not always lend themselves to a definitive answer. And often the speed at which events move is such that preliminary legal advice is required within a period of hours, or even minutes.

Surveys of State Department officials have consistently ranked the Legal Adviser's influence within the Department as "substantial."[6] That influence waxes and wanes, however, depending upon the depth of the personal relationship that the Legal Adviser develops with the Secretary of State and other top Department officials, and the role the Legal Adviser perceives is most appropriate for his Office. Some Legal Advisers have taken a restrictive view of their role and have felt that L's advice must be confined to issues of pure law, while others have felt comfortable opining on broader policies that may have indirect legal implications. One might suspect that Secretaries of State who, themselves, are lawyers, would be more inclined to perceive the importance of international law and assign a broad Advisory role to L. Of the sixty-four Secretaries of State since Thomas Jefferson first held the office in 1790, fifty-two have been lawyers, including most recently James Baker, Warren Christopher, and Hillary Clinton. Recent Secretaries of State who were not legally trained include Condoleezza Rice, Colin Powell, Madeleine Albright, George Shultz, Alexander Haig, and Henry Kissinger. Yet, during our discussions at the Carnegie Endowment, the Legal Advisers indicated that they did not perceive any relationship between the Secretary of State's legal background (or lack thereof) and a proclivity to hold international law and L in high esteem.

The Office of the Legal Adviser also serves as a training ground of sorts for future professors of public international law. L alum, including the Legal Advisers, have contributed substantially to the body of public international law scholarship, with more than 1,000 articles and books authored by former L lawyers. A select bibliography of the articles and books authored by the Legal Advisers is available in the Annex.

# 3   The Path to L

I N THIS CHAPTER, EACH OF THE TEN LEGAL ADVISERS (IN CHRO-
nological order of service) describes his background and how
he came to be appointed to the post.[1] As indicated in their
narratives, the approach of each Legal Adviser to the role of international law was distinctly shaped by their previous legal experience, and
in some cases by their previous service with the U.S. Government.

## Herbert J. Hansell (Carter Administration)

I believe I was nominated to be Legal Adviser at the outset of the Carter
Administration because Cyrus Vance and Warren Christopher, President Carter's appointees to be Secretary of State and Deputy Secretary,
each had known me and my legal experience quite well.

I had encountered each of them often in the course of our respective
legal and civic service careers. Vance and I had worked together in connection with creation of Amtrak, and also in raising funds for Yale Law
School, of which we both were graduates. Christopher and I had worked
with one another as directors of the lawyers' Committee for Civil Rights
Under Law, a national organization created at the instance of President
Kennedy to involve private-sector lawyers in the pursuit of equality for
minorities; and when he was Deputy Attorney General in the Johnson
Administration, we also had discussed the possibility of my serving in
the Justice Department.

I first learned that Vance and Christopher were considering me as a prospect for nomination as Legal Adviser in a telephone call from one of them in December 1976. At their invitation, I met with them in Washington, DC. Moving rapidly to staff the State Department, they promptly advised me that they wished to submit my name for nomination. I requested a short period to consult with family, law firm colleagues, and clients. I was encouraged to accept by John Reavis, revered former Managing Partner of my law firm, and by my partner Erwin Griswold, who described the Legal Adviser as "the second best legal job in government" – the best in his view of course being Solicitor General, which he had been.

A principal reservation in my mind was that, although I was honored and flattered by the offer and had broad experience in domestic and foreign corporate law and business finance, and also in federal and local government, I had not acquired broad knowledge of public international law. Vance and others reassured me that the highly talented L staff could be counted on for a rapid education and strong support (which proved to be correct beyond all expectations). Thus satisfied, I accepted, and arrived in L on Inauguration Day, January 20, 1977.

### Roberts B. Owen (Carter Administration)

In light of my pre-State Department career, my appointment as Legal Adviser in mid-1979 was hardly a predictable event. I had graduated from the Harvard Law School in 1951, spent a Fulbright Scholarship year at Cambridge University in England, and in 1952 joined the Washington, DC firm of Covington & Burling. Although I then worked extensively with former Secretary of State Dean Acheson (who returned from the State Department to the firm just as I arrived there), over the next twenty-odd years my work focused heavily on litigation, with some but not great involvement in international law.

It thus came as a surprise when I received a call in mid-1979 from then–Deputy Secretary of State Warren Christopher, whom I had never previously met, asking whether I would have any interest in becoming the Legal Adviser. Because I had had some exposure to L, particularly through old friend (and former Legal Adviser) Abram Chayes, I knew the post to be one of the world's most interesting legal jobs – and said as much to Christopher – but I also felt compelled to acknowledge at the outset that I was hardly a scholar in the field of international law. Chris replied that he consulted various people with whom I had worked in the past, including Abram Chayes, Judge Gerhard Gesell, and Lloyd Cutler, who evidently considered me qualified, and literally minutes later I found myself in a joint job interview conversation with Secretary Cyrus Vance and Christopher. During our talk an awkward moment occurred when I felt obliged to disclose that just hours before I had been offered a position on the Federal bench – a career option that I wanted to consider – but both of my interviewers did a charming job of persuading me that I should defer any judgeship notions until after I had had the truly unique experience of serving as the Legal Adviser.

In hindsight, they were right about the experience and its rewards. It was a remarkable, although sometimes stressful adventure, and because the main focus of my work during my 1979–1981 tenure happened to be (as explained later) on the resolution of "the Iranian Hostage crisis" via the Algiers Accords, my prior experience in litigation and negotiation may have been more helpful to the cause than pure scholarship. In any case, it was a hugely rewarding experience and a great privilege to have served.

I might add a post-L postscript. Early in 1995, as a direct result of my L experience, Warren Christopher – by now President Clinton's Secretary of State – asked whether I would take on an amorphous pro bono project for the Department. Dubbed "Senior Adviser to the Secretary of State for the Former Yugoslavia," I became deeply involved, first, as chief arbitrator in multiple political disputes in war-torn Bosnia and, second, as a member of Ambassador Richard Holbrooke's shuttle diplomacy team, negotiating the war-ending Dayton Accords with Slobodan Milosevic. Thereafter, under an appointment by the President of the

International Court of Justice, the Bosnian arbitration work (still on a pro bono basis) continued on and off for more than a decade, well into my retirement, but again it was well worth the effort.

### Davis R. Robinson (Reagan Administration)

Like many stories, how I became Legal Adviser has a number of random but related strands. Initiated into the world of philately at age five, I developed an abiding interest in history, geography, and world affairs. Majoring in history at Yale, I took the Foreign Service examination in the fall of my senior year and entered the U.S. diplomatic service shortly after graduation in 1961. Initial postings were to Egypt and Jordan. Taking a leave of absence from the State Department, I attended Harvard Law School where I took a number of courses in international law–related subjects. I then returned to the Foreign Service with assignments as Attorney-Adviser in the U.S. Arms Control and Disarmament Agency and as Staff Assistant to the Secretary of State. In 1969, for financial reasons, I resigned from the career Foreign Service in order to engage in the private practice of law, where I worked for the next decade in firms on Wall Street and in Washington, DC. As a result, a mixture of experience in world affairs and in law came into place.

Another strand in the story is more personal in nature. As a child growing up in Greenwich, CT, I attended school with several students named Walker and Bush and, many years later, one of these Walkers became my wife. Shortly after our marriage, George Herbert Walker Bush, a first cousin of my wife, ran for Congress from a House of Representatives district in Houston and, upon election, moved to Washington, DC just before I returned there to begin my assignment to the U.S. Arms Control and Disarmament Agency.

In 1979, George H. W. Bush decided to make a run for the office of President of the United States. At an early stage, I became involved in his campaign for the Republican nomination. Having attended Philips Exeter Academy, where my father had taught English for several years, my wife and I in early 1980 went to Exeter, NH to support George H. W.

Bush's effort in the crowded and fateful New Hampshire primary, where Ronald Reagan ultimately turned the tide to his favor.

Returning to Washington to resume the private practice of law, I assumed that my foray into the American political scene was finished. However, after the Republican Convention of 1980 nominated Ronald Reagan and George H. W. Bush as the Republican Presidential and Vice Presidential candidates, a close confidant of Ronald Reagan, who had met me in New Hampshire earlier that year, asked if I would consider taking a leave of absence from my law firm to participate in the national campaign effort. I decided to accept this offer. Thereafter, I was named one of the three heads of the campaign's operations center where I became well acquainted with many of the closest advisers to the former Governor of California.

Following the election victory, I was asked to serve as a volunteer member of the transition team at the Department of Commerce, but I did not then anticipate participating in the new Administration. However, out of the blue in late February 1981, I was invited to an interview with the newly appointed Secretary of State, Alexander Haig, during which the retired General inquired about my interest in serving as the Legal Adviser to the Department of State. With my background both as a Foreign Service Officer and as a lawyer, this position, if attainable, would take full advantage of my experience, skills, and life-long interests.

My appointment as Legal Adviser thereafter took several months to wind through the intricacies of the State Department, the White House, and the Senate. Ultimately, it all came to pass in July 1981, resulting in a challenging and supremely rewarding four-year tour in what I regard as the premier legal job in the U.S. Government, in large measure thanks to the quality and dedication of the finest legal staff in Washington, DC.

### Abraham D. Sofaer (Reagan and Bush (41st) Administrations)

In early 1985, I was called by a friend who lived in DC, who asked me if I would be interested in serving as Legal Adviser to Secretary of State

George P. Shultz. It seems that Deputy Secretary of State Kenneth Dam, whom I had met when we were both professors of law, suggested that Secretary Shultz consider me for appointment to the job on the basis of a book I wrote on the early history of the exercise of the war powers in the United States. I had read speeches by Secretary Shultz on the need to deal more firmly with terrorism, and I greatly admired his stance on that and other issues. In particular, I agreed with his call for an "active defense" that involved using force to preempt attacks. Although I was honored to serve as a District Judge, I told my friend I would be prepared to resign to join Secretary Shultz. A meeting was arranged between the two of us at a New York hotel, on an evening that he planned to be in New York.

Secretary Shultz and I spent about an hour together, talking about the State Department and his view of the proper role of the Legal Adviser. He told me he wanted a lawyer who did all the jobs a lawyer was supposed to do. But he said he wanted his Legal Adviser to be in the flow of the Department's work in order to observe policymaking and to weigh in when necessary. He also contemplated that the Legal Adviser would have a diplomatic portfolio of his own, with legal issues that required negotiation. He had actually read my book, and he said he admired it. We discussed how so many of the issues that are currently at the heart of executive/legislative disputes sprang from the very beginning of the constitution's history.

When he had finished describing the job, he said I would be invited to the morning meeting of principals. I did not know then how important that was to being able to do the job properly, but I surmised that it was a good thing and nodded. He then asked me if I had any requests or concerns. I told him that my sense of the job as he described it was that my role would be determined over time, depending on his needs and his view of my capacities, and that I saw no point in trying to negotiate understandings. He grinned and offered me the job. I grinned and accepted. He told me, with amazing accuracy, how much time it would take to get me confirmed, and that I should not worry about rumors but just assume that everything would work out. I nodded, we shook hands, and the next time we met was at my swearing in ceremony.

## Edwin D. Williamson (Bush (41st) Administration)

As an associate and then a partner at the firm of Sullivan & Cromwell, I heard quite a lot about the firm's lawyers leaving to do government service, particularly in the State Department. John Foster Dulles, President Eisenhower's Secretary of State until Dulles' death in 1957, and his brother Allen W. Dulles, the first (and longest-serving) Director of Central Intelligence, had both been partners in the firm. Arthur Dean, who negotiated the Panmunjon Treaty ending the Korean War and President Kennedy's Nuclear Test Ban Treaty, was the Chairman of the firm during my associate years and my early years as a partner. John R. Stevenson, who served as Legal Adviser in the first Nixon Administration and the Chief Negotiator of the Law of the Sea Convention in the second term, was the firm's hiring partner when I was hired as an associate. Davis Robinson was an alumnus of the firm, although he was not at the firm when he became a Legal Adviser. In addition, several other partners had served at one time or another in the government or left to become judges.

Although the aura of government service hung pretty heavily at the firm, and we talked a lot about it, we worked pretty hard and never seemed to get around to doing much about leaving the firm and heading to Washington, DC. Furthermore, I was quite happy in my capital markets practice, essentially doing large financings in the public debt and equity markets, which had a large international element in it (I spent three years at the end of the 1970s as the resident partner in our London office). Somewhat out of the blue, however, in 1988 my then-Chairman asked if I would be interested in moving to the firm's Washington, DC office, where we needed another corporate partner. So, responding to a combination of the call of duty and the adventure of moving to the banks of the Potomac, I moved down to Washington in summer 1988.

Once settled in Washington, I renewed some old law school acquaintances, one of which was with Abe Sofaer, who had been a year behind me in law school. I talked to Abe about the possibilities of seeking a position in the George H. W. Bush Administration, in case he should win the election. When Bush won and I told my wife that I might see if I could find a position in the new Bush Administration, she hit the roof. She had been dragged to Washington, kicking and screaming (not quite literally, but close), from her beloved native New York City. The last thing she was going to do was to cut the umbilical cord – my partnership in Sullivan & Cromwell – to all that she held near and dear. So, I dropped any idea of doing anything in the Bush Administration and continued with my quite satisfying practice at the firm.

Abe had been asked by Secretary of State James A. Baker III to stay on as Legal Adviser. Abe and I had lunch on a fairly regular basis, and in January 1990, he decided that nearly five years at L was long enough, and he had told the Secretary that he wanted to leave. He asked if I wanted him to recommend me as his successor, and I responded quite positively. (By then, my wife had gotten a little more settled in Washington and was less anxious about the prospect of not returning to New York City.)

For what seemed an eternity (I have found the period between being told that one was under serious consideration for a government position and actually getting the nod very unsettling because one cannot breathe a word of the possibility of the appointment, and must continue with one's practice as though nothing was going on, despite the fact that being appointed would mean disrupting that practice), I finally had an interview with Robert Kimmitt, Secretary Baker's trusted aide, who was serving as Under Secretary for Policy. This ultimately led to an interview with Secretary Baker and eventually to my being nominated by the President to be Legal Adviser. My most vivid recollection of the interview with Secretary Baker was his concern as to whether I would be happy just being a lawyer, and not getting into policy issues. I assured him that I would be. I said that I thought the thing that I liked best about my practice was being at the heart of major transactions, but knowing when the lawyering stopped and the business decision making started. I did the former, but the latter was the job of my client. I saw no reason why it should be any different in the foreign policy arena (although I suspected that perhaps the line between lawyering and policymaking was a little fuzzier in government than in the private sector). Thus, I tell people that my deal with the Secretary was that I would not practice foreign policy and he would not practice law, though the former part of the bargain was a bit more binding than the latter!

So, finally, on April 20, 1990, I was told that I had been selected, and on June 20 my nomination was announced. Fairly soon after the announcement, Senator Daniel Patrick Moynihan put a hold on my nomination, because of a totally unrelated dispute he had with the State Department over the issuance of visas to Canadians, and notwithstanding that I was practically a constituent, having moved down to Washington from New York less than two years earlier. He did permit me to have a hearing, which was held on August 1. As I was leaving my office that night, someone asked if I had heard that the Iraqis had invaded Kuwait. Notwithstanding our entry into a state of war with Iraq, Moynihan kept his hold on my nomination. He finally relented in the middle of September, and I was confirmed by the Senate on September 20 and was sworn in on the following Monday, September 24, 1990.

## Michael J. Matheson (Acting Legal Adviser Several Times, Most Notably During the Bush (41st) Administration)

I first joined the Legal Adviser's Office as a summer intern in 1967. After graduating from law school and completing my tour of duty in the military (as an attorney in the Air Force General Counsel's Office), I went back to L as a career attorney, where I worked on environmental law, United Nations affairs, and arms control. I then became Assistant Legal Adviser for African Affairs, working on legal issues concerning apartheid, Rhodesia, and Namibia; and then–Assistant Legal Adviser for Political-Military Affairs, working once again on arms control, as well as law-of-war negotiations and the deployment of U.S. forces abroad. In 1983, I became a Deputy Legal Adviser, and from time to time during the rest of the 1980s supervised the Office's sections on political–military affairs, African affairs, international claims, law-enforcement and intelligence, economic affairs, and others. Much of my work involved the Iran–United States Claims Tribunal and the negotiation and interpretation of arms control agreements.

I was Principal Deputy Legal Adviser in June 1990 when Abraham Sofaer ended his term as Legal Adviser, and I served for the next three months as Acting Legal Adviser until Edwin Williamson was sworn in, at which point I reverted to my position as Principal Deputy. As it happened, Iraq invaded Kuwait during this period, which meant that I was heavily engaged in coordinating the U.S. legal position on sanctions, the use of force, and the involvement of the United Nations Security Council. These issues continued to occupy me in the following years, particularly with respect to the creation of the postwar regime and the United Nations Compensation Commission. When Edwin Williamson left the Office in November 1992, I was once again Acting Legal Adviser until Conrad Harper was sworn in as Legal Adviser in May 1993. During this period, L was charged with creating a process for the prosecution of war crimes in the former Yugoslavia, which resulted in the creation of an International Criminal Tribunal. This process, along with the creation of a similar tribunal for Rwanda, occupied much of my time in the succeeding years.

Conrad Harper left the Office in June 1996, and I was once again Acting Legal Adviser until David Andrews took over in September 1997. During this period, I was involved in bringing to a conclusion the negotiation and ratification of the United Nations Mines Protocol that had occupied much of my attention for several years. Finally, when David Andrews left office in April 2000, I was once again Acting Legal Adviser for a few months prior to my retirement from the State Department. During this entire period of the second Clinton Administration, I was frequently involved in the legal questions presented by the United States use of force against Iraq and Serbia, and the United Nations involvement in Iraq, Bosnia, and Kosovo.

In all, I was a career attorney in the Legal Adviser's Office for more than thirty-eight years, working under both Democratic and Republican administrations. I had the privilege of serving under eleven different Legal Advisers and was deputy to five of them. I was Acting Legal Adviser for a total of more than two years.

### Conrad K. Harper (Clinton Administration)

After getting my L.L.B. from Harvard Law School, I worked at the NAACP Legal Defense and Educational Fund in New York, and then worked my way up to partner at the firm of Simpson Thacher and Bartlett in New York City. Within days of President Clinton's first inauguration, Secretary Christopher telephoned me. We had never met, but I knew of his formidable reputation as a lawyer and a diplomat. He asked me to consider an appointment as Legal Adviser. I said that I was not interested. My lack of interest proceeded largely from a lack of knowledge. The conversation ended cordially.

An hour or so later, Arnie Miller called. We had known each other during the Carter Administration when he had helped Secretary Califano find potential appointees for the Department of Health, Education, and Welfare (HEW). He was now helping Secretary Christopher in a similar way. Arnie understood that I had spoken with the Secretary. Arnie continued, "The Secretary did not like your answer." Arnie planned to be in New York the next morning and asked whether we could meet. I agreed.

I then requested one of the librarians at Simpson Thacher to provide me with information on the Office of Legal Adviser. Among other materials, she sent the excellent and still useful article by Richard H. Bilder, *The Office of the Legal Adviser: The State Department Lawyer and Foreign Affairs*, 56 AJIL 633 (1963). By the next morning, fortified by my reading of the materials from the firm's library and by the good advice of my wife, I met Arnie for breakfast and indicated my willingness to change my mind and be considered for the position. A few days later, and immediately following the funeral of Justice Thurgood Marshall at the National Cathedral – a service attended by the President, the Cabinet, the Supreme Court, and thousands of others, including me – Secretary Christopher and I had lunch in the Secretary's private dining room at the Department. He was kind enough to renew his offer. I accepted.

### David R. Andrews (Clinton Administration)

My journey to the Legal Adviser's office began in 1969. The journey included a brief stopover in the administration of President Jimmy Carter at the U.S. Environmental Protection Agency from 1976 to 1980 and at the Department of Health, Education, and Welfare (later to become the Department of Health and Human Services) from 1980 to 1981, and culminated in my confirmation by the U.S. Senate to the position of Legal Adviser to the State Department in August 1997.

In 1969, I was a second-year student at the University of California at Berkeley's School of Law, Boalt Hall. Among the luminaries of international law was Professor Stefan Riesenfeld, and I was fortunate to be selected as one of Professor Riesenfeld's research assistants. This was the beginning of a thirty-three-year friendship with Steve who was not only a friend but also a mentor and job counselor. As a result, early in my legal career, I was fully aware of the role and importance of the Legal Adviser in our government. Nevertheless, I did not consider the possibility of ever becoming the Legal Adviser, and, frankly, I did not aspire to the position.

At graduation in 1971, I became an associate in a large law firm, as did most graduates with large federal loans to pay off. In 1974, I was a third-year litigation associate at McCutchen, Doyle, Brown, & Enersen in San Francisco. Steve called to ask if I might be interested in a fellowship to do research at the Max Planck Institute for Comparative Public and International Law in Heidelberg. Professor Hermann Mosler, the codirector of the Institute had asked Steve to send one of his students to do research on the act of state doctrine. I was of course interested, but needed Steve's help to convince firm management to allow me to take a sabbatical leave. He did and my wife, my two children, and I departed for Heidelberg in February 1974 where I was a visiting Fellow and Professor of Law until September.

Shortly after my return to McCutchen, I was offered the position of Regional Counsel for the U.S. Environmental Protection Agency Region 9 and accepted the position. In 1976, Jimmy Carter was elected President and I was asked to move to Washington to take the job as Legal Counsel and Special Assistant for Policy to the Deputy Administrator of EPA. In 1980, I moved to the Department of Health, Education, and Welfare as Principle Deputy General Counsel. At the end of the Carter Administration I returned to the McCutchen law firm in San Francisco.

Shortly after President Clinton was elected, I was contacted by the White House regarding my interest in the number two position at EPA. In 1991, I had been elected to a two-year term as chairman of McCutchen and respectfully declined to be considered for the EPA position. In 1995, I was again contacted by the White House, but this time in connection with newly vacated position of Associate Attorney General, the number three position in the Department of Justice. Once again, I respectfully told the White House I was not interested.

In February 1997, I was again contacted by the White House regarding the Associate Attorney General spot. Once again I said I was not interested. Approximately two weeks later I received a call from a friend who had been the Director of White House Personnel in the Carter Administration. He was calling about the Legal Adviser's position at State and urged me to meet with the new Secretary of State, Madeleine Albright. Subsequently, President Clinton nominated me for the position of Legal Adviser, I was confirmed by the Senate in August 1997, and on September 2, 1997 I was sworn in as the nineteenth Legal Adviser to the State Department.

## William H. Taft (Bush (43rd) Administration)

I first met Secretary Powell when he was a candidate for the White House Fellows program in 1972. I was serving on a regional panel to select persons to go to the final round. The panel was expected to forward the names of the two best candidates out of the dozen or so that we interviewed that day. When the panel caucused, the Chairman said, "Well, we will send forward Colin Powell and who else?" It was obvious to all of us that this was an extraordinary man or, as General Wickham put it to me once years later when he was Army Chief of Staff, and we were discussing Colin's career path, "Colin Powell is a national treasure."

I got to know then–Colonel Powell better later in 1972 when he was selected as a White House Fellow and assigned to the Office of Management and Budget. I was the Executive Assistant to the Director, Caspar Weinberger.

In 1981, President Reagan appointed Mr. Weinberger to be Secretary of Defense, and he asked me to join him at the Pentagon. Between 1981 and 1989, I served as General Counsel at the Pentagon and later as Deputy Secretary. I worked closely with then–General Powell during this time, particularly so when he was Secretary Weinberger's Military Assistant and I was the Deputy. We were the two channels through which work could be sent to the Secretary, so we were in virtually constant communication. We became good friends and respected colleagues.

When President Bush announced that Secretary Powell was his choice to lead the State Department in December 2000, I called him up and said I would like to be part of his team. A few days later he called back and said he would like me to be the Legal Adviser. If you tell the captain you want to be on his team, you don't argue about the position he asks you to play; at least I don't. Having been the General Counsel in two cabinet departments, including the Pentagon, I knew how to manage a government legal office. Through my experience at the Pentagon and in private practice I was familiar with many aspects of the Legal Adviser's work, although obviously there were subjects on which I had much to learn. My close personal relationship with the Secretary and his commitment to the rule of law assured that the Legal Adviser's Office would be a strong player in the conduct of the department's business during our time there, as I believe it was.

### John B. Bellinger III (Bush (43rd) Administration)

I was born in 1960 in Paris, France, where my father, an Army officer, was then working for the Supreme Headquarters Allied Powers/Europe (SHAPE). I was raised primarily in the Washington, DC area and at various military bases in the United States and Germany. My mother was a Russian analyst at the CIA, so I had public service in my genes.

I graduated from St. Albans School in Washington, DC in 1978, from Princeton University's Woodrow Wilson School of Public and International Affairs in 1982, and from Harvard Law School in 1986. At Harvard, I was an editor of the Harvard International Law Journal. I also received an M.A. in Foreign Affairs in 1991 from the University of Virginia, where I wrote my thesis on the Western European Union.

From 1986 to 1988, I practiced law with Shaw, Pittman, Potts, & Trowbridge, having been attracted to the firm in part by former Deputy Legal Adviser John Rhinelander. In 1988, I applied and was selected to be special assistant to then–Director of Central Intelligence William Webster, a former federal judge who had been appointed by President Reagan to lead the CIA after the Iran-Contra scandal. I worked at CIA from 1988 to 1991, and this experience cemented my permanent interest in national security law.

From 1991 to 1995, I returned to private law practice with Wilmer, Cutler, & Pickering, where I worked primarily on financial institutions and securities matters but also helped senior partner Lloyd Cutler advise current and former officials, including former Secretaries of State George Shultz, Henry Kissinger, and James Baker, in connection with various Congressional and Independent Counsel investigations. My experience as lawyer for these Secretaries of State was to prove useful a decade later!

In 1995, the call of public service proved irresistible to me, and I returned to government to a series of five positions, culminating in my appointment as Legal Adviser. From 1995 to 1996, I served as General Counsel of the Commission on the Roles and Capabilities of the

U.S. Intelligence Community (the Aspin-Brown Commission), created to make recommendations on the structure and mission of U.S. intelligence agencies after the Cold War. In 1996, I served as Special Counsel to the Senate Select Committee on Intelligence, where I drafted changes to the National Security Act to implement the recommendations of the Aspin-Brown Commission. From 1997 to 2001, I served as Counsel for National Security Matters in the Criminal Division of the Department of Justice, where I coordinated criminal investigations with national security or foreign policy dimensions with other parts of the government, and in this capacity I worked closely with L and with the National Security Council (NSC) Legal Office.

Although I was a political independent and had not been active in the 2000 presidential campaign, based on my experience as a national security lawyer, in January 2001, I was recommended to and selected by then–Counsel to the President Alberto Gonzales and then–National Security Adviser Condoleezza Rice to serve as Legal Adviser to the NSC, with a joint appointment in the White House Counsel's Office as Senior Associate Counsel to the President. I served in this position until January 2005, and during this period I worked on a daily basis with Will Taft, with many other L lawyers (including two who were detailed to the NSC Legal office) and with the General Counsels and senior policy officials of all of the national security departments and agencies in the federal government.

When President Bush nominated then–Dr. Rice in November 2004 to succeed Colin Powell as Secretary of State, Dr. Rice in turn asked me, having served as her NSC Legal Adviser for the previous four years, to manage her Senate confirmation process and to codirect her State Department transition team. This was a quite fascinating experience because it allowed me to work closely with her to set a vision and plan her objectives for her tenure as Secretary of State. I and the other members of her small transition team set goals, inter alia, for her four years, for her first year, for her first hundred days, for her first trip, and for her first week in office. For my parochial part, I urged that she emphasize and demonstrate her commitment to international law, which I believe she did, starting shortly after her taking office.

I moved with then–Secretary Rice to the State Department in January 2005, serving initially as Senior Adviser to the Secretary and occupying an office fashioned from a small reception room immediately outside her office. Secretary Rice asked me to remain as part of her team and asked me whether I would be willing to serve as Chief of Staff or as Legal Adviser. This was a difficult decision for me because I was interested in helping the Secretary as much as possible in managing the Department, but because I considered myself primarily a lawyer and I had enormous respect for L, I said that I would prefer to serve as Legal Adviser.

After I was confirmed by the Senate in April 2005, Secretary Rice asked whether I would consider remaining in the small office outside her office while serving as Legal Adviser. Again, I was somewhat conflicted, but I told her that I felt that it was important for me to be with the L "troops" on the sixth floor. Nevertheless, Secretary Rice asked me to continue to be part of her small "personal staff," which included attending a small 8:00 AM "inner-office" staff meeting each morning and a "wrap-up" meeting at the end of each day. Attendance at these meetings provided me with constant access to the Secretary and allowed me to raise not only legal issues but also policy matters on which I had views.

# 4 The Carter Administration – Herbert J. Hansell (1977–1979)

**W**HEN CYRUS VANCE, WHO HAD BEEN NOMINATED TO BE Secretary of State by President Carter, asked me to be his Legal Adviser, we talked about what he wanted to accomplish as Secretary and he outlined a number of goals, three of which I thought would be appropriate to talk about today. Each of these goals raised a number of interesting legal questions, and I have chosen two questions regarding each goal that I thought would be most useful to discuss.

These three goals were all accomplishments of President Carter and Secretary Vance that I worked on with them. The first was the establishment of official diplomatic relations with the People's Republic of China and the corresponding establishment of unofficial relations with Taiwan. The second was the peace treaty between Egypt and Israel. The third was resolving the Panama Canal Treaty negotiations.

## Establishment of Diplomatic Relations with the People's Republic of China

The establishment of diplomatic relations with the People's Republic of China and the simultaneous termination of formal government relations and creation of unofficial relations with Taiwan were accomplished by a series of measures: a joint communiqué of the United States and the People's Republic of China; formal notice of termination of a mutual defense treaty that existed between the United States and the formerly recognized government of China (the Republic of China); several Presidential Executive Orders; and the Taiwan Relations Act to implement the regime of unofficial relations with Taiwan.

The joint communiqué[1] also confirmed, as bipartisan U.S. policy, the fundamental basis for United States–People's Republic of China relations that had been established by President Nixon in the Shanghai communiqué: the United States acknowledged the position of Chinese on both sides of the Taiwan Strait that there is but one China and that Taiwan is part of China. By reason of this bipartisan affirmation, the "one China" recognition has remained established U.S. policy since then.[2]

The two issues raised by these transactions that I will talk about today are first, whether the President had the power to terminate the mutual defense treaty with the Republic of China without Congressional authorization; and second, how legally to extend to a non-State (Taiwan) all (except diplomatic relations) of the U.S. Government benefits and agreements and arrangements that Taiwan had previously enjoyed as a recognized State – including such privileges as the ability to obtain visas, Export-Import Bank and OPIC financing, and so forth.

The termination of the mutual defense treaty was an essential ingredient of granting recognition to the People's Republic, which would not agree to exchange official recognition without termination of the treaty. President Carter could pursue two possible procedures for terminating the treaty. One was to give notice of termination under the provision of the treaty that provided for one-year notice of termination; the other would be simply to abrogate the treaty, on one or more of several possible grounds.

Termination of the treaty by the President without Congressional authorization was bitterly opposed by a group of Senators and Congressmen, led by Barry Goldwater. After considerable study in L, I opined that the President did have the authority to terminate the treaty without any authorization either by the Senate or by joint Congressional action. Goldwater, and seven other Senators, as I recall, and about a dozen

Congressmen immediately filed suit in Federal District Court to prevent the termination of the treaty.[3] Amazingly enough, they won in District Court, but the Court of Appeals reversed the decision;[4] Goldwater took the case to the Supreme Court, which directed that the complaint be dismissed on "political question" grounds.[5]

There is a related anecdote that I think is worth sharing. Because of the opposition to the treaty's termination within the Congress, which was all on the Republican side, Secretary Vance and I thought it would be politically useful to obtain the support of a highly respected Republican lawyer. We asked Herbert Brownell, who had been President Eisenhower's Attorney General, to look at the question independently, which he did, and he fully supported our position on termination, which was very helpful in our dealings with the Congress.

Change of diplomatic recognition to the People's Republic of China and establishment of a regime of unofficial relations with Taiwan presented the issue of how to extend to Taiwan, as a non-State, the statutory programs and benefits available to States and governments with which the United States has official diplomatic and governmental relations. Achievement of that objective was critical to winning public and Congressional acceptance of the disestablishment of relations with the Republic of China.

Initially we were concerned that it might be necessary to identify every statute that created such a program or established such a benefit and amend each one individually, which, of course, would have been an immense undertaking. I asked Professor Steve Reisenfeld, a distinguished and widely revered international law scholar, then the Counselor in L, to investigate how we might deal with that problem in ways other than amendment. He ultimately convinced me and the Secretary and the Deputy Secretary (both excellent lawyers) and the Department of Justice and the White House Counsel's office that we could adopt what we called a "blanket amendment," namely, a policy that any reference in any federal statute to a foreign government or State or foreign country or nation would be deemed to include Taiwan. That posture was adopted, first in a Presidential Executive Order[6] issued by President Carter and subsequently in the Taiwan Relations Act,[7] and it has worked satisfactorily in the ensuing twenty-five years.

## The Egyptian–Israeli Peace Treaty

The second of the Carter Administration's major diplomatic initiatives that I would like to discuss is the Egyptian–Israeli Peace Treaty.[8] At the beginning of the Carter term, of course, a state of war existed between Israel and Egypt, arising out of the 1973 Middle East War. The United States had been mediating negotiations between the two countries for some period of time, with three objectives: first, to establish peace between the two sides, if at all possible; second, to effect Israeli withdrawal from territories that had been occupied in the 1973 war and establish secure and recognized borders; and, third, to develop a resolution of Palestinian issues.

The U.S. mediation had continued from the beginning of the Carter term until September 1978, a year and a half later, when the President convened the Camp David negotiations.[9] Those negotiations produced two frameworks: one framework for a treaty of peace between Egypt and Israel; and a second framework for a broader Mideast peace, which chiefly involved resolution of the Palestinian problem and the status of the West Bank and Gaza. The elements of the second framework were based on the land-for-peace formulation of Security Council Resolution 242.[10]

The peace treaty, of course, generated a number of legal issues, as well as political and military issues;[11] one of the most important and interesting was the so-called conflict of obligations problem. Egypt was a party to a mutual defense treaty among the Arab nations, which obliged each party to come to the aid of any other signatory engaged in military conflict with Israel. The Israelis were concerned about that provision, because it would mean that, even though Egypt had a peace treaty with

Israel, the Egyptians would be obliged to go to war again with Israel in the event of a conflict between Israel and one of the other Arab States.

That issue proved to be one of the most difficult of all issues in the peace treaty negotiations. Ultimately, it had to be settled at the Chief-of-State level among Presidents Carter and Sadat and Prime Minister Begin, by some artfully drafted language that minimally satisfied each party: a peace treaty provision that in the event of a conflict between the parties' obligations under the peace treaty and another document, the peace treaty obligations would prevail, accompanied by an agreed minute, to satisfy Egyptian concerns (focused on their relations with the other Arab States), that there would be no assertion by reason of the peace treaty that the treaty prevailed over other obligations or that other obligations prevailed over the treaty. Now, if that sounds as though a bit of legal mumbo jumbo was involved, in fact there was; but it passed muster with the three heads of state, to resolve the conflict of obligations issue.

The second Camp David framework provided for negotiations concerning future status of the West Bank and Gaza and resolution of the Palestinian problem. It was important to Egypt that there be an undertaking to deal with Palestinian issues, because Egypt had become a pariah in the Arab world for negotiating a separate peace with Israel that didn't include settlement of all other issues remaining as a result of the 1973 war. Negotiations for Palestinian self-government in the West Bank and Gaza commenced following the signing of the peace treaty and continued throughout the remainder of President Carter's term without resolution.

Of the many legal issues involved in those negotiations, the most troublesome at the time was the question of the legality of the Israeli settlements in the occupied territories. The parties, and particularly the Congress, pressed the State Department for a U.S. view on that legality issue, and after extensive study, I gave Congress an opinion to the effect that, although Israel could remain in occupation until the state of war ended, the establishment of civilian settlements in the occupied territories was inconsistent with the Fourth Geneva Convention.

## Panama Canal Treaties

Before the Carter Administration took office, there had been considerable unrest in Panama over U.S. occupation of the Panama Canal Zone and its ownership of the Canal. The agitation in Panama had led three preceding U.S. administrations to accept the need to renegotiate the U.S. role in Panama, and the United States had committed to negotiate a new treaty fixing a date for American withdrawal from Panama.[12]

In the course of negotiations during the first Carter year for the new Panama Canal Treaty, two critical legal issues confronted the U.S. negotiators. The first of these issues was how to preserve U.S. security interests in continued availability and use of the Panama Canal following U.S. withdrawal from Panama.

After lengthy and difficult negotiations, those security issues were resolved by agreement on two treaties.[13] In addition to a withdrawal treaty,[14] there would be a second treaty[15] assuring in perpetuity the neutrality of the Canal and U.S. rights to defend the Canal and to claim expeditious Canal transit in wartime.

A number of questions regarding implementation of the neutrality treaty that arose during Senate debate on ratification of the two Panama Canal Treaties found expression and resolution in Senate adoption of amendments, conditions, reservations, and understandings, necessitating further acrimonious negotiations with Panama before the treaties were ultimately finalized and signed.

A second critical legal issue was whether the President could dispose of U.S. property (the Canal) by treaty subject only to Senate consideration, or whether he had to obtain Congressional authorization by both Houses.[16] Both the Attorney General and the Legal Adviser were called on by Congress to deliver legal opinions on the matter, and both opined that the President could act by treaty. Notwithstanding those opinions, two suits challenging the President's power to act by treaty were filed in Federal District Court, one by a group of Senators led by Senator Helms,[17] and one by a group of Representatives.[18] The District Court dismissed both suits, and both dismissals were affirmed by the U.S. Court of Appeals.

## Discussion

*Question*: All of the issues covered today, even though some of them happened twenty-five years ago, are issues that are still in the front pages of the newspapers. One of them is the possibility of China invading Taiwan at any moment. Since we now have a statutory authority rather than a treaty authority establishing the obligation to defend Taiwan, does that mean that the President has less discretion in choosing to break that authority?

*Mr. Hansell*: Well, after the *Goldwater v. Carter* case,[19] it is clear that the President can unilaterally terminate a treaty; but violating a federal statute would be another matter.[20] The President would have to make the difficult argument that his Constitutional Commander-in-Chief authority trumps the foreign affairs authority of Congress under the circumstances. Another fascinating international law issue embedded in that question is that we have a conflict between a Congressional statute and an international agreement (the joint communiqué with the People's Republic of China[21]) entered into by the United States. That raises the question whether an Act of Congress, which takes effect domestically, can alter in any way our international obligations undertaken in a separate bilateral agreement with a foreign State.

There is a side question as to whether or not the joint communiqué is indeed a binding international agreement (I have always regarded it as a binding). So there is a legal issue. As a practical matter, I think there is no doubt that in the White House, and probably in the Congress as well, the view is that the Taiwan Relations Act[22] does constrain our relationship with the People's Republic of China insofar as Taiwan is concerned.

However, that conflict that you mentioned, between the international commitment to recognize the "one China" principle and the Taiwan Relations Act,[23] remains.

*Mr. Robinson*: I thought that the international law was fairly clear that a joint communiqué under those circumstances would be viewed as an international agreement for purposes of the Vienna Convention.[24] I also thought that the U.S. Supreme Court ruled very reluctantly, after many years of attempting to avoid the question, that if there was any conflict as between a statute and an international treaty, then the later in time would govern for domestic law purposes, even though it might violate the international obligations of the United States.

*Mr. Hansell*: I agree with both of those propositions. Although I think the communiqué[25] was a binding international agreement, as a domestic matter, there is no question that the Taiwan Relations Act[26] would govern. Internationally, as you say, the legal effect is a separate issue.

*Mr. Robinson*: I'd like to ask, Herb, whether you were aware that you left for one of your successors, that is, me, one of the single most pleasurable experiences in my four years, which was the fact that the recognition of the People's Republic of China failed to settle the prerevolutionary bond issues. So I ended up having to go to Beijing to explain the American legal system to the Chinese Government, because the first time that Secretary Shultz met with Deng Xiao Ping, there was the threat that a Chinese 747 aircraft was about to be attached at San Francisco Airport in satisfaction of the default that had been entered down in Alabama. Apparently Shultz met with him and I was told that Deng Xiao Ping became highly annoyed and said, "If one bit of our property is ever attached, there will be no more trade, no more investments." And Deng Xiao Ping added, "Why don't you just call that judge down in Alabama and tell him to lay off the People's Republic of China." And apparently Shultz replied, "Oh, we have the separation of powers, you have to understand." And Deng Xiao Ping said, "Well, what is the separation of powers?" Shulz answered, "I'll send my lawyer to explain it." So I thank you for that.

*Mr. Sofaer*: I thought it would be useful to mention one more thing. We have talked about the Egypt–Israel Peace Treaty,[27] which is probably one of the most important historical events of the last century. In that peace treaty negotiation, as I understand it, although it was an effort to settle everything, it became clear that they could not settle everything and they settled only the peace between Egypt and Israel and left the other issues involving the Palestinians and others to another day.

It might be an interesting exercise to compare that with Camp David II, where they went right down to the wire and refused to package what I, from the outside, saw as a vast array of issues on which they *had* reached agreement. Instead, they decided that they would roll the dice and try to get everything – and as a result they got nothing.

*Mr. Hansell*: Well, there were two frameworks, as I said, arising out of Camp David, the first for the peace between the two countries and the second for the package of additional issues that you were addressing. It was clear that they were to be separated.

*Mr. Sofaer*: But when Sadat went to Camp David, he swore he would not leave without having the Palestinian issue also settled.

*Mr. Hansell*: Obviously – and that was his problem. He was the pariah within the Arab world because he settled Egypt's peace but not any of the other issues.

# 5 The Carter Administration –
Roberts B. Owen (1979–1981)

WHEN HERB HANSELL LEFT THE DEPARTMENT IN 1979 and I stepped into his shoes, I spent the first week or two on the basics – learning what Secretary Vance and Deputy Secretary Christopher wanted from this 120-plus-person lawyer group, how the bureau was organized, how good or bad was the morale, how L's lawyers related to their clients in other bureaus of the Department, how L related to the General Counsel's offices of other departments, and, apart from general supervision, what were the particular issues to which I thought I could make a personal contribution.

## The Iranian Hostage Crisis

This short and relatively relaxed learning period came to an abrupt halt when suddenly, and completely unexpectedly, the United States was plunged into a major international crisis – not outright war, to be sure, but close to the precipice – when a mob of Iranian "revolutionary students" attacked and seized the U.S. Embassy in Tehran on November 4, 1979, and captured fifty-two members of the Embassy's diplomatic staff.[1]

Immediately, meetings were convened in the White House and the State Department to discuss how the United States should react. At first it was hoped that the new (post-Shah) Revolutionary Government of Iran would promptly step in and restore order, as in fact it had in a similar episode earlier in the same year, but very soon it became clear that the Ayatollah Khomeini government would not only not restrain the "students"; in fact, it quickly endorsed their conduct, thus committing the clearest possible breach of its international obligation, under the Vienna Conventions on Diplomatic and Consular Relations, to protect the Embassy and its personnel.[2]

We immediately began to consider lawful reprisals, of course, including the use of force, but there was a deep concern about taking any action that would cause the young and apparently impetuous captors to harm or kill the hostages. The focal issue quickly became how best to exert pressure on Iran to restore order without the United States either paying ransom (a potentially disastrous precedent) or increasing the hostages' danger. The aim was to convince Iran's leaders that their holding of the hostages would create, for Iran, costs that far exceeded any possible value to be gained from their unlawful conduct.[3]

Implementing this basic policy involved a huge amount of L's time – for example, working with Treasury and Justice to freeze Iranian assets in the United States and other parts of the world, devising trade and travel restrictions that would legitimately interrupt Iranian commerce, and assisting Justice in making sure that, as the U.S. courts faced massive numbers of new lawsuits brought by U.S. claimants against Iran, the courts would not act in such a way as to inflame the situation. We also worked with Justice and the private bar to set up teams of trial lawyers to appear in Iranian courts if Iran tried to put any hostages on trial. Importantly, great and very successful efforts were made to enlist nations throughout the world to support our entire hostage-release campaign. Needless to say, other governments were quick to realize how important it was to the entire international diplomatic world that hostage taking not be tolerated.

On a personal note, one time-consuming project flowed out of L's recommendation to the Secretary and the President that the United States bring the World Court into play. Within days after the Embassy seizure, we were authorized to ask the International Court of Justice (ICJ), first, to convene an immediate hearing on a request for an

emergency interim order calling on Iran to release the hostages forth-
with, and then, after full briefing and argument on the merits, to enter
a final judgment in our favor. Although it was generally recognized that
if the Court entered the contemplated interim order, it was unlikely that
Iran would obey, we nonetheless believed strongly, and correctly as it
turned out, that quick condemnatory action by the World Court would
help us mobilize world opinion against Iran's irresponsible actions. In
fact, shortly after the hostage taking, we made a quick personal call on
the President of the Court, and he summoned his fourteen colleagues for
an emergency hearing in record time. After listening to six hours of U.S.
argument, with hostile questioning from the Soviet and Syrian judges,
the Court on December 15 – setting another world speed record – issued
a unanimous interim order in our favor. As Abe Chayes later remarked,
this and the Court's favorable Final Judgment in 1980, constituted a new
high watermark for U.S. involvement with the ICJ.

In a moment I want to add a sort of technical footnote to the World
Court hostage-case story, but first I should say a word about L's involvement in the final solution to the hostage crisis. In October 1980, almost
a year after the Embassy seizure, Iran found itself at war with Saddam
Hussein's Iraq, and it desperately sought support from the international
community. Iran was quickly rebuffed, however, the general diplomatic
response being that so long as you defy the international community with
your illegal hostage taking, you will get no help from law-abiding countries. And that rebuff, I have always believed, marked the beginning of
the end of the crisis.[4] Shortly thereafter, Iran initiated negotiations, using
the Government of Algeria as an intermediary, and Warren Christopher
and I then spent several hectic weeks in Algiers negotiating what came
to be called the Algiers Accords under which Iran agreed not only to
release the fifty-two hostages but also to sponsor a claims mechanism –
the Iran–United States Claims Tribunal – allowing U.S. nationals with
valid claims against Iran to recover. While for its part the United States
agreed to unfreeze some (not all) of Iran's frozen assets, it is clear that,
taking into account the pay-back to U.S. claimants, Iran's hostage-taking

adventure brought with it not only international condemnation but a substantial financial outlay as well. Interestingly, right after the hostages' release on January 20, 1981 (just as Christopher and I were exiting the public service), some incoming Reagan Administration lawyers considered renouncing the Algiers Accords on the ground that perhaps they involved an illegal U.S. payment of ransom to Iran. As soon as they delved into the facts, however, they found – to our considerable satisfaction – that the United States had actually made money on the exchange, and the renouncement idea was quickly dropped.

Without wanting to appear too partisan, I am reminded of one other reaction of the new administration to the hostage situation. In April 1981 the new Secretary of State, Alexander Haig, convened a Departmental ceremony to honor both the now-freed hostages and a few individuals who had participated in the release process. With the former hostages the most important part of his audience, Haig's principal message of the day was that if the Reagan Administration had been in power during the hostages' captivity, it would have strictly adhered to the principle that one must never, never negotiate with terrorists because to do so will inevitably lead to concessions and encourage further terrorism. In other words, Haig was directly telling the former hostages, his new diplomatic colleagues, that if their release had not occurred on January 20, they would not be sitting here in the Department auditorium; they would still be languishing in captivity in Tehran. It was a strange message, particularly in view of the fact that the United States managed to avoid any substantial concessions during the release negotiations.

Our team was also pleased that throughout the crisis the United States had taken the high road and obeyed the law – which reminds me of an early-1980 episode when American patience with the stalemate was beginning to wear thin. In the middle of the night I got a call from a very prominent Washington lawyer who said, "I just don't understand you State Department people. Here is Iran holding our diplomats hostage, and at the same time, right there on Massachusetts Avenue, there is the Iranian Embassy purring along with its full diplomatic staff.

All you have to do, obviously, is send in the Marines, lock up the Iranian diplomats, and, boom, the crisis will be over. What is holding you back?" (There were those in the Administration who also shared such a view.) The short answer, of course, was that Secretary Vance was a good law-abiding lawyer who had concluded that Iran's wrongdoing would not justify wrongdoing by the United States. That effectively ended the debate. I might add that, in appearing before the World Court, we found it useful to point out that so long as diplomatic relations continued between the two countries, the United States did in fact protect the Iranian Embassy, and that when the United States then severed relations, we turned the Embassy over to a protecting power and let the Iranian diplomats go home, all in precise accordance with the rules.

Now, having touted our virtues, let me close by noting one criticism of our conduct that was voiced by the ICJ in its final opinion. I have long considered the criticism invalid, and this may be a good forum in which to answer the charge.

In April 1980, while our ICJ case was awaiting Final Judgment, President Carter concluded that our hostages remained in imminent danger and launched an ill-fated military rescue mission – à la the famous Israeli rescue raid at Entebbe.[5] Regrettably, the mission fell apart due to harsh desert weather and equipment malfunctions.[6] In any event, because the world, including the United States, had long regarded as lawful an Entebbe-type rescue effort to save the lives of endangered hostages,[7] it came as a surprise that, when the ICJ later handed down its Final Judgment against Iran (after another lengthy hearing), its opinion gratuitously included a reprimand to the effect that the U.S. rescue effort displayed disrespect for the Court's judicial process.[8]

The ICJ's theory, apparently was that, while such a hostage-rescue attempt might have been lawful before the United States filed its ICJ suit, once the case was pending the United States was legally obliged first, to assume that the Court's processes could and would protect U.S. interests *pendente lite* and second, not to indicate a lack of trust in or respect for the Court's processes – for example, by undertaking a unilateral hostage-rescue effort. Obviously this reasoning might make sense if the Court actually could have given the hostages protection from danger, but, of course, Iran, by simply ignoring the Court's interim order requiring immediate release, had already demonstrated irrefutably that the ICJ's interim judicial process was *not* protecting the hostages from the whims of their captors. (Obviously as a practical matter, for better or for worse, the ICJ does not have a force equivalent to U.S. Marshals to enforce its interim orders.) It has always been my view, therefore, that once the ICJ's impotence in the hostage context had been made clear by Iran's actions, leaving the hostages in continuing danger, the United States became entitled to assert its preexisting right to attempt to rescue its endangered nationals, whether the case remained pending or not.

Let me add as a final note that in my view, which was shared by such respected international legal scholars as Professors Oscar Schachter and Abram Chayes,[9] the ICJ's pronouncement about the U.S. hostage-rescue effort was and is potentially harmful to the Court's own role and jurisdiction. If other states, as potential ICJ litigants, were to focus on the fact that the filing of a case before the ICJ could inhibit their preexisting right to engage in otherwise lawful self-help measures, such states might well decide to avoid the Court entirely, thus reducing the role that the UN wants the Court to play. We may never know whether the Court's reprimand of the United States, in the hostages, case has had or will have such an effect.

### Discussion

*Mr. Matheson*: I think that you and Warren Christopher did a very good job of negotiating the Algiers Accords under very difficult circumstances. One aspect of your handiwork that all of us have had to deal with is, of course, the Iran–United States Claims Treaty.[10] I wondered if, on reflection, you have any thoughts about whether that treaty worked out as you expected or as you desired. As you know, it still exists in a semi-comatose form.

*Mr. Owen*: I may have made a number of errors in writing that document, but the clearest one was not writing in a provision for the tribunal to come to a halt at some appropriate time. We just assumed that the judges would appropriately bring their work to an end. They chose not to do so and it has turned into a freeloading operation.

*Prof. Scharf*: As a part of this, let me ask you, taking a lead from Mike Matheson's question, whether you, in your wildest dreams, thought, on January 20, 1981, that some twenty-five years later there still would be no diplomatic relations between Iran and the United States? Because I should think that, ultimately, when diplomatic relations are reestablished, the tribunal will finally terminate.

*Mr. Owen*: Things do have a way of dragging on in international law and diplomacy.

*Mr. Robinson*: Having thanked Herb for some of the residue that he left, I would like to thank you, also, for some interesting aspects of my work which followed yours. One was the turf fight with the Department of Justice as to which of us would represent the U.S. Government in the Iran–United States Claims Tribunal. This issue had to go to the President himself, and it was ruled in favor of the State Department about four or five days before 2,800 small claims were due in The Hague. Having won the fight, L had not only to prepare those 2,800 small claims, but also to have them translated into Farsi. I recall that the last airplane leaving for Amsterdam was a TWA flight out of New York, and we had an armored truck carrying all those 2,800 small claims to New York, and they held up the aircraft on the tarmac so that the truck was able to go up and enter the 2,800 small claims on time.

*Mr. Owen*: Regarding the "turf fight," I should tell you the story of when I was confronted with the problem of presenting the argument on preliminary measures in the International Court of Justice. The Registrar of the Court called me up and asked me how much time I thought I needed to make that presentation. I said, "Well, the facts are not in dispute; the law is not in dispute; everybody knows what the law is and Iran probably won't even show up, so I think thirty minutes would probably be enough." The Registrar fainted and said, "Oh, no! We were thinking in terms of six days of argument!"

So we negotiated it back to three mornings. At that point, Attorney General Benjamin Civiletti got wind of the fact that there was to be a major argument in The Hague and he called up the President and said, "I think it would be appropriate for the Attorney General to present the argument."

But then White House Counsel Lloyd Cutler weighed in and said, "No. It would be appropriate for the Attorney General to go and make twenty minutes of opening remarks to emphasize to the Court how important the case is to the United States; but the Legal Adviser should handle the other five hours and forty minutes of argument." That was the final arrangement.

*Mr. Robinson*: Well, all I can say is that following the mining of the Nicaragua harbors case,[11] the Department of Justice did not have the same level of interest in participating in presentations to international tribunals.

# 6 The Reagan Administration – Davis R. Robinson (1981–1985)

**I** WOULD LIKE TO FOCUS ON THREE TOPICS. THE FIRST RELATES to some personal perspectives on the role of lawyers in the formulation of American foreign policy. The second compares L's experience in connection with Grenada and Nicaragua, two instances involving United States use of force. And the third comments on L's experiences in U.S. international adjudication during my tenure. Of course, my term in office is now long ago, and there have been major changes in the world since then. The United States, for example, has gone from contending with one large elephant to dealing with 1,000 snakes.

The main lesson that I drew from my days in L is that, if the U.S. Government is to realize the full benefit of the potential contribution of its international lawyers, the lawyers need to participate from the beginning of a takeoff in policy and not just in a crash landing whenever things go wrong. This is especially so where the use of force by the United States is involved, and that applies in my judgment whether that use of force is overt or covert. In this connection, I will compare the overt Grenada "rescue mission" with the supposedly covert mining of the harbors in Nicaragua.

A lot of my days in L were devoted to U.S. participation in the peaceful settlement of disputes by international adjudication, and I will also comment on that subject. My watch included the establishment of the Iran–United States Claims Tribunal,[1] the hearing of the Gulf of

Maine maritime boundary delimitation case before the first Chamber of the International Court of Justice,[2] and the jurisdictional phase of the Nicaragua case before the International Court of Justice (ICJ).

First, I would like to share some personal perspectives on the Office of the Legal Adviser.[3] The role of the Legal Adviser's Office is not an easy one because, first of all, it is responsible for assuring compliance with many of the increasingly complex U.S. statutes and regulations that deal with foreign affairs. The Office is also responsible for overseeing compliance of the United States with many of the international treaties to which the United States is a party. In my day, as I recall, there were about 10,000 of these, including what in the United States are referred to as executive agreements.

A further task of the Office of the Legal Adviser is to uphold the dictates of customary international law,[4] a demanding chore because of the ongoing debate in the U.S. Government and in the international law community as to exactly what is encompassed in that rather amorphous body of law and, furthermore, as to whether customary international law is binding on the President of the United States as a matter of domestic Constitutional law[5] – that is, whether the President is theoretically subject to impeachment if the tenets of customary international law are violated.[6]

When I assumed office, I knew from my personal experience as a former Foreign Service Officer, including from my tour as an Attorney-Adviser in the Office of the General Counsel of the United States Arms Control and Disarmament Agency, that some policymakers will on occasion assume the following attitude: "Oh, let's not involve the lawyers. First, they are likely to say no. Second, they will take forever – they are so slow. And, if you're not careful, once they get involved, they will run away with your store." All of this I would argue is not the case so long as the attorneys are brought into a matter from the start.

In the Department of State, there are traditionally varying degrees of status among the Assistant Secretary level of Presidential appointees.

The regional Assistant Secretaries, for example, are always the "Cinderellas," because they are usually invited to every ball. They normally receive every report and every cable that applies to their respective regions and they are invited to every relevant meeting with the Secretary or the Deputy Secretary. The functional Assistant Secretaries of the Department of State, however, are often the "ugly sisters," who have to struggle for inclusion. The lawyers, being lawyers, are sometimes perceived as the ugliest of all and, therefore, need the support of the incumbent Secretary in assuring that they are always appropriately involved, and, most importantly, are engaged early in the policy process rather than late. In order to fulfill its important mission, the Office of the Legal Adviser must, in sum, both in reality and in appearance, constitute a constructive force in assisting the decision makers in the Department of State.

Separate from the issue of L's position within the Department of State is the role of L in the U.S. Government as a whole. L is generally the repository of the ultimate knowledge and expertise within the U.S. Government with regard to the many international agreements to which the United States is a party as well as with regard to customary international law. But the Office of Legal Counsel in the Justice Department sometimes seeks to claim a piece of this role even though its purview is generally supposed to pertain to U.S. statutory and Constitutional interpretation and not to treaty interpretation. A major episode during my watch was an all-out effort by the Department of Justice to gain control over U.S. representation before the Iran–United States Claims Tribunal in The Hague. Turf issues within the U.S. Government are often serious and difficult, and this one certainly fit the bill. Ultimately, the President himself had to confirm State's historic role where international tribunals are concerned. He ruled, within days of the Tribunal's opening for business, that State would, as had traditionally been the case, take the lead.

During my tenure, although there were Interagency Groups of many kinds on many subjects in the field of national security, there was no

General Counsel's Interagency Group. As a result, the General Counsels of State, Defense, and CIA were sometimes not fully informed as to what each of them was doing that had importance for the other two. This lack of coordination in my opinion had serious consequences, for example, for the Intelligence Oversight Act,[7] which required the Legal Adviser to the Department of State, the General Counsel of the Department of Defense, and the General Counsel of the CIA to certify that nothing had come to their attention that gave any of them reason to believe that international law had been violated in the preceding calendar quarter. Lack of knowledge and information often made that certification worrisome. Because of the need to certify, I perceived that there was a disincentive to keep the lawyers from other agencies in the loop.

## Grenada Contrasted with Nicaragua

In the case of Grenada,[8] I and one other lawyer in the Office of the Legal Adviser were informed in advance of the commencement of the "rescue mission."[9] We were given approximately seventy-two hours to make a thorough review of applicable international law and to develop the best argumentation in support of the action. The facts of the Grenada case presented an unprecedented circumstance. The Head of State had been murdered and the acting successor (the Granadian-born British Governor General) was under house arrest. In our legal justification for the "rescue mission," we consciously avoided argument that might imply any weakening in the legal restraints that apply to the use of force for fear of any American-implied acceptance of the Brezhnev doctrine.[10] For example, we did not claim that we were exercising an inherent right of self-defense under the United Nations Charter.[11] Furthermore, we did not assert any broad doctrine of humanitarian intervention. Rather, we built our legal argumentation upon three well-established principles that together we believed supported this military action. The first of the three pillars involved a telephone invitation to the United States to intercede that came from the Governor General as the then lawful authority on the island even though he was under house arrest. The second pillar involved a request from the Organization of Eastern Caribbean States, a regional organization that we regarded as having the competence to ask for assistance in the maintenance of peace and security in Grenada. And the third pillar in our legal justification for the "rescue mission" was the right of the United States in these particular circumstances to protect the safety of U.S. nationals residing on the island. We relied not solely on any one of these three pillars but rather on the combination of all of them.

An hour or so after the President made an early morning television announcement of the "rescue mission" in Grenada, I found myself in the White House Situation Room. A telephone call shortly arrived from Senator Howard Baker, who at the time was in the Senate Chamber. He told the person who answered something along the following lines: "Senator Patrick Moynihan is speaking on the floor and he's up in arms about the rescue mission. He is arguing that the mission is illegal because he sees it as in violation of the Rio Treaty,[12] the Charter of the Organization of the American States,[13] and the Charter of the United Nations.[14] What is the Administration's legal position?" The person on the line then said something like: "Oh, we will give you Robinson, the Legal Adviser to the Department of State; he has the answer." Because we were prepared in advance, I was, then and there, able to provide the Senator with the Administration's legal justification for the rescue mission. I was not in the least embarrassed by the merit or quality of that argument. In fact, I used to quip with one of my predecessors (who was also one of my professors at Harvard Law School), Abram Chayes, who wrote critical legal op-ed articles about Grenada and other actions of the Reagan Administration. I said, "Abe, on a scale of one to ten, I think that our three-prong argument in the Grenada case was a ten compared to your ex post facto 'quarantine' argument in the Cuban missile crisis." Reasonable people can, of course, differ about the merits of any United States use of force, but, regardless of that fact of life, being in on the takeoff, I would argue, greatly improved the legal position of the United States with the American public and with the world community.

In the case of the mining of the harbors of Nicaragua,[15] the opposite transpired. The Legal Adviser's Office had no advance notice of that action. Certainly, Director William Casey of the CIA did not, through the inter-Agency process, ask for L's opinion. Here, this supposedly covert intelligence operation quickly became open and notorious, splashed across the headlines of newspapers around the globe. As is all too well-known, covert operations can run awry and, therefore, it makes good sense to have the legal justification of any such action prepared well in advance. I would argue strongly that if L had been involved in the takeoff in the case of the mining of the harbors of Managua, we could have provided constructive advice as I believe L did in the earlier Grenada situation. The input of L would, I believe, have added a significant dimension to the decision-making process and also improved the implementation of the President's ultimate decision. However, as it transpired, instead of being ready for the firestorm that followed the public disclosure of the mining of the harbors, the Administration was legally caught off guard. Thus, all that the lawyers could contribute was assistance in after-the-fact containment of a train wreck. I remember one Secretary of State under whom I served stating: "I have only one rigid rule and that is, don't ever let me be blind sided." I can only have wished that this sensible rule had applied to L as well.

### The Peaceful Resolution of Disputes by International Adjudication

On the subject of the peaceful settlement of international controversies by adjudication, I believe that the Iran–United States Claims Tribunal effort has demonstrated both significant creativity and substantial success. The Tribunal's precedents have made major contributions to the international law of expropriation and breach of contract.[16] Likewise, the *Gulf of Maine* adjudication in the ICJ[17] brought to rest a long-standing thorn in the sides of two exceptionally close neighbors.

This latter case revolved around the depiction of a maritime boundary that would separate the fishery zones and the continental shelf areas

of the United States and Canada in the North Atlantic. The focus of
the dispute was Georges Bank, one of the great fishing grounds in the
region. The controversy had been on the agenda of nearly every meeting
between the President of the United States and the Premier of Canada
since the end of the World War II. Politicians had tried for years and
years to negotiate a solution to the problem. When the fisheries agreement negotiated during the Carter Administration proved to be unsatis-
factory to the New England fishermen, the political powers in both countries, after a lot of to-ing and fro-ing, decided to throw the matter into the
laps of the lawyers. Consequently, the *Gulf of Maine* case was submitted
to the first special Chamber of the ICJ. The result, which I would argue
was more advantageous to the New England fishermen than the earlier
discarded fisheries agreement, split the difference in a way that the politicians had been unable to bring about after years of trying. I remember
well one of the judges from the Chamber, during a reception that took
place after it had rendered its decision, calling me aside and announcing: "Now, my dear Robinson, you must not be upset by the award. I
had only one objective, and that was equal disappointment for both the
United States and Canada." While one would have hoped for proper
application of the law to the facts as the primary goal, the decision in
*Gulf of Maine* did politically solve the greater part of the problem.

In comparison to the positive attributes of the *Gulf of Maine* case and
the Iran–United States Claims Tribunal, the case that Nicaragua brought
before the ICJ against the United States proved the most disillusioning
experience of my life. In this matter, we State Department lawyers were
on a very short leash, which was not the case in *Gulf of Maine* where
L was simply told, with proper consultation and reporting, to resolve
the matter in the best interests of the United States. In the *Nicaragua*
case,[18] we were not allowed to make certain arguments that we as attorneys found persuasive. Some political forces in Washington argued that
the United States should not have shown up in The Hague at all, even
though that was contrary to the history of a nation known for its preem-
inent support of the Rule of Law and even though jurisdiction issues are

commonly litigated in U.S. courts. In finding jurisdiction to hear the case, the World Court overlooked both fact and legal precedent.[19] The President and Registrar of the Court paid scant attention to the United States' distinguished judge, Stephen Schwebel, who, we know from his writings, asked for access to the files of the Court with respect to the acceptance or nonacceptance in Nicaragua of its compulsory jurisdiction. He was not allowed that privilege whereas, from the opinion of the Court, one can surmise that the President of the World Court was given access to all of these records. The lawyer in charge of the Nicaragua case has since admitted in a remarkable article that a Judge of the Court was in communication with Nicaragua before its application was submitted. After the fact, events have confirmed, as we then believed, that Nicaragua's application was based on a fraudulent affidavit. The whole affair, to say the least, has proved most disquieting.

In conclusion, if the appropriate lawyers of the U.S. Government had been fully engaged in advance, taking into account security and secrecy concerns, then I believe that we could have done, with respect to the mining of the harbors of Nicaragua, what we did in the case of the Grenada rescue mission.

### Discussion

*Question*: Can you to specify what L could have done to avoid the adverse ICJ ruling?

*Mr. Robinson*: I think that, once we were in the World Court after the event had occurred, the result would have been the same no matter what arguments the United States had then made because of the bias of the majority of the members of the Court. But had we lawyers in L been informed in advance of the planned mining of the harbors of Nicaragua, and had we been in a position to show that the Soviets were sending weapons into Cuba, which were then transshipped to Managua and, thereafter, through the Sandinistas, were forwarded to the El Salvadorian insurgents, we then would have found ourselves making, in my view, a meritorious argument that the mining was in the exercise of self-defense. I personally believe that, with such factual support, we could have constructed a rationale that would have been legitimate. In sum, if all of the brain power in the Government's international law community had been called upon in advance, this entire episode would have ended up much, much better than it did.

*Mr. Williamson*: A very strong argument was made to me that we ought to reopen the *Nicaragua* case and raise some issues of fraud and questions about the evidence that was presented. But I just did not quite see how I could do that, since we had pulled out from the merits phase of the case. I was sure that we would be told that, if we had stayed in the case, we could have made those arguments.

*Mr. Robinson*: The affidavit from the Foreign Minister of Nicaragua that was the basis of the case, and that accompanied Nicaragua's application, was, in my opinion, a fraud, as I have earlier indicated. He affirmed, as I recall, that the Nicaraguans were not providing any kind of weapons assistance to the El Salvador insurgents. We know now, as we believed then, that that assertion was simply not true. After the fall of the Ortega Government, former Sandinistas testified about what in fact had taken place. I believe that one of the main lessons of the mining of the harbors case is that the United States should have amended its acceptance of the compulsory jurisdiction of the Court a long time before and not exposed itself to the risk of a prejudiced full Court.

*Mr. Williamson*: This whole question of what one does about the ICJ is an important one. Many of their current decisions, like the recent *Mexican Avena* case,[20] create problems when the decisions concern anything to do with national security or the use of force. It is a dangerous institution.

*Mr. Robinson*: I think that, if the U.S. Government were willing to devote the resources and the time, the United States and other like-minded nations could institute rules of conduct for the ICJ judges that go way beyond those that are currently in effect. We should not, for example, have former judges representing parties before the World Court, and there should be strict qualification standards for election to the Court.

*Mr. Williamson*: Here's another slight change of subject. On the Grenada issue, why didn't we argue protection of the U.S. nationals with essentially an Article 51 self-defense argument?

*Mr. Robinson*: We did not want to make that argument for fear of undercutting Article 2(4) of the United Nations Charter. The so-called Brezhnev Doctrine of the Soviet Union[21] was in vogue with the Russians at that time, and we were very concerned that, if we relied solely upon the potential harm to U.S. nationals, we would have undercut the restrictions of Article 2(4) and might be seen as somehow endorsing or replicating the Brezhnev Doctrine. Now, of course, the United States got out of Grenada very quickly, I think after just about one month. And, as you will recall from my earlier comments, our legal argument consisted of three pillars. We decided that we would rely on the combination of the three pillars rather than just on any one pillar.

*Mr. Matheson*: I think that the Grenada episode was similar in many ways to the use of force in Panama and Kosovo in that there were a number of factors that seem to give credibility to our desire to intervene, although no one factor by itself formed an independently adequate legal basis, so we chose to take several factors in combination and argue that, with this unique combination of circumstances, intervention was justifiable.[22]

*Mr. Sofaer*: And there's nothing wrong with that because this is really the approach that I think governments have always adhered to as I will describe in my remarks.

# 7 The Reagan and Bush Administrations – Abraham D. Sofaer (1985–1990)

**M**Y FIVE YEARS AS LEGAL ADVISER TO THE U.S. DEPART-
ment of State fell within two Administrations: that of
Ronald Reagan, under Secretary of State George P.
Shultz (1985–1988) and that of George H. W. Bush, under Secretary
of State James Baker (1989–1990). When my service began, the Cold
War was still intense, and fundamentalist terror had begun in earnest.
Iran had released U.S. hostages, but its allies in Lebanon had seized oth-
ers, and its conflict with Iraq destabilized conditions in the Persian Gulf.
Dealing with these and other challenges was made more complex, more-
over, because, in his second term, President Reagan faced a Democratic
Congress that resisted many of his policies.

The highlights of my activities can be divided into four general areas:
first, the settlement or adjudication of ad hoc international problems and
controversies; second, issues concerning the then-critical and conclusive
confrontation with the Soviet Union; third, participating in the shifting
and insufficient U.S. response to terrorism, in particular the fundamentalist terrorism with which the world is now painfully familiar; and fourth,
growing out of these efforts, the development and articulation of the U.S.
position on the use of force under the UN Charter.

## Withdrawal from the ICJ's Compulsory Jurisdiction

My first, and one of my most controversial decisions, was to recommend that the President terminate the U.S. submission to the mandatory

jurisdiction of the International Court of Justice (ICJ). This issue arose when the one-year suspension the United States had declared on our submission came to an end soon after I joined the State Department. By then, the ICJ had refused to allow El Salvador to intervene in the case brought by Nicaragua against the United States, despite El Salvador's position that the United States had come to its defense against the Sandinistas' cross-border infiltrations aimed at bringing down El Salvador's democratically elected government. This ICJ decision led the United States to withdraw from that case. It had long been clear, however, that the U.S. submission, due to its reservations, subjected the United States to suit in the ICJ by other States but enabled any State that the United States sued to secure dismissal based on reciprocal rights. Secretary Shultz and President Reagan accepted my recommendation, and the United States gave notice of its intent to terminate its submission to the ICJ's mandatory jurisdiction on October 7, 1985.[1]

Critics of this action argued that, despite the disadvantages incurred by its submission, the United States should have allowed itself to continue to be vulnerable to suit while having no ability to ensure a successful suit against other States in order to set a good example to the rest of the world. This argument gave little if any weight to the interests of the United States, which I believe lawyers serving the United States should protect. Maintaining the U.S. submission was also likely to preclude any chance of adopting a substitute submission that provided reciprocal rights. Furthermore, the United States viewed the ICJ's decision in the *Nicaragua* case as an unjustifiable assertion of jurisdiction over a highly charged, political matter, and one that improperly purported to narrow the "inherent" right of States to engage in individual and collective self-defense.

Nevertheless, the United States remained committed to utilizing international litigation to resolve disputes on the basis of the consent of States, truly given, including litigation in the ICJ. We demonstrated this commitment during my tenure by submitting an investment dispute with Italy to a panel of the ICJ[2]; by resurrecting the Permanent Court of Arbitration (PCA) as a forum for adjudicating international disputes in agreeing with Britain to submit a dispute to the PCA over the fees charged U.S. airlines at Heathrow Airport[3]; by appearing in the ICJ in an advisory opinion case involving the authority of UN committees[4]; and by fashioning and submitting to the other four permanent members of the Security Council a proposed treaty for a new mandatory regime for the ICJ, which we believed would greatly enhance the Court's role.[5]

## Negotiating the Settlement of Disputes

Among the disputes I was privileged to settle on behalf of the United States was the claim of Egypt to the beach resort of Taba and other border areas between Sinai and Israel. After three years of negotiation, and with the help in particular of Deputy Legal Adviser Alan Kreczko, the parties developed a *compromis* pursuant to which they submitted the border issue to an ad hoc international tribunal. The tribunal's decision in Egypt's favor was implemented, however, only after they separately agreed on several political issues concerning the areas in dispute, which required two additional years to resolve. The final agreement represented the last step in implementing the Egyptian–Israeli peace treaty. We simultaneously settled the claims against Egypt for the murders by a crazed Egyptian border guard near the Sinai beach area of Ras Burqa of seven Israelis, one of whom was also an American. We supported Egypt's desire to submit the compensation requests to judicial determination in accordance with Egyptian law, even though we knew the amounts awarded, although reasonable under Egyptian standards, would be insufficient to meet international standards; we found private individuals, Jewish and Muslim, to make up the difference between the Egyptian awards and the amounts sought. Ambassador Frank Wisner provided crucial assistance and guidance.

Another dispute I was able to settle was for claims against Chile for killing the former Chilean Ambassador to the United States, Orlando Letelier and his American assistant Ronni Moffit, in a bombing on

September 21, 1976, near Dupont Circle, in the heart of the U.S. capital. We negotiated a settlement of the civil claims for damages acceptable to the Pinochet regime and the claimant families. Chile was unprepared to concede responsibility, so we agreed on a payment *ex gratia*, that is, without conceding legal responsibility, as is often done in such cases. Chile was also unwilling to agree to submit the determination of damages to any U.S. tribunal, and Principal Deputy Legal Adviser Mike Kozak came up with the idea of relying on the arbitration clause of the Bryan-Suarez Treaty,[6] to which Chile agreed.

On May 17, 1987, Iraq accidentally fired two Exocet missiles at an American frigate, the USS *Stark*, killing thirty-seven sailors, injuring many others, and almost sinking the ship. In early 1990, not long before Saddam's invasion of Kuwait, we were able to convince Iraq to pay, *ex gratia*, more than $1 million to the families of each seaman who lost his life and to pay some $65 million to repair the ship.

As Agent for the United States, I argued against Iran's effort to secure the return of a submarine it had purchased from the United States, but which was undergoing repairs when the hostage crisis began. At that time, we were attacking Iran's naval vessels for mining shipping lanes in the Persian Gulf. We were not about to provide Iran with a submarine it could use to sink U.S. or other vessels. The Tribunal rejected Iran's request for return of the submarine and ordered the United States to pay its value. We convinced Secretary Shultz and President Reagan to reject efforts to refuse to make payments to Iran for judgments issued by the Iran–United States Claims Tribunal in The Hague. We managed to settle most of the intergovernmental claims pending at the time, including the many thousands of "small" (under $250,000) claims, a settlement that was upheld in the case of *Abrahim-Youri v. United States*, 139 F.3d 1462 (1998).

On July 3, 1988, the cruiser USS *Vincennes*, while on patrol in the Straits of Hormuz Gulf, mistakenly shot down Iran Air Flight 655, killing all 290 on board. President Bush apologized for this tragedy and agreed to pay compensation to the victims' families. My Iranian counterpart and

I agreed on the amounts to be paid, and Iran eventually accepted that the payments would be made directly to the families through the Red Crescent Society. The United States later agreed to transfer a substitute airplane of equivalent value as compensation for the plane.

## Confronting the Soviet Union

One of the two major themes of my service was the Reagan Administration's effort to confront and ultimately defeat the Soviet Union (characterized by Reagan as the "Evil Empire"). The Cold War had been going on for many years when Ronald Reagan became President; confronting the Soviet Union began with Harry Truman and was a bipartisan policy. But President Carter's responses to the invasion of Afghanistan (one of which was the U.S. boycott of the 1980 Moscow Olympics), and to the seizure of U.S. diplomats in Iran (he promised not to use force and later used it ineffectually) were viewed by many Americans as inadequate and likely to encourage our enemies. The Soviets, by contrast, robustly implemented the Brezhnev Doctrine during the 1970s and into the 1980s, pursuing a policy of active military intervention abroad and seeking to overthrow democratic regimes by supporting violent revolutionary movements sympathetic to socialist ideology.

Upon assuming office, President Reagan announced his own doctrine, declaring that the United States would oppose Soviet efforts to overthrow nonsocialist regimes by assisting them in fighting Soviet-sponsored insurgencies. Pursuant to the Reagan Doctrine, the United States challenged the Soviets in several theaters.[7] In addition, the United States built up its armed forces and military capacities, and diplomatically pressured the Soviets to adopt more humane policies with regard to the civil and political rights of persons under their control. The military confrontations began with the U.S. intervention in Grenada, prior to my tenure. Some international law scholars equated that brief and virtually bloodless restoration of freedom with the ruthless and devastating Soviet invasion and occupation of Afghanistan. Other conflicts extended into

my tenure, including efforts to undermine Soviet influence and involvement in Africa, Central America, and Central Asia. In Afghanistan, we
joined forces with Afghanis and several Muslim States, eventually driv-
ing the Soviets out of the country, and reducing their appetite for future
implementation of the Brezhnev Doctrine.

## Central America

The most controversial uses of force during the Reagan Administration
were aimed at countering insurgencies intended to undermine democratically elected regimes in El Salvador, Honduras, and potentially throughout Central America. These insurgencies were supported by the Sandinista regime in Nicaragua, which was funded and armed by Cuba and the
Soviet Union. Congressional policies fluctuated wildly, especially with
regard to the controversial policy of providing military ("lethal") support for the Contras, who were attempting to undermine the Sandinista
regime.

The Legal Adviser's Office supported the Reagan Administration's
positions at the ICJ, in the UN, and before Congress, and attempted
to ensure that legislative directions were obeyed. Unfortunately, officials within the Administration kept the Office uninformed with regard
to several efforts that violated United States and/or international law.
Had we been involved, we could have altered or prevented those actions,
most notably the Iran-Contra affair, which contributed nothing positive
in confronting Communist subversion.

## Anti-Ballistic Missile Defense

A central aspect of President Reagan's response to Soviet aggression was
his rejection of the policy of mutually assured destruction (MAD), incorporated in the ABM Treaty.[8] At a 1986 United States–Soviet summit in
Reykjavik, Iceland, President Reagan announced that he was prepared
to share the ABM defenses he wished to develop, test, and deploy, in

exchange for complete nuclear disarmament. ABM systems would be developed, shared, and retained by both Superpowers, as a hedge against cheating. The Soviets rejected this proposal.[9]

The President proceeded to pursue his goal of missile defense (derisively called "Star Wars" by the Administration's opponents). The program was ambitious and based on a wide range of unproved technologies. Disputes generated from both outside and inside the Administration raged about the program. Progress depended in part on the extent to which the ABM Treaty limited development, testing, and deployment of ABM systems and components based on "physical principles" other than those on which the systems described in the Treaty were based (commonly referred to as the "other physical principles" or OPP). Secretary Shultz asked me to examine the Treaty and its negotiating record to determine the latitude it allowed the United States in implementing the Administration's proposed program. The United States had the power to terminate on six months notice; but what could the United States do without terminating?

I worked on the project for several months, in close cooperation with Ambassador Paul Nitze, a key negotiator of the ABM Treaty and serving at the time as Special Advisor to the President on Arms Control. We concluded that the Treaty was ambiguous with regard to its regulation of OPP systems and components, and that the negotiating record supported the view that, although the parties agreed not to deploy OPP systems or components without each other's consent, the Soviets refused to agree to refrain from development and testing of such systems or components.[10] When this conclusion was announced, it set off a storm of protest from the arms control community, many of whom regarded the ABM Treaty as the cornerstone of strategic stability in the Cold War.

Thereafter, I was asked to review the record of the treaty's submission to the Senate to determine whether the President was bound by that record to adhere to the interpretation that prevented testing and development of OPP systems or components. I concluded that, although the Carter Administration had presented the treaty to the Senate for its advice and consent based in part on the narrower interpretation of what could be undertaken with regard to OPP systems and components, this presentation was insufficient to alter the underlying scope of the agreement with the Soviets, or to bind the President as a matter of domestic law.[11] In my view, if we were correct that the Soviets were not bound by the narrower interpretation of the treaty, the United States could not be bound as a matter of reciprocity. This conclusion was attacked even more vigorously than our interpretation of the meaning of the treaty, as it was seen to represent a challenge to the powers of the Senate.

Although Ambassador Nitze and I both concluded that the President had the power to implement a new interpretation of the ABM Treaty, we also agreed that for him to do so without the Senate's consent would be unwise and ineffective. We privately recommended that the President adhere to the narrower interpretation of the treaty until the Senate agreed to support implementation of the new interpretation. We did not include this advice in the written opinion on the treaty, because we believed it would effectively preclude the President from using the authority we believed he possessed. Our views were firmly conveyed, however, and were firmly rejected.

Instead, the Administration attempted unilaterally to implement the new interpretation, despite the mixed record of how the treaty was presented to the Senate, and despite the political reality that both the Senate and House were at the time controlled by the Democratic Party. This policy was futile and alienated several key senators who might have been willing to consider the merits of the broader interpretation had the President agreed to implement it only after securing Congress' support. In the long run, the failure of the branches to agree on a more flexible policy regarding the development and testing of OPP systems and components led – as the Soviets had predicted it would – to the treaty's termination due to its lack of flexibility in the face of materially changed strategic realities.

The Reagan Administration's strategy with regard to the Soviet Union had more to it than confrontation. When Mikhail Gorbachev became Soviet General Secretary in 1987, and Eduard Shevardnadze his Foreign Minister, President Reagan – at the recommendation of Secretary Shultz – worked to develop a negotiating framework in which the leaders of the two Superpowers could cooperate with one another without public exploitation of such moves for political purposes. Several crises between the United States and Soviet Union were successfully resolved through such quiet diplomacy, enabling the United States to have far greater impact on Soviet policies than confrontation alone would have made possible. I played a role in some of these cooperative efforts.

## The Daniloff Affair

On August 23, 1986, the FBI carried out a "sting" operation against a Soviet official in New York who lacked diplomatic immunity named Gennady Zakharov. Zakharov had accepted information marked "classified" from an FBI informant. In a typical Cold War response, the Soviets were able to get Nicholas Daniloff, a U.S. reporter for *Newsweek*, to accept materials with "classified" markings from a KGB informant. Daniloff had been urged by a U.S. intelligence official in Moscow to respond to a contact from a prior source of information, in the hope that contact with that source could be reestablished. He agreed to this limited role, but due to the carelessness of the U.S. official the Soviets were able to entrap him by providing him with papers with classified markings, the same ploy used to trap Zakharov. The Soviets arrested Daniloff and charged him with espionage.

President Reagan's initial response to this crisis was to insist that Daniloff be released. The Soviets knew Daniloff was innocent of spying, Reagan stated, whereas Zakharov was a professional diplomat who knew precisely what he was doing. Former Secretary of State Cyrus Vance, acting as attorney for *Newsweek*, provided me with the information that Daniloff had received from the Soviets and the history of the case. He urged me to help save Daniloff from years of incarceration based on Cold War tit-for-tat behavior. I read the papers and advised Secretary Shultz that, however unfair the Soviet treatment of Daniloff, the record of the case against him would be sufficient, based on my prior experience as a federal prosecutor and trial judge, to convict him of espionage if he were tried in a U.S. court.

Shultz took me to the President to explain this position. The President initially resisted my analysis on the ground that the Soviets knew better. He was shaken, though, by the realization that Daniloff could spend most if not all the rest of his life in jail, due to unwise and poorly executed U.S. intelligence operations. Secretary Shultz authorized me to communicate my views and the evidence to the Justice Department for its own appraisal. Associate Attorney General Stephen Trott, now a Judge on the Ninth Circuit Court of Appeals, confirmed that Daniloff would indeed be convicted in a U.S. court, based on the evidence the Soviets had developed against him. That opinion convinced the President to allow us to negotiate an exchange in which both Zakharov and Daniloff pleaded *nolo contendere* to espionage charges and were released.

This negotiation was important, not only because it erased a potentially disruptive element in United States–Soviet relations, but also because it enabled Secretary Shultz to develop some trust in his relationship with Foreign Minister Shevardnadze. To protect this relationship, Shultz publicly treated the releases of Zakharov and Daniloff as a one-for-one trade; privately, however, he successfully insisted that the Soviets also release several prominent figures as part of the bargain, including Elena Bonner, wife of Soviet dissident Andrei Sakharov.[12] My Special Assistant, Elizabeth Keefer, provided invaluable assistance in implementing the legal aspects of this complicated negotiation; Assistant Secretary Roz Ridgway led the European Bureau team in crafting the diplomatic measures necessary to implement the deal.

## Terrorism

Terrorism was a formidable problem by the time I joined the government in 1985. The vast majority of States had ratified the Montreal Convention and other multilateral treaties making attacks on civilian aircraft and some other forms of terrorism illegal. But hijackings and other forms of attack continued nonetheless. Terrorists received significant diplomatic and practical support from many States that insisted that all measures must be considered permissible in combating the denial of what was characterized, for example, as "the most elementary human rights, dignity, freedom and independence."[13]

Lebanon had become a nightmare for its citizens and for the world; the U.S. Embassy there was bombed on April 18, 1983, killing sixty-six, including seventeen Americans. The United States sent Marines into Lebanon to provide security, but more bombings occurred, including the destruction of the Marine barracks on October 23, 1983, killing 241 U.S. servicemen. Other bombings that year killed fifty-eight French troops, and twenty-nine Israelis. President Reagan said the United States would not be driven out of Lebanon by these terrorist attacks, but after several ineffectual bombardments of terrorist camps, the United States withdrew.

Fundamental differences in how to deal with terrorism developed within the Administration. Between April and June 1984, Secretary Shultz made three speeches advocating an "active defense" intended to prevent and preempt terrorist attacks. Others in the Administration opposed this view, arguing that force should be used only when a series of prerequisites had been met. All emphatically agreed, however, that no concessions should be made to terrorists. President Reagan accepted the Algiers Accords by which Iran was given back most of its frozen funds in return for the release of U.S. hostages, among other things. But this was done with a sense of regret, purportedly in light of the prior Administration having negotiated and signed the agreements. The record of activity on these issues during my tenure included several resolute actions;

the program was undercut, however, by actions that violated or reversed declared policies.

## TWA Flight 847

On June 14, 1985, only four days after I was sworn in as Legal Adviser, Palestinian terrorists hijacked TWA Flight 847. They boarded the plane in Athens, where security was inadequate. Greece immediately violated the Montreal Convention on aircraft hijacking by releasing one of the terrorists arrested at the airport in exchange for the release of three Greek citizens. The plane ended up on the ground at the Beirut Airport, where the hijackers tortured and killed a young Navy diver, Robert Stetham, and threw his body to the tarmac.

The Office was asked to provide legal options to secure the release of the hostages. The Lebanese Government was unwilling to act against the terrorists. This made the United States free, in my view, to use force to liberate the hostages or to attack the perpetrators. The costs of pursuing either of these options would, however, have been prohibitive, with little or no chance of success. Efforts therefore focused on attempting to reach a negotiated settlement.

The hijackers made several unacceptable demands, including release of the so-called al-Dawa prisoners, a group of seventeen terrorists held in Kuwait for the bombing of the U.S. and French Embassies in Kuwait City, killing six and injuring more than eighty. One demand the hijackers made, however, was consistent with established U.S. policy: that individuals taken from Lebanon to Israel as prisoners during Israel's intervention in that country be repatriated. The State Department had repeatedly announced that removal of these individuals from Lebanon violated the applicable provisions of the Geneva Convention. I brought this fact to the attention of Secretary Shultz, arguing that we should not change our position on the propriety of returning these individuals, merely because the terrorists had seized hostages in an effort to bring about that result, among several other inappropriate ones. I proposed that we could responsibly state that, if the terrorists released the hostages, we would adhere to our previously stated position and do everything possible to secure the return to Lebanon of those prisoners held in Israel.

My position was rejected at the State Department, but the President quietly made this offer to President Assad of Syria. The Government of Israel agreed to cooperate, and a deal was brokered on this basis that led to the release of the passengers and crew. This was an appropriate arrangement, consistent with U.S. policy; but the fact that it was done secretly may have led some in the White House to think that other, indefensible deals could be made with terrorists, so long as they were kept secret.

### Seizure of the *Achille Lauro*

A major terrorist incident occurred when a group of PLO thugs seized the Italian cruise liner *Achille Lauro* in the Mediterranean. It was scheduled to visit the Israeli port of Haifa, and the terrorists planned to attack Israeli citizens on the beaches and in the port. They were discovered during the voyage, however, and took control of the ship, herding the passengers into custody and taking away their valuables. One passenger, an elderly handicapped Jewish man named Leon Klinghoffer, resisted and, at one point, bit the hand of a terrorist who was mistreating him. The terrorists pulled Klinghoffer out of his wheelchair, shot him in the back, and threw him into the sea.

Two major legal issues arose. First, the mastermind of the operation, Abu Abbas, came to Egypt from Tunis and negotiated a deal whereby the ship was brought to Alexandria and turned over to Egyptian authorities. In exchange, the terrorists were allowed to leave Egypt with Abbas in a military plane for sanctuary in Tunis. We identified the plane and launched fighters from an aircraft carrier to intercept it. Undersecretary Michael Armacost called me up to his office, where he was following the interception in real time. He asked me, as our fighters closed on the Egyptian aircraft, whether we could legally attempt to force it down.

I told him the situation seemed analogous to stopping a getaway car after a bank robbery. The plane was not a civilian airliner and was in international airspace. Egypt was a friendly power and had made its bargain with the terrorists in good faith to avoid further deaths or injuries. But Egypt had not asked us to agree to respect the deal they had made to allow the murderers of an American to escape without prosecution.

The President authorized that the plane be ordered to land, but he did not authorize the use of force in the event it did not comply. The plane did agree to land as directed, but the only place we could find for such a landing was a NATO base in Italy. While the aircraft was on its way there, my staff and I reviewed the accord under which we operated at the base. It clearly precluded any non-NATO operation without Italy's consent. Therefore, when the Italians surrounded the plane as soon as it landed, we had no legal alternative to turning over the terrorists.

An important precedent was established, since some of the terrorists taken into custody by Italy were tried in the Italian courts and received substantial sentences. The leaders, however, including Abbas (who we believed planned the operation), were hustled out of the country in disguises, and put on a plane for Iraq, through Romania. We attempted to have them arrested by drawing up extradition requests based on criminal complaints filed against them in the United States, which we transmitted before they landed in Romania. Our efforts were futile, however, as Romania allowed them to land and take off for Iraq as we expected.

In doing the work to try to get Italy (and Romania) to turn over Abbas and his confederates, we encountered the argument that we could not properly regard the terrorists as pirates, because their aims had been political rather than financial. This position, rooted in the proposition that political violence should be given greater leeway than common criminality, was advanced in a Harvard study from the 1920s and incorporated into some relevant conventions.[14] We rejected this proposition, certainly as it related to U.S. law. Nevertheless, the issue deserved attention, as the position favoring political violence would result in treating hijackings of vessels far less severely than most States had agreed to treat hijackings of aircraft. Italy and Egypt agreed to take up the issue, and their Legal Advisers (Liugi Ferrari Bravo and Nabil El Araby) led a successful effort to prohibit all attacks on maritime targets in the Maritime Terrorism Convention.[15]

## Responding to Libyan-Supported Terror

In December 1985, terrorists attacked airline passengers at the Rome and Vienna airports, killing five Americans, and wounding many more. One was a young girl, Natasha Simpson, whose body was pictured in the press lying in a pool of her blood. The terrorists were killed by security personnel after they opened fire on the passengers. They had in their possession Tunisian passports that had been confiscated by Libyan officials from foreign workers expelled from Libya. Coincidentally, Libya's leader, Colonel Muamar Qadhafi, announced that he regarded the killers as "heroes."

Secretary Shultz asked me whether we had legal authority to attack Libya on the basis of these attacks. I said that the U.S. view of international law justified a responsive use of force for the purpose of deterring future attacks. A State should not be able to avoid responsibility by assisting terrorists in attacking Americans abroad, instead of using its regular forces to attack within U.S. territory. I suggested, however, that this view be authoritatively articulated before we actually used force on this basis, adding that in any event we had not fully exhausted nonforcible options. Secretary Shultz was not happy with this advice but accepted it. The President imposed on Libya all remaining sanctions short of force, and issued the following statement:

> By providing material support to terrorist groups which attack U.S. citizens, Libya has engaged in armed aggression against the United States under established principles of international law, just as if he [Qadhafi] had used its own forces. If these [economic and political] steps do not end Qadhafi's terrorism, I promise you that further steps will be taken.[16]

Libya was undeterred by this warning. The United States learned of a planned attack on civilians lined up for visas at the U.S. Embassy in Paris. It was thwarted through excellent work by U.S. and French intelligence officials. We were not so fortunate in Berlin. There, the Libyans coordinated a terrorist attack on the LaBelle disco on April 5, 1986, killing two U.S. servicemen and a Turkish national, and wounding some fifty other Americans. We also learned of other attacks being planned. After carefully considering appropriate targets, the United States attacked Libya on April 15, striking training camps and related facilities, as well as one of Qadhafi's residences. Some claimed that the attack on Libya was illegal, despite the strong evidence of Libya's responsibility for the disco attack (which the President ordered be made public) and the fact that additional attacks were being planned.[17] The precedent has, however, been relied on by subsequent Administrations in formulating and implementing use-of-force options.

## The Iran-Contra Affair

In contrast to the many actions taken by the Reagan Administration that served to combat terrorism, the Iran-Contra Affair seriously damaged its record.[18] During 1986, while the Administration was developing, declaring, and implementing policies to deal with terrorism based on "active defense" and noncompromise, officials in the White House – with the President's approval – adopted a secret plan to secure the release of U.S. hostages held in Lebanon by selling arms to Iran. The rationale for this initiative included an effort to improve U.S.–Iranian relations, but the program centered on sales of arms explicitly conditioned on the release of hostages. This effort therefore violated both the letter and spirit of the Administration's policies, particularly the President's assertion that deals would not be made that rewarded terrorist misconduct. The plan undermined U.S. credibility, and the deterrent value of the measures and arguments we had adopted. It also failed to lead to a better relationship with Iran, and instead caused its terrorism-sponsoring government to regard the United States with even less respect than before the affair and angered the Iranian government when they discovered they were being charged prices for the arms greatly in excess of fair market value. (The profits were subsequently used to fund the Contras in fighting the Sandinista Government in Nicaragua.) Finally, the effort had precisely the effect on terrorism that official U.S. policy predicted such arrangements would cause: the hostage holders in Lebanon released three hostages at Iran's request but then seized three new ones.

The Office of the Legal Adviser had nothing to do with the Iran-Contra Affair. After the arms sales were publicly revealed, Secretary Shultz briefed me on the situation. This enabled me to determine that CIA Director William Casey and others were intent on deceiving Congress with regard to the roles of the CIA and the White House in the arms transfers. I reported this to the Attorney General, supplying him with proof from contemporaneous documents. The President ordered an investigation of the people and records associated with the affair, which resulted in the discovery of a memorandum describing the arms sales and the diversion of profits. Although this disclosure ended the effort to hide the truth as to what had happened, the arms-for-hostages project was abandoned only after Secretary Shultz brought to the President's attention ongoing negotiations over demands by Iranian negotiators for the release of convicted killers in Kuwait, among other things. Great damage had been done by that time to the Administration's antiterrorism program.

## Pan Am Flight 103

On December 21, 1988, Pan Am Flight 103 was blown up over Lockerbie, Scotland, killing all 270 aboard, including 189 Americans.[19] At that time, suspicion based on intelligence focused on terrorists in Iran and Syria as the responsible parties; that suspicion has never been disproved. A lack of definitive proof of culpability was not, however, the reason no military action was taken in response to the bombing. Even after the investigation into the incident was complete (by which time I had left the government), and Libyan agents were identified as responsible, the George H. W. Bush Administration decided to rely exclusively on UN sanctions and criminal prosecutions rather than to use force against State sponsors of terrorism. Years of economic sanctions did have some effect, and Colonel Qadhafi ultimately agreed to allow the trial of the two defendants charged with the bombing in The Netherlands, under Scottish law. One defendant was convicted, and compensation was paid by Libya to the families of those killed.

The decision to rely exclusively on economic sanctions and criminal prosecution in the Pan Am 103 bombing reversed the policy of active defense, which President George H. W. Bush had opposed during the Reagan Administration. President George H. W. Bush resumed the practice of pursuing terrorists as criminals and punishing States responsible for their actions through means other than force. This policy was followed during the eight years of the Clinton Administration, which used force only sporadically and symbolically in response to terrorist attacks. The leader of Al-Qaeda in Afghanistan, Osama bin Laden, considered the United States as weak and unwilling to make sacrifices for its own defense, citing several failures to act resolutely. In 1996 he issued a *fatwa* declaring war on the United States, and carried out at least five major attacks prior to the attacks of September 11, 2001. The attacks of September 11 caused President George W. Bush to shift back to active defense and prevention as guiding principles in dealing with terrorists and their State sponsors.

## Use of Force

Perhaps the most important advice a Legal Adviser can be called on to give is whether a proposed use of force is lawful. In responding to such requests during my tenure, I relied on the advice and reasoning of several former Legal Advisers, and on the language, history, and purposes of the relevant UN Charter provisions.[20] My views (and those of my predecessors) differed from the views of the current ICJ majority, and of most international law scholars, with regard to both the meaning of self-defense, and whether a State may use force where it believes that a thorough evaluation of all the relevant considerations, in light of the Charter's purposes, establishes that the use of force is reasonable.

The ICJ narrowly construed the "inherent" right of self-defense in Article 51 of the Charter in its decision in the Nicaragua litigation.[21] El Salvador had asked the United States to join it in collective self-defense against Nicaraguan aggression. The ICJ concluded that the aggressive actions of Nicaragua were not substantial enough to give rise to El Salvador's right of self-defense, and therefore that the United States could not join in the collective exercise of that right. Although it recognized that El Salvador had the right to respond to lesser aggressions by using proportionate measures, this newly created category was not considered to qualify as "self-defense" under Article 51, and therefore the United States could not lawfully join in cross-border activities into Nicaragua. This unprecedented and artificial interpretation of the UN Charter directly threatened the scope of the Reagan Doctrine and U.S. efforts to assist other States defend against antidemocratic insurgencies. We rejected it.[22]

The United States rejected similarly restrictive views with regard to the meaning of "attack" under Article 51 and engaged in bombing of terrorist camps in Libya after that country supported or used terrorists in attacks on U.S. nationals in Europe. Those seeking to limit the doctrine of self-defense argue that a State may exercise its right of self-defense only if the "attack" is carried out by another State and occurs on the territory of the State claiming the right to defend itself. Parenthetically, the ICJ aligned itself with at least one of these positions in its advisory opinion on the security barrier Israel is building to protect against attacks by Palestinian suicide bombers by stating that Israel's right of self-defense can only arise if the attack is committed by another State.[23] No U.S. President has ever accepted or is likely to accept either of these limitations. President Clinton, for example, considered Iraq's effort to kill former President George H. W. Bush in Kuwait as an attack on the United States, and both he and President George W. Bush treated Al-Qaeda attacks on U.S. nationals abroad as justifying the use of force in self-defense against both the terrorists and the regimes involved.

## Intervention in Panama

The Bush Administration undertook a major military action in Panama in 1989 and replaced Manuel Noriega and his government with Guillermo Endara. The action was condemned in UN General Assembly Resolution 240/44 on December 29, 1989, by a vote of 75–20. In defending this action, the Administration relied on the combined weight of several factors, rather than on any single one of the factors as adequate in itself. The factors cited by the President and others in this regard were: first, attacks by Noriega's forces and with his approval that resulted in the death of an American soldier, several injuries, and increasingly hostile confrontations with the families of military personnel; second, a formal declaration of war issued by the Panamanian Parliament at Noriega's request; third, an explicit threat by Noriega that the United States would soon see its soldiers' bodies floating down the Canal; fourth, the illegitimacy of the Noriega regime, in that he had disregarded the results of an internationally supervised, UN-sponsored, election in which Endara was the victor; fifth, a specific request from Endara, after he went to a U.S.-controlled base and was sworn in as President, approving the U.S. intervention; sixth, Noriega's involvement in drug trafficking, including the exportation of drugs to the United States; and seventh, the threat that Noriega's conduct posed to the viability of the U.S. commitment to relinquish sovereignty over the Canal to Panama. Noriega's decision to seek refuge in the residence of the Papal Nuncio in Panama led to one of the most challenging and enjoyable professional experiences of my life: exchanging letter briefs with the Pope's legal staff in Rome on the so-called right of refuge; the Pope's lawyers were superb and eventually convinced Noriega to leave.

This approach to use-of-force decisions was strongly criticized by many scholars, but it is firmly rooted in U.S. practice reaching back to the Kennedy Administration, when Abe Chayes published an article advocating the "common lawyer" approach to such decisions. The approach reflects the methodology of national security analysts and political leaders and was employed by President Clinton in defending NATO's action in Kosovo.[24] Its legitimacy is also implicit in the UN Charter's prohibition on the threat or use of force "against the territorial integrity or political independence of any State, or in any other manner inconsistent with the Purposes of the United Nations." The U.S. action in Panama breached the physical boundaries of Panama but did not affect its territorial integrity. Moreover, the intervention was undertaken to advance several Charter-based purposes, and it did so, resulting in the full grant of sovereignty over the Canal to Panama, under a legitimate, democratically elected leader. Of course, it's not a solution to say that you look at all the factors. You still have to be honest about the process. You have to talk about procedure and the importance of justifying what you do and not just acting unilaterally without going to the international tribunals to seek justification; and you have to realize that not everyone is going to agree with you just because you think what you did was reasonable. However, the pressure on the international community for humanitarian interventions, and for effective deterrence of terrorist violence, should bring this approach greater acceptance over time.

### Discussion

*Question*: After the U.S. bombing of Tripoli in 1986, you published an article explaining the legal rationale for preemptive use of force against terrorist-supporting States, and subsequently commentators have labeled this the "Sofaer Doctrine." Is the "Bush Doctrine" of preemptive war any different, other than in name, from your original doctrine?

*Mr. Sofaer*: Actually, the issue of preemption was articulated by Secretary Shultz, starting in 1984, the year before I came into the office. He made three speeches in that year articulating the principle, with the clearance of the White House, over the opposition of Secretary of Defense Casper Weinberger. By 1986, Shultz's position was being implemented, but unfortunately, by the end of my term, the Pan Am 103 case signaled a reversal, making the FBI and DOJ the central agency for the antiterrorism effort rather than the Department of Defense. That policy continued through the Clinton Administration and was only changed back to the way Shultz initially had wanted it in the George W. Bush Administration after 9/11.

*Mr. Robinson*: I would like to comment on the way the Pan Am 103 case was handled. I had the pleasure, after I was out of office, of attempting to help the families of the Pan Am 103 victims. Despite the fact that we did not have an extradition treaty with Libya and there was no chance of ever trying the perpetrators in the United States, the Justice Department went ahead with a Grand Jury, and two Libyan officials were indicted. This turned out to be very bad for the families, because they could never get any kind of information as to what the U.S. Government had found in its investigation due to the Grand Jury's secrecy rule, Rule 6(e). I've often wondered why we pressed so hard with those indictments, when we knew that, in fact they would never come to fruition in a U.S. court; yet the strategy caused hardship to the families.

*Mr. Williamson*: That part of the Pan Am 103 story occurred on my watch, and I'll address that in my comments.

# 8 The Bush (41st) Administration – Edwin D. Williamson (1990–1993)

I WANT TO TALK ABOUT THE LEGAL POSITIONS WE TOOK WITH respect to the use of force in the first Gulf War, both domestically and internationally.[1] I chose this topic because it is still being debated now, and I thought we would want to review how we got to where we are today. I'll also talk about a couple of other subjects as well.

## The Persian Gulf War

The development of these legal positions had already started by the time I took office in September 1990. I always like to tell a story that happened around my confirmation hearing on August 1: one of the statements I had planned to make (but ended up omitting at the urging of one of my editors) was that since Senator Biden was always interested in talking about the War Powers Resolution,[2] I was going to say that because we were then in a period without any major hostilities, perhaps it would be a good time to discuss it. That night, as I was leaving the office, somebody said, "Hey, Edwin, did you hear that Iraq has invaded Kuwait?" So I guess my editor had a good intuition. Anyway, I took office on September 20, and several resolutions had already been passed by the UN Security Council relating to the Iraqi invasion. The second of those resolutions, Resolution 661,[3] affirmed the right of individual and collective self-defense on the part of Kuwait. Additional resolutions were adopted, imposing increasingly stringent sanctions on Iraq, until we got to Resolution 678,[4] which was the key resolution. It recalled and reaffirmed the previous resolutions and demanded that Iraq comply with all of them. And then, if after a month Iraqi still failed to comply with these resolutions, Resolution 678 authorized member States to use all necessary means to implement these Resolutions and to "restore international peace and security in the area."

That last phrase in Resolution 678 was borrowed from Resolution 83,[5] which was passed shortly after the North Koreans invaded South Korea in June of 1950. In that case, it was the basis for the United Nations' authority to push North Korea back beyond the original border rather than having to stop at the 38th parallel. Similarly, the goal of Resolution 678 was to get Iraq to pull back to its August 1 position. But once the battle had started, we did not think that Resolution 678 required the coalition to stop at the Kuwait–Iraq border.

As you remember, there was a quick ceasefire announced in early March 1991, which was noted in Security Council Resolution 686[6] adopted on March 2. (I refer to Resolution 686 as a ceasefire resolution, though it really dealt with short-term issues.) Then later, throughout March, we negotiated Resolution 687,[7] which was passed on April 3. I consider Resolution 687 the first UN Resolution that was done in lieu of an armistice agreement.

Resolution 687 again reaffirmed the previous resolutions, and it laid out some very clear obligations on Iraq going forward. It dealt with weapons of mass destruction, kept up the sanctions on conventional weapons, and imposed other sanctions. While that process was going on and very shortly after Resolution 687's adoption, we lifted the no-fly restrictions with respect to helicopters. I think that was the most significant military mistake of the first Iraq war. In other words, the mistake was not that we stopped fighting in early March, but rather that we lifted the no-fly restriction in late March, thus permitting Saddam Hussein to brutally suppress the uprisings of the Shiites in the South and the Kurds in the North.

I worried very much about our ability to go in to Iraq to take further action, because we had not specifically dealt with the resumption of the use of force in Resolution 687 and Resolution 678 only allowed us to use force to restore peace and security in the area. And at that stage, all the conditions of Resolution 687 were in place. Iraq had sent its agreement over saying, "We accept all these conditions and so forth, and it looked like the armistice was still intact."

But when the impact of putting down the Kurds and the Shiites became apparent a few days later, Resolution 688 was adopted.[8] Resolution 688 recognized that the repression had led to the flow of refugees toward and across international borders and to cross-border incursions, which, the Resolution recited, threatened international peace and security. So from that point on, I felt much more confident that we still had the use-of-force authority from Resolution 678 – international peace and security had not been restored to the region.

So after years of operating under those resolutions, in the summer and fall of 2002 we were again discussing what authority would be needed from the UN to go back into Iraq. Resolution 1441[9] very much fits into what I call the classic definition of a treaty: a disagreement reduced to writing. It includes the recitations and the findings that Iraq was in material breach of Resolution 687. Implicit in that finding was the assertion that the authority of Resolution 678 still existed; and, therefore, there was no need for any further Security Council action to authorize the use of force.

I think this is important, because I would also argue that Resolution 678 was a political resolution. At the time it was passed, we did not need any authorization to use force, because we had ample authority under the right of collective self-defense to do what we did. I thought that the self-defense argument, even a preemptive self-defense argument, was much harder to make in fall 2002 and spring 2003. Howver, there was no need to make that argument because to find an authorization to use force in 2003 it was enough to show that Resolution 687 had been flagrantly violated and therefore international peace and security had not been restored. That by itself was a perfectly sufficient argument.

On the domestic front, we worked closely with the Justice Department and White House Counsel on the response to *Dellums v. Bush*,[10] in which a group of Congressmen tried to get a court to issue an injunction against the use of force in Iraq. Judge Greene, having decided, I think, that he could run the U.S. telecommunications industry, decided this war stuff ought to be a piece of cake, as well. He did a very clever thing and declared that the case was not ripe for decision, but then laid out, *without* a decision, all of the reasons why it would be wrong for us to go to war without a Congressional authorization. That led to further discussion of what to do, and a political decision was made to go to Congress for authorization before taking action. We lawyers assured the President that he did not have to go to Congress for any further authorization. Therefore, in the President's statement accompanying his signing of the joint resolution authorizing the use of force,[11] he made it clear that this did not constitute any change in the longstanding position of the Executive Branch either on the constitutional authority to use armed forces to defend vital U.S. international interests or on the constitutionality of the War Powers Resolution.

## Dissolution of the Soviet Union

In all of the interactions between L and our clients at the State Department, I very much took the view that we at L were lawyers; that if asked about policy issues, we would certainly respond, but that we did not expect our policy views to be sought. But in the breakup of the Soviet Union in 1989, it became pretty clear that the policymakers didn't really know how to deal with a lot of international law issues. They kept using what they thought were legal terms, such as *recognition* when they really meant *diplomatic relations*. So we found ourselves very much in the driver's seat, at least in laying out the policy rationale and explaining the basis for it.

There was an interesting contrast between the Soviet situation and the Yugoslavian situation two years later. We were presented with the Soviet situation first – with the question of whether to go the clean slate route or to require that each constituent country coming out of the breakup of the Soviet Union continue with all treaty obligations. Everybody talks about treaty obligations, but one has to bear in mind that there are also often treaty benefits. So the questions are: who gets those benefits, and who has those obligations?[12]

Rather than follow the approach of the Restatement of Foreign Relations Law,[13] which adopts the clean slate approach pretty much across the board, we took the other position that all of the evolving constituent countries had to abide by the treaties as long as that could be accomplished consistent with the object and purpose of each treaty. Now, in some cases that approach does not work and in some it does. In particular, two positions had to be assigned. One was who would be the nuclear power under the Non Proliferation Treaty (NPT). We certainly did not want fourteen nuclear powers. Second, the permanent seat on the Security Council, which the Charter says shall be held by the Soviet Union, needed to be assigned.[14] We decided that where these treaty structures had an indivisible, unre-creatable asset or obligation, we would find one dominant continuing country to take that on; that country, obviously, was Russia, for both nuclear state status and Security Council permanent membership. There was agreement among the republics that that would happen, which helped very much.

In the Yugoslavian situation, things were a lot messier because there was no devolution agreement among the republics. Serbia-Montenegro claimed the position as the continuing country. But the United States was not particularly interested in endorsing that, because Serbia had been engaged in continuing violations of international humanitarian law in Bosnia. So we adopted a rule that all the constituent countries of Yugoslavia (including Serbia-Montenegro) had to go through the front door and apply for membership in the UN.[15] That gave us a little handle on keeping Serbia-Montenegro at bay until they behaved themselves.

On its face, this appeared in sharp contrast to Russia's slipping into the Soviet Union's permanent seat on the Security Council without much ado, but we rationalized it on the basis that the permanent seat was indivisible and unre-creatable, whereas Yugoslavia's ordinary UN membership was recreatable.[16]

## General Comments

One of the interesting things about these conversations is the spillover from one administration to another. Abe talked about Pam Am 103, and, obviously, I worked some on that. We did the first round in the ICJ.[17] Davis talked about his Canadian disputes, which reminds me of my first meeting with the Canadian Legal Adviser. I was given this list of things we needed to resolve, most of which involved private-sector commercial grievances against Canadian governmental action, and I thought, "how am I going to get politicians to pay attention to these issues?" That transformed me into a strong supporter of investor-state arbitration under investment treaties. Let's provide a forum for the private sector to sort out their disputes with another government and keep those disputes out of the diplomatic channels.

Abe did not get a chance to get into the *Alvarez-Machain* issue,[18] which unfolded on his watch. In that case, the DEA abducted a Mexican doctor involved in the torture murder of an undercover DEA agent in Mexico. The Supreme Court ruled that the violation of Mexico's territorial integrity did not require dismissal of the case. After the trial court dismissed the charges at the end of the prosecution's case for insufficient evidence, Dr. Alvarez-Machain brought a $20 million tort suit against the United States and the agents involved in his kidnapping. The Supreme Court recently dismissed the suit on the basis that the Alien Tort Statute does not create a cause of action of arbitrary arrest and detention, but left the door open for suits alleging torture.

## Discussion

*Mr. Sofaer:* The *Alvarez-Machain* case is another example, Edwin, of what Davis had raised earlier – the strong correlation between disastrous policies and failure to consult in advance with the international lawyers. In the *Alvarez-Machain* case, not only was the Legal Adviser's office not consulted, but the Justice Department didn't even consult the White House. They went ahead and seized this doctor from Mexico in a secret operation and brought him to the United States, took the case all the way up the Supreme Court, and then lost the trial. It had a negative affect on our foreign policy, and several countries required that we provide assurances that we would not kidnap citizens from their territory. It's a classic case of how you can get the country into a mess by doing something without talking it through with the relevant people.

*Prof. Scharf:* Can I ask a question that relates to the bridge between Abe and Edwin? Davis alluded to the fact that when the bombing of Pam Am 103 occurred, he thought it was a mistake that the government went for indictments. I was working under Edwin at L when the indictments were issued, and I didn't think it was a mistake. The indictments could have laid the foundation for potential use of force under the Sofaer-Shultz doctrine.[19] More importantly to the way things turned out, they provided a basis for obtaining Security Council-imposed sanctions on Libya.[20] And when Libya sued the United States before the ICJ,[21] they provided the factual background for the U.S. argument. So the indictments in that case were less about trying to get these two Libyans prosecuted in U.S. court than about setting the stage for other international strategies against Libya.

*Mr. Sofaer:* The first thing you have to take into account is that if we had made an immediate military response to the bombing of Pan Am 103 back in 1988 or 1989, before the year-long investigation was completed and the indictments were issued, we would have gone after the wrong countries because we initially thought Iran and Syria were the culprits.

Second, I think it's arguable that the indictments were really a way of not resorting to force; in a way, the whole use of criminal law in the terrorism area has been a device to give leaders the argument that they are doing something about terrorism without having really done something about it.

*Mr. Andrews*: I think Abe is right in saying that the indictments were a mechanism to show momentum with respect to this case. I can't answer the original question but I think the indictments laid the foundation for what we were able to accomplish with respect to the case during the Clinton years, which I'll talk about shortly.

*Mr. Matheson*: Let me comment very briefly. I don't think the indictments were well-integrated in any foreign policy decision process. There was no coordination between Justice and State about the approach. But once the indictments were handed down, curiously enough, a lot of people in the State Department saw this as a very useful opportunity to impose a punitive regime on Libya in the form of sanctions, because they felt that Libya would never surrender these people and, therefore, if they had sanctions in place, the sanctions would continue on into the foreseeable future.

*Mr. Sofaer*: It was what we did with Iraq as well, for years, using sanctions as a way of continuing to hammer them without actually using force to do it.

*Mr. Matheson*: But the fact is that the process of indictments in the U.S. system is not well integrated with foreign policy concerns. Take, for example, Noriega.[22] The Noriega indictment occurred with essentially no integration into a sensible foreign policy strategy, yet it was one of the factors leading to the use of force in Panama.

# 9 The Bush (41st) Administration – Michael J. Matheson

FIRST, I WANT TO SAY THAT I REALLY FEEL THAT THIS GROUP of public servants has contributed more to international law and U.S. foreign policy than any other group I know, and I'm very thankful to be included in it. Much of the work of the Legal Adviser's office, of course, is in giving legal advice and good counsel to senior officers in the handling of matters within their primary responsibility; but I think it is also the case that the Legal Adviser's office is given important projects over which it has primary responsibility, where it has to make both legal and policy judgments – where it has to develop positions within the Executive Branch and to conduct necessary negotiations with the Congress and with foreign governments. Today I want to discuss three examples of this that occurred during the time that I was Acting Legal Adviser and Principal Deputy.

## The 1991 Persian Gulf War Legal Regime

The first occurred in the aftermath of the 1991 Gulf War, at a time when the Security Council was engaged in constructing a postwar regime to preserve the peace and, also, to deal with various aspects of the conflict. Of course, the legal vehicle for this postwar regime was a series of resolutions adopted by the Security Council under Chapter 7 of the UN Charter, an authority that had largely been dormant during the period of the Cold War. Edwin has already mentioned the key one of these resolutions, Resolution 687, the famous mother of all resolutions.[1]

That resolution was basically drafted in L, and I think it represented a creative and, in some ways, a very aggressive use of international law to find new ways to deal with many of the difficult problems of the day. In the case of Resolution 687, this included trying to resolve the boundary dispute between Iraq and Kuwait, which had been one of the ostensible causes of the war; the problem of elimination of Iraqi weapons of mass destruction; and the problem of providing compensation for the large volume of lawsuits that occurred as a result of the invasion and occupation of Kuwait.

This last matter, the compensation matter, was essentially assigned to L as its primary responsibility. This required L to get involved in the resolution of both legal and policy issues: what forms of loss would be covered, where the resources for compensation would come from, which categories would have priority, who would make the decisions, and how those decisions would be made.

We found it was necessary to create an interagency process to sort out the equities of the various agencies of the U.S. Government in the process. We needed to have a public process to deal with the interests of the U.S. nationals and corporations that had claims, and an international process both to gain support for the U.S. claims process and to negotiate the instruments necessary to carry it out.

In many ways, the problems posed by these losses during the Iraq War were greater than those of any comparable international compensation process that had occurred up to that time. There were hundreds of thousands of claimants, the great majority of whom were individuals who had an urgent need for compensation. The amounts claimed totaled well over $200 million, and it was clear that the usual method by which such international claims problems are resolved (a formal case-by-case adjudication process in the adversarial mode, like the Iran–United States Claims Tribunal) would be wholly inadequate to deal with the problems presented here. So instead, the Legal Adviser's office proposed and ultimately the Security Council agreed to an innovative system, which had a number of new features.

The UN Security Council decided the basic issue at the outset, the issue of liability. Iraq was held by the Council to be responsible for the war and for all the losses that resulted. That meant that it was unnecessary to litigate the question of liability in any of the following adjudications and claims. Compensation was to be funded through a deduction from future Iraqi oil export revenues, which was potentially a very rich source of revenues, and a new institution was created – the UN Compensation Commission, which was designed to adjudicate these claims in a nonadversarial system. That is, it didn't give Iraq any procedural rights that would allow it to obstruct or delay the process, as Iran was able to do with the Iran Claims Tribunal.

Priority both in adjudication and in the payment of claims was given to the most needy categories, particularly the hundreds of thousands of individuals who suffered from the occupation. To deal with this huge volume of claims, it was decided to adopt various modern techniques for mass claims resolution: sampling, computerized analysis, and standardized determinations for classes of claims.

Now, of course, not all claimants were entirely satisfied with the results here, and it is true that with the Saddam regime, the Security Council has drastically reduced the overall income from Iraqi oil revenues. So it's probably the case that full recovery for all of these large categories of claims is not likely in the foreseeable future. But still the process did produce considerable and, in some ways, unprecedented results. The process has already resolved more than 98 percent of the claims. It has awarded more than $50 billion. It has paid approximately $20 billion already, and that includes relatively prompt payment of large sums to the most-needy categories of individuals.

## Creation of the Yugoslavia Tribunal

The second example I want to give of a project in which L had primary responsibility was the creation of the International Criminal Tribunal for the former Yugoslavia.[2] By the end of 1992, there was considerable international attention to the atrocities that were being committed in the former Yugoslavia. After the Clinton Administration took office, Secretary Christopher asked L to devise and implement a plan for the creation of an international prosecution process.

At the time, it wasn't clear what the legal and institutional basis for such prosecution would be. The Nuremberg and Tokyo tribunals had been based on the authority of victorious belligerent powers, the Allies, and their custody over the individuals accused of the crimes, who were basically enemy POWs.[3] This precedent didn't apply very well in the case of the Yugoslav conflict, which at that time was far from over. The major powers were not parties to the conflict, and the perpetrators were as yet neither defeated nor apprehended.

There were a number of European proposals for the creation of a tribunal by negotiation of a treaty among the States in the conflict and among other States who might support the process. But this idea of creating a tribunal by treaty had a number of serious drawbacks. It would have taken years to negotiate and bring such a treaty into force. The tribunal would have had jurisdiction over only the territory of those States that ratified the treaty, and that would exclude, in all likelihood, the former Yugoslav republics that were the object of the whole exercise. Furthermore, States that did not ratify the treaty would have no obligation to cooperate by surrendering persons or providing evidence to the tribunal.

So instead, the Legal Adviser's office proposed that a tribunal be created by a decision of the Security Council under Chapter 7. This would be based on a judgment by the Council that such prosecutions would contribute to the restoration and maintenance of the peace. The idea of doing it this way had some important advantages. The tribunal would be created immediately, as a formal matter. It would have jurisdiction over crimes in any of the former Yugoslav republics, whether or not they consented to the process. All States would be bound to cooperate in the surrender of persons and evidence. The fact that the Council had created the tribunal would make it much more likely that the mandatory powers of the Council under Chapter 7 would be available to support the process and deal with recalcitrant States – and that would include the use of sanctions and the possible use of military force.

L's proposal was readily accepted within the U.S. Government, but it took some persuasion to get it accepted by the other members of the Security Council. There were some doubts among other members as to whether it was lawful or appropriate for the Council to use its Chapter 7 authority to create a criminal tribunal and to prosecute individuals. However, after a series of consultations in New York and in the capitals, with the Legal Advisers of the Permanent Five, the Council ultimately did adopt a statute very similar to that originally proposed by the United States.[4]

Of course, the creation of the tribunal was important in a number of different ways. It created a precedent for further international prosecutions of such crimes later; and, also, it dealt with the definition and expansion of the Chapter 7 authority of the Security Council. But the creation of the tribunal was, of course, only the first and, in some ways, the easiest step. There was a lot of work that had to be done by L and by other bureaus, which became more involved in the process over succeeding years.

## Landmines Protocol Negotiations

The third example I want to discuss of a project under L's primary responsibility during this period is negotiation of the UN Landmines Protocol.[5] The Legal Adviser's office had long had primary responsibility within the U.S. Government for the negotiation of instruments on conflict, obviously in close cooperation with the Department of Defense. In the 1980s and the early 1990s, it had become pretty clear that the indiscriminate use of antipersonnel landmines was one of the most serious threats to the welfare of the civilian population during the conflicts of that period, which included those in Afghanistan and Cambodia and Angola. So L was charged with creating a strategy that would both serve humanitarian ends and satisfy U.S. military requirements. After studying the matter, we realized that the U.S. military was not going to give up all of its uses of antipersonnel mines; but at the same time, the U.S. military had already been adopting various limits on its own mines that we saw might become the basis for a useful international regime. Specifically, the Department of Defense was already eliminating its undetectable plastic mines. It was also eliminating mines that had more than a very short active life, at least if they were not kept within a marked and monitored field. The reason was that the military considered such mines a threat to U.S. forces, which would be expected to advance over territory where the mines might be laid.

All of this enabled us to convince the Department of Defense that we should propose to incorporate these limits that the U.S. military had already decided on into an international treaty regime, and that these limits should be applied to all forms of conflict, whether international or internal.

It was not an easy idea to sell to other governments. The major mine users, Russia, China, India, and Pakistan, didn't really want to have any limits on their mines at all. And many States were opposed to any limitations on internal conflicts, which they considered to be an intrusion into their domestic affairs. There was lot of process and negotiation in Geneva and Vienna and various capitals for about three years, but it finally resulted, in the end, in the adoption of a protocol that was almost exactly what the United States had proposed in the first place.

After this protocol was adopted, later in the decade, there was a movement by those States that had no further use for antipersonnel mines to ban them completely, and this resulted in the Ottawa Convention.[6] However, the UN Protocol negotiated by L is still very important because the major mine users, who have not accepted the Ottawa Convention, are nonetheless committed to the restrictions in the UN Landmines Protocol.

These three projects are representative of many issues and problems in which L was given primary responsibility over the years. L is not limited to pronouncing on legal issues, but has to consider all aspects of a problem – legal, policy, political – and deal with all of the relevant elements involved. That is one of the aspects of the Legal Adviser's office that makes it a very interesting place in which to work.

## Discussion

*Mr. Sofaer*: What is the legal status of the Land Mines Protocol, Mike, right now?

*Mr. Matheson*: It was ratified by the United States and by most of the countries in the world. Most countries are party to both the Ottawa Convention and the UN Protocol. The critical category of States that are parties to the UN Protocol but not to the Ottawa Convention are all major landmine users.

*Mr. Sofaer*: What Mike and the office did in coming up with the Yugoslavia tribunal was very creative and would have been a great way to move the process forward as a model for an international criminal court. Unlike the ICC that emerged over our objection from the Rome Diplomatic Conference, the United States could have supported a permanent ad hoc tribunal whose jurisdiction was determined by the Security Council.

# 10 The Clinton Administration – Conrad K. Harper (1993–1996)

L ET ME BEGIN BY RETURNING TO ONE OF THE TOPICS MIKE Matheson has touched on. The statute of the Yugoslav tribunal was in its infancy when I took office. It had been adopted by the Security Council on May 25, 1993; a day or two before then, I was sworn in.[1] I had not realized that my first year at L would be dominated almost entirely by this undertaking that Mike and his colleagues had crafted, but that turned out to be the case; we found ourselves with a marvelous document, but then our project was to create a reality.

## Operation of the Yugoslav Tribunal

You would assume perhaps that the international legal community would be a rich source of people ready for such an undertaking, but it turned out, at least on my watch, not to be the case. The first challenge was to get anything started. Nobody today has said anything about the difficulty of getting the United Nations to do *anything*. But we realized early on that if this tribunal was going to begin to work, and that the designated location turned out to be The Hague, people had to be there; materials had to be there; and somebody had to get those people and materials to The Hague to start working – and that somebody, of course, was the United States. By the time, a year later, when Richard Goldstone was selected as the chief prosecutor, approximately twenty-three of the forty staff members who were there in The Hague were, in fact, detailees from the U.S. Government. We also supplied the computers, the forensics experts – and I could go on and on. The involvement of the Legal Adviser's office at the implementation/operational level in getting this institution up and running cannot be overstated.

At another level – that is to say, getting the judges – again, we had an interesting challenge. What would be your ideal profile for these judges? Of course we thought there ought to be a U.S. judge on the Tribunal, and we thought that such a judge that had experience with criminal cases would make some sense. But then where do you find that person, and whom would you have the confidence in for such an undertaking? As it turned out, luckily, early on, we found the right person in Gabrielle Kirk McDonald, who fit the profile. She had not actually practiced criminal law, but she had been a U.S. District Judge. She had retired from that position early enough, when she still had all of her wits about her. We found that she had the people skills that are so important in an undertaking like this, and she rapidly got approval at the United Nations.

But for the job of prosecutor, the problem was much more difficult.[2] What is the profile for the ideal prosecutor for such an undertaking? The ideal would be somebody who had actually done it before – but there was nobody around that had actually done it before who was still sufficiently able to contemplate doing it again. There were a few survivors from the Nuremberg and Tokyo experience, and we talked to them, but, because of their advanced age, none of them was really a likely candidate.

And at that time there was a curious parochialism (which I think has now dissipated to some degree) among prosecutors as a group worldwide. They may be highly skilled in the laws of a particular State in which they hold office, but the idea of undertaking international humanitarian law has never occurred to them. Most had simply not considered the notion of prosecuting violators of the Genocide Convention. So it was a great problem trying to find the right person.

Again, we had some success. From Venezuela, Ramone Escobar Salone was selected. He wasn't necessarily our top candidate, but he was selected and for a brief time there was a chief prosecutor. But then he received an offer from his own government to go home to become interior minister. He decided that was better than being chief prosecutor in The Hague, and he took it.

We did not want even to contemplate the idea of a U.S. prosecutor, for fear this would look like a U.S. rather than a UN undertaking – but we were coming very near to doing exactly that, because we felt we had no ready candidates elsewhere; I even talked to some potential U.S. candidates. Then someone suggested Richard Goldstone – and in many ways, he had the profile we wanted. He headed the Goldstone Commission that investigated apartheid crimes in South Africa. He had a tremendous reputation in the highly divisive society of South Africa, and he had been a judge. Again, he had never practiced criminal law; but he seemed to have the qualities of good faith and good judgment one would seek for this position.

As it turned out, Goldstone was far beyond what any of us anticipated he might be. Beginning in July 1994, Richard got permission from President Mandela to forego for the moment his appointment to the Constitutional Court in South Africa and to take up the reins in The Hague as chief prosecutor. And he was the almost cosmic force that was unleashed on this initiative. He was never shy about holding us or anybody else not only to our obligations, but to our intentions to make this thing work.

There were some sticky problems. One of them was getting cooperation within the intelligence community. And then there was the question of how much intelligence information could be shared with The Hague and, furthermore, whether any of it would ever be available for evidentiary purposes. We had to work that through. We had the related issue of the obligation to render suspects to the tribunal under domestic law; that required a statutory fix in many countries. There was just one thing after another that needed to be addressed on the operational level, but happily, we were able to do it. Over time, the institution, working through its rules – a blend of common law and civil law and heretofore unknown provisions – came to work quite well.

It's been suggested earlier today that maybe sometimes governments undertake a criminal indictment in lieu of taking a vigorous action, such as the use of force; and certainly that charge was made with respect to the establishment of the Yugoslav war crimes tribunal. My own sense from the very outset was that the most salutary thing you can do is set up an institution, because it then takes on a life of its own and establishes its own rationale, and it becomes a player in the process. That is exactly what has happened with this tribunal, and perhaps no more important occasion demonstrated this than the Dayton Accords negotiations in 2005. You will recall that it was decided to hold those meetings in Dayton and the question was who would attend from the areas of the conflict. The worry, of course, was that Bosnian Serb leader Radovan Karadzic and other malefactors might not only show up but might wreck the undertaking. Happily, since they had been indicted by the war crimes tribunal, we were able to take the very high-minded view that, of course, it was not appropriate for someone under that cloud to participate in the international peace conference.

*Mr. Owen*: [interjecting] I have to say I wish you people would have arrested Karadzic and the other indictees.

*Mr. Harper*: Well, I wish I could say I had some control over that.

*Mr. Matheson*: Actually, L and the State Department were pressing throughout this period to get NATO and the NATO countries to accept the fact that it was part of the mandate of the NATO forces to arrest indicted war criminals.[3] But it was a hard sell because the military was not initially prepared to commit U.S. troops to that task.

*Mr. Owen*: That's the trouble. The U.S. military was not listening to you.

*Mr. Harper*: Well, in 1994, as if there were not enough horrors in the world, the massacres in Rwanda started. President Clinton has already apologized, so I don't have to add to the apology for the default of our government in that episode. But one thing we did eventually do was set up the Rwanda Tribunal.[4] Again, we had a model, which, of course, was the one that Mike and his colleagues had drafted earlier for Yugoslavia. The operational challenges for the Rwanda tribunal were if anything greater than they were for Yugoslavia. Early on, the decision was made that the seat of the tribunal could not, in fact, be in Rwanda. Nor could it be in The Hague. Establishing the Tribunal in Arusha, Tanzania; and recruiting a Deputy Prosecutor, Registrar, judges, and senior staff, created extraordinary challenges – it was like The Hague all over again. And once again, the United States and L undertook to do a lot of it. I have the feeling that the Rwanda Tribunal has always been a stepchild and hasn't had the attention or the resources that that horror should command. Nonetheless, L's involvement in that project cannot be overstated.

## Shoot-Down of Iranian Airliner by the USS *Vincennes*

But let me take a leap now to the *Vincennes* shoot-down, because it leads to some of the things that all of us have touched on. The time now is July 1988 and through an error one of our Aegis guided missile cruisers, the USS *Vincennes*, shot down an Iranian airliner, with all aboard perishing.[5] Of the 290 people aboard, 248 were Iranian nationals. President Reagan virtually immediately apologized and offered *ex gratia* payments, but that did not satisfy the Iranians. So amid everything else, another lawsuit was filed against the United States in the International Court of Justice (ICJ).[6] Here, a perhaps unintended consequence of Bob's handiwork on the Algiers Accords[7] came to our rescue – because The Hague was the only place where the Iranian Government and the U.S. Government actually were meeting in a way that permitted the conduct of business. We did have a lot of business that wasn't necessarily related to the Iran–United States Claims Tribunal jurisdiction, and one item of it ultimately turned out to be this case.

We were approaching the ICJ's jurisdictional hearing on the *Vincennes* case, which was set for September 1994 – and we knew we were going to find it extremely difficult to convince the Court to dismiss on jurisdictional grounds. But the month before the hearing, Assistant Legal Adviser Ron Bettauer, U.S. Agent to the ICJ Steve Mathias and I were in The Hague having one of our periodic meetings with our Iranian counterparts. When we got to the agenda item relating to this case, my Iranian counterpart, Dr. Eftikar (one of the shrewdest persons I have ever dealt with) said, "Why don't we clear the room." Everyone cleared out, and Dr. Eftikar and I had a conversation in which we basically decided to trust each other, shook hands, and said, "Let's get rid of the *Vincennes* dispute. We can also take care of some bank claims and some other things that involve U.S. claimants; but let's not have this hearing next month."

So we did that. Now, it took eighteen months for everybody to do the paperwork, and, of course, there were a lot of charges and counter-charges by Tehran and Washington during this time about this, that, and the other thing – but nobody ever mentioned the *Vincennes*. There came a time where the agreements were quietly signed and slipped through, and Congress was advised.[8] I considered that to be a real triumph in international law, where lawyers actually got together and accomplished something that probably nobody else could have done, because we were able to speak the same language.

### ICJ Advisory Opinion on Legality of Nuclear Weapons

The final issue I will discuss is the ICJ advisory opinion on the legality of nuclear weapons.[9] The World Health Organization (WHO) requested that the ICJ write international law for general use on this subject.[10] I had serious reservations about this jurisdictionally, believing that the WHO really couldn't ask the court for something outside of its powers. But the jurisdictional issue was, in effect, cured by the General Assembly's asking the court to opine on whether the use or threat to use nuclear weapons violates international law.[11]

In the end, forty-one nations prepared materials on this matter for the ICJ. Twenty-four nations and the WHO actually presented oral arguments for it. The mastermind behind our approach, of course, was Mike Matheson. I love the theater of the ICJ. You show up with a prepared speech, which has been provided in advance to the judges and the opposing party. There is a monitor that is showing the text, but you act as if this is all news to everybody; it is great fun.

For this case there were fourteen judges, because one of the judges had recused himself. Of course, there were no additional ad hoc judges, given that this was an advisory opinion and not a contentious case. And I have to tell you that sitting in that marvelous courtroom in the Peace Palace, I think all of us who were there that day were touched by how real the problem was. A woman from one of the Pacific Islands talked about how one beautiful day, it started snowing. It turned out that it wasn't snow, but radioactive ash from an atomic test. The impact of this nuclear fallout on her society, on her family, her friends and herself, gave a reality to what we were talking about which was quite stunning.

But there were also periods of comedy. My favorite was the appearance of the delegation from Australia, which made two arguments. The Attorney General stood up and argued for the proposition that international law was not violated by the right to use nuclear weapons. The Solicitor General of Australia then argued just the opposite. So it was clear Australia was going to win.

Another power struggle within a delegation arose with the assertion by the UK Attorney General of his primacy in arguing for the UK position over the long-time UK Foreign Ministry Legal Adviser.

Japan took the prize for sheer courage; this was a State entitled to argue that these weapons should be banned under all circumstances. And yet, in a show of really remarkable governmental courage, Japan's lawyers took the view that although the danger was deplorable, and they hoped that nuclear weapons would never again be used, they could not argue that such weapons be banned in all circumstances internationally.

In any event, the court came down with its decision about eight days after I left office, in mid-July 1996. There were several opinions; Mike has written a quite comprehensive journal article that explains them[12]; but the essence of it was that the court found itself unable to conclude that in all circumstances, nuclear weapons were prohibited under international law.

### Discussion

*Question*: Would you comment on L's role in the controversy surrounding Bosnia and Rwanda, over whether or not these things could be labeled genocide early on and the delay in using that word?

*Mr. Harper*: In my view they were genocides. But there were a lot of policy concerns about being that blunt, including what obligation we had under the Genocide Convention to act – so there was a tap dance. But I never had any doubt in my own mind, and I made it clear that was my view. But the Legal Adviser doesn't make the ultimate decisions, even about characterizing something as an international crime.

*Mr. Matheson*: That is perfectly right. And even when they decided to use the term, for some reason the policymakers were more comfortable with the euphemism that it was "acts of genocide," which was, somehow, better from their point of view than just saying that it was genocide.

*Mr. Sofaer*: But did anyone claim that failure to use the term *genocide* meant that we did not have the authority to act in Rwanda? It seems to me use of the term would not have made a difference. It was a straight policy call.

*Mr. Matheson*: Of course, we could have gone to the Security Council for the authority to introduce forces. But we didn't because of various political factors.

On a different topic, I think Conrad's description of the one-on-one *Vincennes* negotiation is very interesting, because there were a number of occasions, both in the 1980s and in the 1990s, in which the Legal Adviser's office was able to negotiate with the Iranians to resolve some very large issues. Hundreds of millions of dollars were transferred, disposition of U.S. arms had been provided to the Shah, and so on. If these things had been negotiated by some policy bureau, each agreement would have been a big issue on the Hill, a big political event. But somehow because the Legal Adviser's office was able to manage them, they were accepted as mere technical exercises and passed almost without notice on the Hill. That's a curious example of how policymakers can use L as an instrumentality for resolving issues in a politically powerful way.

*Mr. Sofaer*: I have a very funny story that relates to that idea in an article that I wrote for the *Houston Law Review* on Iran-Contra.[13] I was sitting across from Dr. Eftikar, negotiating about these armaments that they had bought, some of which they had taken title to, at the time when the guys in the White House were secretly trying to sell armaments to Iran, of which I had no knowledge. Eftikar said to me, "Well, what's the matter? Why don't you just give us the arms? You know, we paid for them, and you could just give us this stuff." I said, "I've told you over and over again that we are not going to let you have any arms." And he said to me, "Are you sure?"

Then later, when I came back from a trip to Israel, Secretary Shultz called me in and told me for the first time about Iran-Contra and the sale of the arms. As Charlie Hill started reading to me from his notebook and I was getting the story, of course, I recalled the image of Dr. Eftikar saying, "Are you sure?"

*Mr. Robinson*: Do we have time for one more Eftikar story? I happened to have the first meeting with him and it took a year to set the agenda and I was under very strict instructions as to an opening statement, because at least as far as I knew, this was the first U.S.–Iranian face-to-face since the hostages. I always carried with me to The Hague a little portable radio. The meeting was set for 9 in the morning in the Peace Palace, and I woke up in the morning and I turned on the BBC world news and heard that the embassy in Beirut had been bombed. The news reporter, of course, speculated that the Iranians were responsible. So I thought, "Now what do I do? Am I still supposed to attend the meeting?" Of course, the time there in The Hague was six hours ahead of Washington, DC. So I decided to go and say what I had been ordered to say. So I did that, and then, of course, we had three days of meetings that went on interminably. It was sad because we were really offering some things that were in the interest of both the United States and Iran, and it seemed to me there should have been easy agreements – but he could agree to nothing. At the end of those three days of meetings (and confident that the Iranian would be unaware of the meaning of a particular ribbon color), I couldn't resist buying him a gift box of chocolates and wrapping them in a yellow ribbon in honor of the American hostages.

*Mr. Hansell*: Conrad, you said that President Clinton had apologized about Rwanda. In what context?

*Mr. Harper*: It was during his visit to Kigali in 1998. The question was put to him, in effect, why did you delay taking decisive action to stop the massacre, didn't you know that they were going on at the time, and Clinton said "yes" and apologized.[14]

# 11 The Clinton Administration – David R. Andrews (1997–2000)

'VE CHOSEN TO DISCUSS THE NEGOTIATIONS SURROUNDING the establishment of the Pan Am 103 trial in the Netherlands and the negotiations surrounding the accidental bombing of the Chinese Embassy during the 1999 NATO intervention in Kosovo.

## Negotiations for the Pan Am 103 Trial

My first full day in office was September 15, 1997. In my first formal meeting with Secretary Albright, she asked me, "Do you think you can engineer a third-country trial for the two Libyans accused of blowing up Pan Am 103?"

She had just returned from a meeting with some of the families of the victims of Pan Am 103 and was quite moved by what she heard. The idea of a third-country trial had been circulating for quite some time, and Qaddafi, himself had suggested a trial in The Hague. The United States, for a number of reasons, was quite reluctant to take up any of these suggestions. The Attorney General, for example, was skeptical of any attempt to negotiate the venue of the trial of the two terrorists. She thought the approach could be viewed as a violation of U.S. counter-terrorism policy.

However by the end of 1997, the sanctions had been in place for more than five years, and the sanctions regime was crumbling. Various countries were violating the embargo on trade, and the prohibition on flights was being violated with alarming frequency. The tenth anniversary of the bombing was coming up. These factors combined with the French decision to go forward with the UTA bombing trial in absentia (UTA Flight 772 was blown up over Chad, and was traced to Qaddafi's son-in-law) forced the United States and United Kingdom to reconsider the idea of a third-country trial.

The Secretary received authority from the President to pursue a third-country trial. She called UK Foreign Minister Robin Cook to discuss the issue, and he said it sounded like a good idea. He suggested that UK FCO Legal Adviser Frank Berman and I get together to discuss it.

Any initiative would have to be prepared on the assumption that it would be accepted, even though there could be no certainty of this. Every detail therefore had to be settled in advance and needed to be confidential until we were ready to go public. At this point, there were only five people at the State Department who were aware of this effort.

I commuted two or three times a month over the first few months to the United Kingdom. The cover for these visits was the ICJ case that was pending against the United States and United Kingdom at the ICJ. Initially it was just Frank Berman and I meeting to work through the issues.

*Mr. Harper*: That was dangerous.

*Mr. Andrews*: It was dangerous to get two Legal Advisers together by themselves. But we very quickly figured out that there were a number of issues on which we needed to get the trial lawyers involved. We brought in the UK Lord Advocate Andrew Hardy, and we started to discuss about three dozen topics that would need detailed consideration and perhaps even translation into treaty, legislative text, or UN Security Council resolutions.

We initially looked at UN Security Council Resolution 883,[1] which said it envisioned a trial before the appropriate UK or U.S. court.[2] It was obvious that a trial by a U.S. court would not be politically acceptable, if for no other reason than the likelihood that DOJ would seek the death penalty. We knew that this would create an unnecessary obstacle to developing the necessary international consensus to push the initiative. We decided early on, therefore, to explore a trial before a Scottish Court.

The next important item was to quiz the Lord Advocate and his trial staff to see whether, in fact, they thought there was a solid case. We spent a couple of weeks going over their evidence and getting assurance that they felt this was a winnable case. After establishing that the Lord Advocate believed that he had sufficient evidence to win the case, discussions between the United States and United Kingdom covered some three dozen topics, all of which needed detailed consideration. Although we were shoulder-to-shoulder with the British and Scots throughout this effort, there were many issues that needed to be resolved.

One such issue was guarantees that the U.S. indictments would not be compromised.[3] The U.S. Department of Justice (DOJ) was willing to let the Scots take the first crack at trying the two Libyans but did not want to be seen as compromising their indictments. We determined there was no international double jeopardy concept but this was really a political consideration. Once the evidence was aired at the Scottish trial, and if the Scots could not get a conviction, it was doubtful we could.

A related issue was the U.S. Government's role in the trial. The Lord Advocate wanted the United States to take an active role in this case. We determined this could legitimately raise the issue of double jeopardy should we want to try the individuals in a U.S. court. The U.S. prosecutors simply monitored the trial

A third issue was the place of the trial. It had been suggested that it be in The Hague. The ICJ certainly was not an appropriate venue, but we had an alternate site near The Hague, which was a former U.S. Air Force base known as Camp Zeist.

Still another issue was the composition of the court, which had to be consistent with that of the criminal courts in Scotland. The jurisdiction of this court would have to be limited to these indictments. And there had to be special legislation that would allow the Scottish High Court to sit in The Netherlands. For that, there would be a treaty between the UK and the Dutch Governments for the site to be Scottish territory for purposes of the trial.

There were several other issues, which I will just run through quickly. Where would the accused be detained pending and during the trial? Where would the accused be imprisoned if convicted? What type of access would be provided to Libyan observers to ensure satisfactory treatment in prison? Would Libya provide funds for defense counsel? How would contempt of court be handled? Would the trial be televised? How would security be ensured for the court premises and personnel? What types of immunities would the court personnel be entitled to? How would appeals be heard? Who would pay for the costs of the trial?

After months of deliberation and negotiations, we signed a Memorandum of Understanding with the United Kingdom. The DOJ was still highly skeptical at this point, but did go along with it. We then set about drafting the implementing documents. First came the amendments to the Scottish legislation. Next, we needed a treaty between the Netherlands and the United Kingdom. This required legislation, which the Lord Advocate, working with the Foreign and Commonwealth Office, managed to craft as an "Order in Council" that created the necessary legislative changes without requiring a vote by Parliament. Finally, we needed the preparation of the U.S.–UK letter to the UN Secretary General to launch the initiative, and the Security Council resolution to authorize it.

We concluded that the UN Secretary General would be the appropriate intermediary to take this matter to the Libyans, because we did not want any direct contact with the Libyans. The letter that the Secretary General was to deliver would be a take-it-or-leave-it proposal for negotiations. Finally, on May 20, about eight months after Secretary Albright and UK Foreign Secretary Robin Cooke authorized the project, we were authorized to begin negotiations with the Dutch. We presented the Dutch a slimmed-down version of the U.S.–UK Memorandum of Understanding. After this initial meeting, the negotiations were completed at an intensive three-day meeting in The Hague in late

July. Matters were somewhat complicated by the fact that a new Dutch Government had just been elected, which came into being after our first meeting in May. For all our careful planning we did not count on this event. Luckily, the new Dutch Government was extraordinarily cooperative and addressed this matter as one of the first items of business.

The United Kingdom–Dutch agreement[4] covered three main issues: first, the process by which the accused were to be transferred from Dutch to Scottish jurisdiction was covered by the existing extradition treaty; second, a contemplated UN Security Council resolution, under Chapter 7,[5] would ask the Dutch Government to hold or detain the suspects prior to transfer – this was the legal basis for Scottish authorities to hold the accused for trial, and allowed the exercise of foreign criminal jurisdiction on Dutch territory. And third, because this was a one-time event, the agreement defined the jurisdictional powers of the Scottish court for purposes of this trial.[6]

We in the U.S. Government managed to convince ourselves that this was entirely consistent with the terms of Resolution 883[7] and that this really would in effect be a trial in Scotland. On August 5, I flew to New York to meet with the UN Legal Adviser Hans Corell to brief him on the issue. A few days later I flew to Paris to meet with the French, who, of course, did not yet know about this initiative. As a permanent member of the Security Council, we had to get their agreement to go forward with the trial, and we did. On August 24, Secretary Albright and Robin Cook briefed the victims' families and on the same day, a letter was delivered by the United States and United Kingdom to the UN Secretary General announcing the arrangements.

In the end, the trial was a diplomatic success story. International law was creatively employed in a manner that facilitated accountability for those responsible for the bombing. Equally important, the initiative provided a means for Libya to take steps to make amends for its terrorist behavior. In the aftermath of the criminal trial, Libya reached settlements with the Pan Am 103 families paying each family approximately $10 million. It also settled with the UTA victims' families. This initiative was credited with started the process of the normalization of relations between the United States and Libya.[8]

## The Bombing of the Chinese Embassy during the 1999 Kosovo Intervention

As we discussed earlier today, the 1999 NATO intervention was controversial because of the absence of Security Council authorization for the use of force to halt the ethnic cleansing.[9] We knew that any attempt to get a Resolution through the Security Council would be vetoed by Russia and China. We had developed a menu of rationales for taking action. Among them were the human rights violations and the human catastrophe that was occurring in the area. The fact that the Security Council was paralyzed meant that NATO had to act for humanitarian reasons, and the fact that the NATO action was collective gave us some solace. The Security Council had previously defined the conflict as an international crisis and a threat to regional peace and security. The UN Secretary General had issued a written statement that acknowledged the breakdown of diplomacy; and, finally, on June 10, the Security Council passed Resolution 1244,[10] which constituted an after-the-fact ratification of our actions.

Midway through the NATO air campaign, in the early morning of May 7, the Chinese embassy in Belgrade was hit by five laser-guided bombs that were dropped by U.S. planes on a NATO raid. Three members of the Chinese mission to Belgrade were killed and twenty-seven others were injured. The intended target was the Federal Directorate for Supply and Procurement in Belgrade, a legitimate target under the rules of engagement.

When the news reached China there were anti-American demonstrations in Beijing, Chendu, and Shengyang, and our embassy in Beijing was heavily damaged. The Consul General's residence in Chendu was burned after rioters stormed the compound with the help of the People's Armed Police. At this end of the world, Secretary Albright and Undersecretary

Tom Pickering made a midnight visit to the Chinese ambassador's residence in Washington, DC to express condolences and ask for protection for U.S. personnel in China. They were courteously received but basically shown the door after a few minutes. Ambassador Sasser in Beijing was trying to reach the foreign ministry to request protection of U.S. property and couldn't get his calls returned. President Clinton likewise tried to call President Jiang, and his calls were ignored.

In the aftermath of the bombing, China immediately suspended high-level military assistance, nonproliferation, and human rights discussions, and later they stopped U.S. Navy ship visits to Hong Kong and pulled out of the World Trade Organization (WTO) negotiations. President Clinton issued an apology and announced that we would make humanitarian (*ex gratia*) payments to the Chinese. Tom Pickering was sent to Beijing as the President's personal envoy to present the President's letter, which contained an explanation for the bombing as well as the offer of *ex gratia* payments. The Chinese firmly rejected the offer and demanded a full investigation and appropriate apology, compensation for the families of those killed and injured, as well as compensation for the destruction of the embassy – and the Chinese wanted all of this in a single package.[11]

The Chinese added that until the demands were met, there would be no further contacts with the U.S. Government at any level. Up to this point, L had only advisory involvement with the legal issues raised by the President's offer. The reason for this was we did not view the explanation of the bombing or the offer of *ex gratia* compensation as a legal requirement. It is settled under international law that a government is not required to pay claims for injuries or damages incidental to the lawful use of force incurred during armed conflict. That said, there is the well-established practice of governments entering into settlements for damages on an *ex gratia* basis.

In June, to our surprise, the Chinese Ministry of Foreign Affairs (MFA) announced the appointment of a delegation and said they were prepared to engage in discussions on the Embassy bombing. The MFA named as the head of this delegation my counterpart, Yin Yubiao, who was the Director of the Law and Treaty Department in the Ministry for Foreign Affairs. Yen and I had known each other for at least a year and a half. We had successfully negotiated a couple items – a difficult Mutual Legal Assistance Agreement and a Memorandum of Understanding memorializing the anticipated outputs from the meeting of our two Presidents in 1998. We had worked together and had a pretty good relationship. The Secretary quickly decided that I should lead the U.S. delegation.

Before starting the negotiations, however, we had to go through the interagency process of obtaining authority to settle the claims. As I noted, we had quickly established that there was sufficient precedent to allow the United States to make an *ex gratia* payment. This still left us with three problems. First, where to find the money; second, how much, and third, how to resolve these claims while putting aside the property issues. On the first issue, finding the money, we quickly decided that seeking a specific appropriation was out of the question, given the time it would take and President's desire to get this matter quickly behind us. The second issue, deciding on a range, was not too difficult. Given past precedents, we had a sense of the range that would likely be demanded. The third issue was trickier. The President's offer of an immediate *ex gratia* payment extended only to the injuries and deaths, not to the property claims. These issues were much more complicated, in part, because of the damage done to our own diplomatic properties in the bombing aftermath. Under Secretary Pickering had made clear during his visit that we could not address the Chinese property issues without addressing our own claims in parallel. Given that the Chinese had made clear that they expected a package resolution, I had to delink the humanitarian claims from the property claims – otherwise there could be no progress.

I departed for Beijing with a delegation from the Department of State and the Department of Defense. Negotiations often involve a bit of theater. That is particularly true in China. Meetings are highly stylized and formal. There are occasions however where it is possible to side step, at least momentarily the theatrics and approach each other on an issue directly much like Conrad described in the *Vincennes* dispute.

As I mentioned Yin and I had developed a good working relationship during our previous encounters. I chose to try and get our position "on the table" early, before we began the theater of the plenary sessions. I suggested a head-of-delegation–only meeting. As you know this is about as close as you can get to a one on one meeting in a diplomatic setting. I told Yin we needed to do two things. First, because our legal positions were at polar extremes and we could expect to make little or no progress if we spent our time dealing with the legality of the NATO campaign or the legal rights surrounding the bombing of their embassy, we should not waste valuable time on those divisive issues. Second, I suggested that the other key for moving the discussions forward was to separate the humanitarian issues from the less important property issues. Yin responded that it was absolutely necessary for him to fully present the Chinese version of what they believed happened and the legal basis for U.S. responsibility. I told him I was prepared to fully respond to his formal presentation, but after the presentations we should focus on the practical aspects of why we were meeting.

The Chinese side opened the plenary with statements accusing the United States of violating the principles of international law and reiterated their rejection of the U.S. explanation of the bombing. This was followed by a well-produced and well-rehearsed computer graphic and video presentation of the destruction of the Chinese Embassy, including graphic video of the dead and injured. They concluded by arguing that U.S. compensation must reflect the "gravity and uniqueness in human history" of this case. Their insistence that all their claims must be settled in one package was repeated. I presented the U.S. response concluding with my proposal to bifurcate the issues and discuss humanitarian payments for the deaths and injuries first. We took a break, after which Yin pulled me aside and asked if I was ready to make a proposal on the humanitarian damages. I said "yes," and we immediately went into a head of delegation meeting. I made our offer and described the methodology that produced the figure, as well as our proposed procedure for giving the payments directly to the victims. After a substantial recess, Yin returned with a counter proposal that he said covered the deaths, injuries and reflected the "gravity" of this event. The Chinese appeared to have moved off of their rhetoric about a package settlement. After overnight consideration I told Yin that I would take his counteroffer back to Washington and would schedule another meeting in a matter of weeks. I also told him we would have to establish a process to discuss the U.S. property claims. That process could be separate from the humanitarian compensation discussions and chaired at a lower level but must run in parallel with our discussions.

Back in Washington the mood was upbeat. The Chinese demand for humanitarian payment was not off the charts and it appeared that we were on the road to putting our relations "back on track."

The strategy for the next round was simple: reach agreement on the right amount and begin technical discussions on the mode of transfer and distribution of the amounts to the families of those killed and to the injured. Because we were talking about an international transfer of a substantial amount of money under strict controls, we decided to add two members of the Federal Reserve Bank of New York to my delegation. At the policy level, the key concern was that all of the money be distributed directly to the designated recipients. The Chinese had already indicated their desire that any settlement money be turned over to the government to be distributed when and how they saw fit.

Roughly two weeks later, I returned to Beijing and presented our response to the Chinese counteroffer. After a brief recess Yin came back with a counteroffer to settle for $4.5 million, a figure well within my authority. I accepted immediately and suggested that we memorialize our agreement in an MOU. I also laid out the key requirements that we would need, including that the money be transferred to the individuals as quickly as possible and that our payment was a full and final settlement of any claims. Yin did not seem to have any problem with any of these points, and we turned over the drafting of the various "technical" documents to our lawyers.

The lawyers met well into the evening. Later that night I received a call that while they were making progress on the documents, they were now being told that there would be no signing until we reached agreement on the Chinese property claims. I immediately placed a call to Yin at home and asked him to meet me at my hotel. We met in the Hotel bar, which had closed but was opened for the two of us. Over mugs of Chinese beer, I told Yin that the conditions were unacceptable, and I considered the position taken by his subordinates to be a breach of our agreement to proceed on the humanitarian issues only. I told him I was prepared to be on the next flight to Washington if he did not stand by our original agreement. Yin said he would review the situation and get in touch in the morning.

The next morning Yin called and suggested a head of delegation meeting. We met, and he stated that we could finish the documents and conclude this phase of the negotiations with one condition: the MOU would have to make clear that the United States would return promptly to begin discussions of the Chinese property issues. I agreed that once I received assurances that the U.S. property claims would also commence.

Yin and I signed the MOU, and several weeks later the United States transferred the funds to accounts specially set up for the victims and families.

Within a short period of time China reopened talks on WTO, and, at lower levels, a dialogue resumed on other issues such as military to military contacts.

I returned in a month or so to start discussions on the property claims. The Chinese side had been clear that these discussions would have to occur on two levels: one, *the Chinese* property claims would be discussed at Head of Delegation level; and two, *the U.S.* property claims, would be discussed at a lower level. I agreed. We spent the next four months discussing property damage issues. We finally resolved both sets of claims in December. The United States paid $28 million for damage to the Chinese embassy. The Chinese paid $2.87 million for damages to the U.S. properties. It took more than a year to get the funds appropriated. The

$4.5 million for the humanitarian payments came from the Secretary of Defense's discretionary fund.

As Conrad described in the *Vincennes* dispute, this was a case where the lawyers actually got together and resolved a dispute that only they could have done.

### Discussion

*Question*: Let us turn to the question of the rationale for the Kosovo intervention? It is generally understood that L was asked, but did not end up supplying a written justification similar to the kind that we've been discussing about some of the other crises. Some have commented that L's refusal to provide a written justification had left certain ill feelings toward L among some of the other parts of the State Department. Can you comment on that?

*Mr. Matheson*: I can shed some light on that. About six months before the actual conflict, at the time when NATO was considering giving an order to threaten the use of force, the political community of NATO got together and had a discussion about what the basis of such threat of force would be.[12] At the end of the discussion, it was clear that there was no common agreement on what might be the justification. There were some NATO members who were prepared to base it on a new doctrine of humanitarian intervention; but most members of the NATO Council were reluctant to adopt a relatively open-ended new doctrine.[13] So at the end of that week, the NATO political community said, here is a list of all of the important reasons why it is necessary for us to threaten the use of force. And at the bottom, it said that under these unique circumstances, we think such actions would be legitimate. There was deliberate evasion of making a "legal" assertion.

And this same process occurred in the U.S. Government. There were some who wanted to articulate that humanitarian intervention is now the basis for U.S. action. There was another theory from the Department of Defense, which wanted to adopt sort of an expanded idea of self-defense, based on the general interest of the United States in the region; but on reflection, nobody was really prepared to throw all the eggs into either of those baskets. So we ended up with a formulation similar to that of NATO, where we listed all of the reasons why we were taking action and, in the end, mumbled something about its being justifiable and legitimate but not a precedent. So in a sense, it *was* something less than a definitive legal rationale – although it probably was taken by large parts of the public community as something like that.

And I think what this all illustrates is that although L doesn't really ever make a decision as to whether to use force or not; nonetheless, it does have a significant impact on how the decision is articulated, and that can be important in terms of what precedents are or are not created for the future. At the time, the concern was that if we articulated the broad self-defense or the humanitarian intervention rationale, it might be misused by others.

*Mr. Sofaer*: You don't need to dress it up like a legal rationale. It doesn't change the basic soundness of the approach, and it's really consistent with what the United States has always done in these situations. It's a common law approach. It's a sad thing that Abe Chayes is not with us anymore. Chayes, in his classic article, argues for this approach and I think it's the right approach. The case for intervening in Kosovo was overwhelming. Even though you did not have a Security Council Resolution, you had the international lawyers saying, "My goodness, we've got to do this. It's clearly the right thing to do and the moral thing to do, both strategically and morally, but yet we have to regard it as nonprecedential." But I don't see how you can legitimately take military action and not allow people to refer in the future to the reasons you gave for taking the military action.

*Mr. Williamson*: I see us as lawyers and I really think that when asked a question, we have to respond with a legal conclusion. There can be various gradations of strength and so forth. I think that a legal conclusion should have been expressed, and I think it would have been a self-defense argument. The NATO treaty[14] makes clear that NATO cannot do anything except in self-defense. In terms of precedent setting, I think that the least damage would have been done through the self-defense argument.

*Question*: Let's address a final question about Lockerbie that ties up the loose ends in our discussion. Do you think the fact that they had the trial contributed more toward Libya's current cooperativeness and departure from its rogue status, than a military response would have?

*Mr. Harper*: Over what period of time? No matter how you parse the question, one has to assume that over time, states change their interests and change their appreciation of their own interests.

*Mr. Andrews*: It's pretty clear that Qaddafi had changed his interests. Sanctions started taking effect, but, also, he wanted to refocus his country on Africa and start reaching out. I didn't take part of any of the discussions, but there were meetings after the trial to discuss settlement issues, and it's my understanding that during that period, it became quite clear that Qaddafi was reaching out to the United States in a number of ways.

*Mr. Robinson*: I would say, however, that from the perspective of the victims' families, if you compare this to instances in which we did use force over the last fifteen years, it sticks out like a sore thumb in recent history. Here we have destruction of an aircraft with almost three hundred Americans, and we did fundamentally nothing for years except issue a public indictment, which we knew full well would not lead to a trial on U.S. soil.

*Mr. Williamson*: I think you have to talk about what kind of use of force. If you're talking about a pin prick, it's one thing. If you're talking about what we did in Iraq in 2003, it's something else altogether.

*Mr. Sofaer*: But at the same time, I think it clearly contributed to moving Qaddafi along to have done this wonderful trial arrangement that David has described here that finally got the thing done.

# 12 The Bush (43rd) Administration – William H. Taft IV (2001–2005)

I WAS THE LEGAL ADVISER FOR THE FIRST ADMINISTRATION OF President George W. Bush, from April 2001 to February 2005. During these years the United States deployed its armed forces and engaged in military operations in Afghanistan, starting in October 2001, and Iraq, starting in March 2003. The legal issues involved in both of these instances were significantly different. I will discuss each of them and the role the Office of the Legal Adviser played in each of them in turn.

## The Use of Force against Afghanistan

Our military operations in Afghanistan beginning in October 2001 and continuing today have been undertaken in self-defense against those responsible for the attacks on the United States on September 11, 2001.[1] Those attacks made clear to all nations what had probably been the case for some years, namely that the organization Al-Qaeda, led by Osama bin Laden, was engaged in a campaign against the United States, its military forces, and its citizens wherever they might be. During the days and weeks after September 11, the Legal Adviser's Office worked with lawyers in the White House Counsel's Office, the Department of Justice and the Department of Defense to establish the legal basis for military operations we expected might be necessary to defend against further attacks. We drafted the UN Security Council Resolution that recognized our right to use force.[2] We were in touch with lawyers in allied governments to share our understanding of their treaty obligations in the circumstances. The member States of NATO, the Organization of American States (OAS), and the Australia, New Zealand, United States Treaty (ANZUS) all adopted resolutions of support for our use of force in self-defense,[3] and many of them joined in military operations with our forces. We assisted the Department of Justice in drafting the joint resolution adopted by Congress in late September that authorized the President to deploy our forces and engage them in hostilities.[4] This resolution stated that it satisfied the requirements of the War Powers Resolution for our troops to be committed to combat.

Perhaps the only peculiar thing about all these resolutions being adopted by the different organizations and the Congress was that the specific enemy against whom they were directed was not a State. The President made clear throughout the process that we would welcome the support of every nation in our conflict with Al-Qaeda.[5] He also made clear, however, that in the event a State was harboring Al-Qaeda we would consider the government of that State hostile and would attack it.[6] This approach was fully supported by the UN Security Council and our allies as well. Because the Taliban regime in Afghanistan continued to support Al-Qaeda, we invaded that country in October 2001.[7] The Taliban regime was overthrown in a matter of weeks and the interim authorities in Afghanistan and subsequently the interim government established under UN auspices in early 2002 then, in turn, supported our forces in their continuing efforts to destroy Al-Qaeda and its Taliban supporters. The legal basis for our activities continued to be our right of self-defense, reinforced by the UN Security Council resolutions recognizing it.

In short, the legal basis for our military operations in Afghanistan has never been controversial, either internationally or domestically. The Legal Adviser's office had no difficulty in establishing that we had a right to use force in self-defense against Al-Qaeda and any government supporting it, as well as any related terrorist organizations. We participated in drafting the necessary UN Security Council resolutions, and they were promptly adopted. There has been some controversy over some of the resolutions, including the Congress' important joint resolution authorizing the use of force against terrorist organizations whose relationship to Al-Qaeda or the attacks of September 11, 2001 was tenuous. And there has been a great deal of controversy over the rights of captured Al-Qaeda and Taliban forces to contest their detention and over how they should be treated.

## Treatment of Detainees in the War on Terrorism

With respect to this subject, it is now well known that the Attorney General advised the President that the Geneva Conventions did not apply to the conflict with Al-Qaeda or the Taliban and that captured members of these organizations were not entitled to any rights beyond what the President decided to provide them as a matter of policy.[8] I reviewed this conclusion with the office staff, and we did not agree with it. Accordingly, I advised the Secretary that the Conventions did apply to the conflict with the Taliban and, originally, that because our conflict with Al-Qaeda was part of the conflict with the Taliban the Conventions applied to it also. On further consideration, we determined that the conflict with Al-Qaeda could be viewed as distinct from the conflict with the Taliban and came to agree with the Attorney General that the Conventions did not apply to it. In the meantime, the President had decided to apply the Conventions to the conflict with the Taliban as a matter of policy,[9] so our differences with the Attorney General appeared to have been resolved. Regrettably, however, this seeming agreement was an illusion.

In the months following the President's decision, the Legal Adviser's Office drafted a lengthy memorandum, which concluded that because our policy was to treat the Al-Qaeda and Taliban detainees consistent with the requirements of the Geneva Conventions, the question of whether they were entitled to this as a matter of law was moot.[10] (This draft memorandum was made public by the Administration in January 2005.) The draft also expressed the view that customary international law required that the detainees in any event be treated humanely and had certain of the rights set out in the Conventions. We thought that because it was our policy to treat the detainees consistent with the Conventions, that this was being done. It developed, however, that at the same time we were working on our memorandum and subsequently the Department of Justice lawyers were working separately with the lawyers at the Department of Defense to authorize certain departures from the Conventions' terms in the treatment of the detainees, particularly with regard to methods of interrogation.[11] My staff and I were not invited to review this work and we were, indeed, unaware that it was being done. In several decisions in summer 2004, the Supreme Court disapproved some of the legal positions that the Department of Justice had adopted,[12] and, on review, that Department later withdrew at least one memorandum it had issued (on a classified basis) in 2002.

It was highly regrettable that the Legal Adviser's Office was not involved in the legal work following the decisions in February 2002. I think that we were excluded because it was suspected, in light of some of the positions we had taken, that we would not agree with some of the conclusions other lawyers in the Administration expected to reach and that we might leak information about the work to the press. It was somewhat ironic that when the fact of the work subsequently did become known, it was clear that we at least were not responsible for this because we had been excluded. I am convinced, however, that if we had been involved and our views considered, several conclusions that were not consistent with our treaty obligations under the Convention against Torture (CAT) and our obligations under customary international law would not have been reached. Later, in 2004, when we worked with the Department of Justice on the revision of the memorandum on the CAT that had been withdrawn earlier in the year, we were able to reach agreement on a very respectable opinion.

## Military Operations in Iraq

In contrast to the situation involving the treatment of detainees in the conflict with Al-Qaeda and the Taliban, the Legal Adviser's Office was the lead office in analyzing and, indeed, establishing the legal basis for our military operations in Iraq in 2003.[13]

Operation Iraqi Freedom was the final episode in a conflict initiated more than twelve years earlier when Iraq invaded and occupied Kuwait.[14] From the time of that invasion in August 1990, until today, the UN Security Council has adopted a series of resolutions that authorize member States to act to assure Iraq's compliance with their terms.[15] The resolutions have required a number of different things from Iraq over the years: withdrawal from Kuwait, destruction of its weapons of mass destruction (WMD) capability, providing access to international inspectors to monitor its compliance with various resolutions, and so forth. The office was responsible for drafting proposed resolutions and analyzing drafts proposed by other States. Our work was carried out in close coordination with the U.S. Mission to the UN, lawyers from DOD and NSC, and policymakers in the Department. The Secretary was often directly involved in the negotiation of the language of the different resolutions both internally in the U.S. Government and with other members of the UN Security Council. We supported him.

During summer and fall 2002, concern over Iraq's WMD programs steadily increased. For some years, the Iraqi regime had not permitted UN inspectors to come to Iraq at all, and it was widely recognized that in many respects Iraq was not in compliance with its obligations to the UN Security Council. Our view was that earlier resolutions authorized the use of force to bring Iraq into compliance, and over the years we and others had conducted military operations in Iraq for that purpose in reliance on those resolutions. Politically, however, it appeared highly desirable in fall 2003 to update our authorities in light of the circumstances and our growing concerns. The UN Security Council also wanted to give Iraq a final opportunity to comply with its obligations before force was used again. We worked hard to draft and negotiate the text of what became Resolution 1441.[16] It was a delicate matter, because we did not want to bring into question what we believed was our existing right to use force in the event of continuing Iraqi noncompliance, while at the same time giving Iraq a genuine opportunity to correct its earlier defaults.

A difficult issue arose in the course of negotiating the text of Resolution 1441. It concerned whether in the event of Iraqi noncompliance a further UN Security Council resolution would be necessary to authorize the use of force or, as was the case with the resolution authorizing States to evict Iraq from Kuwait if it had not withdrawn by a specific date, States were authorized to act without further action by the UN Security Council. This issue was settled by drafting the resolution to say that in the event of noncompliance the Council would meet to discuss the situation without saying that it had to take any further action. This, in our view, left intact our authority to use force without further authorization from the UN Security Council, if Iraq failed to comply. We stated that this was our understanding of the situation in our Explanation of Vote on Resolution 1441.[17] Other States expressed a different understanding of what the resolution required at the same time. We felt that the language that we had drafted provided better support for our position than for theirs. What was important, we thought, was that no one could be in doubt about our interpretation and the basis for it.

In early 2003, it became apparent that Iraq remained in default on its obligations under Resolution 1441. Inevitably, the different interpretations of the resolution were brought forward again. The United States thought it would be useful in this situation to get a further resolution authorizing the use of force to bring Iraq into compliance, and we were urged by some of our close allies to seek one. We felt that such a resolution might possibly convince the Iraqi regime that its failure to comply would indeed result in military operations against it and, by convincing Iraq of the risk it was running, avoid the need to use force. We did not, however, at any time agree that a further resolution was necessary before we acted. Those who argued then and later that in attempting to obtain a specific resolution authorizing the use of force in early 2003 and failing to get it we had conceded that such a resolution was necessary were simply not listening to what we were saying.

As everyone now knows, Operation Iraqi Freedom was initiated in March 2003. Congress had previously passed a resolution authorizing the deployment of our armed forces,[18] so the legal basis for our action was well established in both domestic and international law. There was little controversy within the Administration about this, as the lawyers from the different agencies and foreign States involved had been in regular contact for many weeks and reached agreement on all key points. An example of how well this coordination worked could be seen when Lord Goldsmith, the Attorney General of the United Kingdom, came to Washington to discuss the interpretation of Resolution 1441. Talking points were prepared by our office and shared with the White House counsel, the Attorney General, and the General Counsel of the Department of Defense. Lord Goldsmith met with each of these officials separately and heard the same analysis of the situation each time. Although some lawyers in the Administration felt that our inherent right of self-defense might provide an additional ground for the use of force in Iraq, it was agreed that this was too tenuous a position to put forward. In addition, doing so could possibly undermine Lord Goldsmith's confidence in our interpretation of our authority to act against Iraq under the UN Security Council resolutions in the event of its continuing breach of its obligations, about which we had no doubts. Lord Goldsmith agreed with our analysis and, when the United Kingdom joined us in Operation Iraqi Freedom, his explanation of the basis for the United Kingdom's participation under international law was the same as ours.[19]

Operation Iraqi Freedom was a success, and, by May 2003, our armed forces and their allies had occupied Iraq. As the occupying power, we had new responsibilities under the Geneva Conventions. Although the Department of Defense had the lead in the occupation, our lawyers continued to play a major role in defining the legal parameters setting out the authorities and responsibilities of the occupying power in the unique circumstances we found in Iraq. There was close cooperation between our lawyers and those in other agencies and in the other States that were contributing to the occupying force. Our work was especially involved in the development and negotiation of additional UN Security Council resolutions that established the terms of the occupation. Successive resolutions prescribed the legal structure for the period immediately following major combat operations (UNSCR 1483),[20] authorized continuing military operations (UNSCR 1511),[21] and provided the framework for Iraq's political transition to a democratic government (UNSCR 1546).[22] In most respects these resolutions embodied the rules of the Geneva Conventions for occupying powers, but they also reflected the fact that after June 30, 2004, Iraq was no longer occupied but a state with an interim government dependent for internal security on foreign forces. The work on these resolutions was conducted virtually nonstop from May 2003 and continues today. Many novel legal issues had to be resolved in what was an unprecedented situation with the UN Security Council using its Chapter 7 authority to provide the terms for the simultaneous conduct of military operations against a substantial insurgency and the transition to a democratic system of government in a country that had been a dictatorship for many decades. I believe that the legal work that was done in connection with this effort will be a model for the future exercise of the Security Council's powers. The contribution of the Legal Adviser's Office to that work has been the key element.

# 13 The Bush (43rd) Administration – John B. Bellinger III (2005–2009)

**W**HEN I MOVED TO THE STATE DEPARTMENT WITH SEC-
retary Rice in 2005, first as Senior Adviser and ultimately as Legal Adviser, I was deeply concerned by
international (and domestic) perceptions that the Bush Administration
not only did not believe in international law but was actively hostile
toward it. These perceptions had been fueled by various Bush Administration actions in the first term, including the renunciation of the Kyoto
Protocol,[1] the "un-signing" of the Rome Statute,[2] opinions on extraordinary interrogation techniques issued by the Department of Justice,[3] and,
perhaps most significant, the decision to invade Iraq without a new UN
Security Council Resolution authorizing the use of force.[4] Throughout
my tenure as Legal Adviser, one of my main goals was to rebut these
perceptions, both by trying to ensure compliance with our international
obligations in the Bush Administration's second term and by engaging in
active "international legal diplomacy" with other countries and international institutions.

From her earliest days as Secretary of State, Secretary Rice supported my mission in both words and actions. In a town hall meeting
of State Department employees during her first week in office, she
stated, in an unscripted response to a question from a young L attorney,
that "This Department, along with the rest of the Bush Administration, will be a strong voice for international legal norms, for living up
to our treaty obligations, to recognizing that America's moral authority

in international politics also rests on our ability to defend international laws and treaties." Similarly, she agreed to speak to the annual meeting of the American Society of International Law in March 2005 – the first Secretary of State to do so in more than thirty years – and agreed again to address the centennial of the Society one year later.

Due to a variety of factors, including Secretary Rice's close relationship with President Bush and perhaps a recognition of the problems caused by failing to involve L's lawyers in the first term, the Legal Adviser's office was able to wield greater influence in the Bush Administration's second term. L's advice was sought not only by Secretary Rice and senior State Department officials but also by the White House and other departments, who came much more to accept its advice on international law issues as authoritative. For example, L's lawyers played key roles in the negotiation of numerous multilateral initiatives, including the negotiation of extremely important UN Security Council Resolutions on North Korea, Iran, and Lebanon. L's lawyers were actively involved in the negotiation of dozens of important new treaties and the ratification of more than a hundred new and previously negotiated treaties. During the 110th Congress, attorneys in L, working with an L lawyer detailed to the Senate Foreign Relations Committee, secured Senate approval of ninety treaties, more than during any single Congress in American history. These treaties included many multilateral treaties, including five international humanitarian law treaties, including The Hague Cultural Property Convention, which had languished unratified for more than fifty years.[5] L's lawyers also successfully negotiated and secured ratification of the Third Additional Protocol to the Geneva Conventions, which created the Red Crystal, and allowed the entry into the International Red Cross and Red Crescent Movement of the Israeli and Palestinian national humanitarian societies.[6] I and L's lawyers also made an enormous push to win Senate approval of the Law of the Sea Convention,[7] persuading policymakers at the White House of the benefits of the Convention and ultimately arranging for statements of support from the President and the National Security Adviser; the Convention was again approved by the Senate Foreign Relations Committee but was never brought to the full Senate.

L also supported international law in litigation in U.S. courts, helping the Justice Department file dozens of briefs on important international law issues in the Supreme Court, Courts of Appeal, and District Courts. For example, L persuaded the Justice Department to reverse its previously held position (dating from the Reagan Administration) and to support the arguments of India and Mongolia in the U.S. Supreme Court that foreign governments enjoy immunity under the Foreign Sovereignty Immunities Act from the jurisdiction of the federal courts to enforce tax liens levied by the City of New York. The Supreme Court, unfortunately, rejected our arguments.[8]

In addition to supporting compliance with international law inside the Bush Administration, I also wanted to make sure that other countries understood that the United States does take international law seriously. At Secretary Rice's urging, I and L's lawyers engaged in intensive efforts in international legal diplomacy. I considered this aspect of the office's work to be a central part of my tenure as Legal Adviser. I traveled extensively during my tenure to engage in dialogue on international legal issues. I visited dozens of countries – meeting regularly with the Legal Advisers and senior officials from governments in Europe, Asia, and North America – and gave hundreds of talks and press interviews on international law issues. I regularly attended the semiannual meetings of the committee of Legal Advisers of the Council of Europe countries, known as the CAHDI, as well as the annual meetings of the UN Sixth Committee.

## The International Criminal Court

One issue to which I personally devoted considerable attention as Legal Adviser was the International Criminal Court (ICC).[9] During the second term, several L's lawyers and I worked hard to develop a pragmatic "modus vivendi" with the ICC and Rome Statute supporters. We made clear that even though the Bush Administration disagreed with aspects of the Rome Statute – a disagreement that I pointed out had been shared by the Clinton Administration – we were nevertheless committed to the Rome Statute's goals of ending impunity for those who commit genocide, war crimes, or crimes against humanity. We repeatedly emphasized that the United States respected the decisions of other countries to become party to the ICC, and that we were prepared to work with the Court in certain circumstances, such as in its investigation of the Darfur genocide and the use of ICC facilities for the trial of Charles Taylor by the Special Court for Sierra Leone. In March 2005, L's lawyers helped Secretary Rice negotiate the U.S. abstention in UN Security Council Resolution 1593, which referred the Darfur atrocities to the ICC.[10] We subsequently made clear that the U.S. was prepared to help the prosecutor in his Darfur investigation. By the end of 2008, other countries recognized that the United States had adopted a more pragmatic approach toward the ICC and human rights groups even applauded the Bush Administration's strong opposition to the efforts by a number of other countries, including Rome Statute parties, to invoke Article 16 of the Rome Statute to defer the investigation of Sudanese President Bashir.

During my tenure as Legal Adviser, L's relations with the Office of Legal Counsel (OLC) at the Justice Department and the Office of the General Counsel of the Defense Department – which had been strained during the first term, largely because of OLC's preparation of a number of memoranda for the Defense Department and the White House on international law issues without the involvement, or over the objections, of L's lawyers – also improved. In contrast to the first term, OLC sought and generally accepted input from L on a number of opinions on international law issues, and Defense Department lawyers began to work more closely with us, including in international meetings, on the legal framework applicable to the detention and treatment of captured terror suspects.

In the remaining part of this chapter, I will focus on two areas of international law that took up significant amounts of my time and the Office of the Legal Adviser throughout all four years of my tenure: our efforts to comply with the decision of the International Court of Justice in the *Avena/Medellin* case,[11] and our efforts to address the many legal issues raised by the detention and prosecution of members of Al-Qaeda and the Taliban, both inside the Bush Administration and with the international community.

## The ICJ's *Avena* Case

L's efforts to achieve U.S. compliance with the decision of the ICJ in the *Avena* case lasted all four years of the Bush Administration's second term and, although little noticed internationally, stand as an outstanding example of L's commitment to ensuring compliance with U.S. treaty obligations, even when politically difficult domestically. The *Avena* case involved fifty-one Mexican nationals on death row in Texas, California, and various other states who had not been informed of their right of consular notification under the Vienna Convention on Consular Relations. Most of the fifty-one Mexicans had exhausted their appeal rights under state law. In 2003, Mexico had brought an action against the United States in the ICJ, alleging violation of the Vienna Convention on Consular Relations (VCCR)[12] and requesting that all of the convictions and sentences be reviewed. My predecessor Will Taft and other members of L argued the case before the ICJ in 2003, essentially conceding violations of the VCCR but arguing that state procedural default rules barred the Mexicans from raising these violations late in the process. In 2004, however, the ICJ ruled that, notwithstanding state procedural default rules, the United States was required to provide review and reconsideration of the convictions and death sentences of the fifty-one Mexican nationals.[13]

In February 2005, within weeks of Secretary Rice's becoming Secretary and while I was still serving as her Senior Adviser, the Bush Administration was forced to decide whether and how to comply with the *Avena* decision. One of the Mexican nationals, Jose Ernesto Medellin, had appealed his conviction to the Supreme Court, citing the ICJ's decision. During this period, although I had been nominated as Legal Adviser, I had not been confirmed, and Will Taft remained as Legal Adviser. I argued to Secretary Rice that the United States had a treaty law obligation under the UN Charter to comply with the *Avena* decision, that it would be good legal policy to comply (because it would help to protect U.S. nationals under the VCCR), and that it would also be an early demonstration of the Bush Administration's commitment to international law in the second term.

The Justice Department, while acknowledging the international law obligation to comply with the *Avena* decision, expressed skepticism as to whether the President could supersede state procedural default rules. They urged that the Bush Administration instead seek legislation that would specifically allow the Mexican defendants to raise the absence of VCCR notifications, notwithstanding state procedural default rules. L's lawyers and I were concerned, however, that it would be difficult to persuade Congress, especially with a Republican majority in the House known to be skeptical about international law and institutions, to pass such legislation in a timely fashion, if at all, while the Mexicans remained on death row. At our urging, Secretary Rice persuaded the President to issue a determination in late February 2005, that state courts give effect to the *Avena* judgment. The significance of President Bush's decision cannot be overstated, given that the President was a former Governor of Texas and a supporter of the death penalty and that Mr. Medellin had been convicted of an especially grisly crime in Texas – the rape and murder of two teenage girls. Ordering review of his conviction and sentence in order to comply with a decision by an international tribunal in The Hague was not a popular decision in Texas.

At the same time, in a Solomonic compromise, Secretary Rice also agreed with the Attorney General's recommendation that the United States withdraw from the Optional Protocol to the VCCR, so that no more actions could be brought before the ICJ.[14] Although the United States had previously relied on the Optional Protocol to bring a successful action against Iran before the ICJ in connection with Iran's failure to provide consular access for the Tehran hostages, withdrawal seemed prudent, given the near impossibility, despite Herculean efforts by the State Department, of ensuring that all state law enforcement officials always provide VCCR consular notifications.

L's involvement in this case did not end there, however. Indeed, it continued for four more years, up to my last hour in office, as Mr. Medellin's case wound back through the Texas courts, to the U.S. Supreme Court, and back to the ICJ. In Texas, the state argued that President George W. Bush lacked the constitutional authority to set aside Texas procedural default rules, and the Texas Court of Criminal Appeals agreed, ruling that the President had acted unconstitutionally. Mr. Medellin then appealed to the U.S. Supreme Court, which also concluded in March 2008 that the President lacked the power to give effect the ICJ's *Avena* decision.[15] The Court further concluded that the *Avena* decision was not self-executing and therefore was not binding of its own force on state and federal courts. Although the Court recognized that no one disputed that the United States had an international law obligation to comply with the *Avena* decision, it nevertheless did not bind state and federal courts as a matter of domestic law.[16]

Following the Supreme Court's decision – and despite the fact that the United States had withdrawn from the Optional Protocol – Mexico again initiated action in the ICJ. It argued that the ICJ retains jurisdiction under its statute to interpret a prior decision where a dispute arises as to its "meaning or scope." Mexico's application to the Court argued that the United States had misinterpreted *Avena* to find some means to implement a decision and not an obligation ultimately to provide review and reconsideration. We rejected Mexico's assertion that there was such a dispute and made clear that the United States fully understood and accepted our obligations under *Avena*. Like Will Taft before me, I personally argued the *Medellin* case before the ICJ, accompanied by L's lawyers Jim Thessin and Steve Mathias, as well as Professor Vaughan Lowe. Unfortunately, in the midst of the ICJ's deliberations, Texas went forward with the execution of Mr. Medellin in August 2008. The ICJ handed down its decision in January 2009, accepting on the one hand the U.S. argument that it did not dispute its obligations under the *Avena* decision, but on the other hand finding that the United States had breached its obligations by allowing Mr. Medellin to be executed.[17]

L remained at the center of every aspect of the Medellin case. From early 2005, L's lawyers argued that the *Avena* decision imposed an international law obligation with which we were bound to comply, and that the Bush Administration should take steps to implement the obligation. In the domestic litigation, we worked hand-in-hand with the Justice Department in preparing the U.S. briefs in the Texas courts and the U.S. Supreme Court. After losing the *Medellin* case, we spearheaded efforts to engage leaders in the state of Texas and other states to press for compliance with the ICJ's decision; L's lawyers flew to Texas for meetings with both the Governor's office and the Board of Pardon and Parole. In June 2008, on L's recommendation, and after overcoming some initial White House reluctance, Secretary Rice persuaded Attorney General Mukasey to cosign a letter to the Governor of Texas requesting that Texas take steps to give effect to the *Avena* decision. When Mexico returned to the ICJ, we sought to demonstrate to the Court the seriousness with which the United States has sought to comply with its obligations under *Avena* and to explain the complications in our domestic law system that made compliance difficult. In addition to personally arguing the case at the provisional measures stage in June 2008 (there was no oral argument at the merits stage), I flew back to The Hague in July 2008 to receive the provisional measures decision and again in January 2009 to receive the ICJ's final decision. I received a six-hour extension from the incoming Obama Administration so that I could be present on January 19, 2009 (the Martin Luther King holiday in the United States) for the reading of the Court's decision, as a final demonstration of the Bush Administration's respect for the Court, and fly back to Washington, DC on Inauguration Day.

## Treatment of Detainees in the War on Terrorism Revisited

In the Bush Administration's second term, L's lawyers also led the efforts inside the Bush Administration to clarify and adopt a more robust legal framework for the detention, treatment, and prosecution of captured terrorists.[18] The Bush Administration's policies and legal decisions on these matters adopted during the first term had stirred up significant criticism both domestically and internationally, and my goal was both to try to move our policies and legal positions to a better place and to engage in greater dialogue with our allies about these issues. We worked very hard to encourage the Bush Administration to adopt clear international rules, including Common Article 3 and Article 75 of Additional Protocol I of the Geneva Conventions. The Supreme Court ultimately concluded that Common Article 3 was applicable to the conflict with Al-Qaeda as a matter of treaty law.[19] Although State Department and Defense Department lawyers had concluded during the Reagan Administration that Article 75 reflects customary international law, L was unable to convince the Defense and Justice Departments to restate this conclusion, in the context of a conflict with a terrorist group, during the Bush Administration.

In 2005, we did persuade the Defense and Justice Departments to make changes to the military commissions in order to provide additional processes. After the President's 2001 Military Order was invalidated by the Supreme Court in the *Hamdan* decision in 2006,[20] L's lawyers tried hard to ensure that the new military commissions created by the Military Commissions Act would withstand international scrutiny and were consistent with international legal norms.[21] Unfortunately, the military commissions continued to be harshly criticized, but the Military Commissions Act was in fact much improved as a result of the hard work by L's attorneys.

In addition to working to clarify the international legal framework for detention, L's lawyers also worked within the Bush Administration to clarify the domestic authority for detention. Until this point, the Bush Administration had relied on the President's constitutional authority as

Commander in Chief, as supplemented by the Authorization for Use of Military Force legislation adopted by Congress in 2001, to hold detainees as "enemy combatants." This authority had become controversial, however, because it provided for potentially indefinite detention without judicial review. L's lawyers prepared draft legislation to provide a legislated framework for detention, subject to judicial review. These proposals were not adopted by the Bush Administration, however.

L was instrumental in helping Secretary Rice persuade the rest of the Bush Administration to move high-level Al-Qaeda detainees held by the Central Intelligence Agency to Guantanamo in September 2006, so that they could be prosecuted for their offenses, given access to counsel and the ICRC, and no longer held in undisclosed locations. L attorneys also tried hard to ensure that the CIA's interrogation program, and the President's Executive Order applicable to it, was consistent with the Detainee Treatment Act in 2005 and the *Hamdan* decision in 2006, which concluded that Common Article 3 applied to the treatment of Al-Qaeda detainees.

Building on work begun by Will Taft, L developed an outstanding relationship with the International Committee of the Red Cross on detainee issues during this period. L met regularly with the ICRC's Washington delegation, organized several offsite conferences for in-depth discussions of the Geneva Conventions, and arranged for ICRC President Kellenberger to meet regularly with Secretary Rice and other senior Bush Administration officials, including President Bush. L also arranged for and facilitated direct discussions between the ICRC and the CIA with respect to individuals who might be detained by CIA.

In addition to its work on the substantive issues relating to detainees inside the Bush Administration, L initiated an intensive dialogue with our European and other allies on the legal issues relating to terrorism. During its first term, the Bush Administration had not done as good a job as it might in explaining its legal decision-making to its allies. This had led the 9–11 Commission to recommend in 2004 that "the United States should engage its friends to develop a common coalition approach toward the capture and humane treatment of captured terrorists."[22] During my time as Legal Adviser, L's lawyers devoted substantial efforts to implementing this recommendation, including through numerous bilateral and multilateral meetings with foreign governments and other legal experts. In particular, we participated in ten rounds of in-depth discussions with the Legal Advisers of the twenty-seven European Union countries, and we hosted two conferences (which we came to call the "West Point Process") of six of our closest allies to try to reach consensus on the legal rules that apply to fighting terrorism. Beyond these direct engagements, L's lawyers helped me with numerous speeches and articles – even an unprecedented series of postings on the *Opinio Juris* blog – to help respond to international concerns and narrow the points of disagreement.[23]

Our discussions with our allies contributed to convergence of our views on many issues. Part of what separated us was rhetoric. The U.S. references to a "Global War on Terror," for example, were often perceived to suggest that we thought war was the principal, or even only, framework for countering terrorism, and that we could lawfully use force against all terrorists at all times wherever they might be located. Other countries understandably bristled at this notion. On the other side, our allies often appeared to argue that combating terrorism was only a law enforcement matter and challenged the readily defensible proposition that States can use force against terrorist groups that attack or imminently threaten to attack them. Both sides clarified our positions during these discussions. We made clear that the "Global War on Terror" was not a legal term of art, and that in many instances, law enforcement can be the appropriate legal paradigm for addressing terrorist threats. Our allies, on the other hand, began to accept the notion that a State can be in armed conflict with a transnational terrorist group such as Al-Qaeda. On other issues, such as detention, the United States moved closer to our allies' positions partly as a result of U.S. domestic legal developments, including new legislation such as the Detainee Treatment Act[24] and the Supreme Court's decisions in *Rasul, Hamdi,* and *Hamdan,* and

*Boumediene.*[25] At the same time, our allies acknowledged that the existing criminal laws and international humanitarian rules, such as the Geneva Conventions, did not neatly apply to the new threats posed by groups like Al-Qaeda.

It is unfortunate that because of interagency disagreements the Bush Administration was unable to change many of its controversial detention policies in the second term, even as we engaged our allies in intensive dialogue on these issues. Nevertheless, because of the hard work of L's lawyers, I believe we were able to lay the foundation for a more cooperative relationship with our allies.

In summary, in the Bush Administration's second term, the Office of the Legal Adviser was able to ensure and demonstrate U.S. adherence and respect for international law and institutions in many important cases. These actions were acknowledged by some, but lingering international discontent over the Iraq war and the Bush Administration's inability to close Guantanamo and change its more controversial detention policies tended to overshadow these efforts.

# 14 Department of State Legal Advisers' Roundtable

**I**N THE EVENING FOLLOWING OUR GATHERING AT THE CARNEGIE Endowment for International Peace, we arranged for the Legal Advisers to participate in a roundtable discussion at the annual meeting of the American Society of International Law (ASIL), and crafted a series of questions to provide a basis for their further elaboration of the role of international law in the development of U.S. foreign policy. In particular, the panel focused on how the Legal Advisers saw their role in ensuring that international law shaped U.S. foreign policy. ASIL President Anne-Marie Slaughter moderated the panel.[1]

## Qualities and Characteristics of an Effective Legal Adviser

*Question*: In the late 1980s, a distinguished panel on which some of you gentlemen served (and some of your predecessors who are no longer with us were also on it) was convened under the auspices of this Society and several other organizations. The report on that panel, which was published in the *American Journal of International Law* in 1990 took up, among other things, the ideal – the Platonic template – for the Legal Adviser. The report noted that Legal Advisers have come from highly variable backgrounds in respect of their previous preparation in international law. It concluded that people have served with distinction (and this panel is evidence of that) without having had a previous advanced degree in international law – that everyone was a quick study, learned on the job, and had great staff support and other qualities to compensate for this. What do you think is the most important quality that a Legal Adviser has to have? Perhaps by way of giving the next Secretary of State some suggestions on where to look – what do you think, from your own backgrounds, was most important to you?

*Mr. Hansell*: When Cyrus Vance asked me to be his Legal Adviser, I first told him, "I don't know very much about public international law." And his response was, "Welcome to the club!" He added, "You're being hired to be yourself. There are a hundred people already in the office who know what they're doing."

*Mr. Robinson*: That's a very, very difficult question. I guess maybe we'll each have to answer individually. I think in my case, I was the first former Foreign Service officer to be the Legal Adviser and I think having had earlier service in the State Department was helpful. I was staff aide to a Secretary of State, and I had served in the Arms Control and Disarmament Agency. I think having some understanding of the Machiavellian nature of the Department of State – where the bodies lie – the structure of the place – was a great advantage.

*Mr. Sofaer*: I would tell the Secretary two things: first, you need a very good lawyer. Find a very good, very smart lawyer. Because he needs to be able to handle that staff at the Legal Adviser's office – they are extremely smart and he needs to keep up with them. And second, he needs to be able to deal with very complex issues. We have talked about some of the more general use-of-force-type questions, but those are far from the most complex issues that you have to deal with when you deal with a treaty that, for example, concerns ancient art objects. You get memoranda that are loaded with analysis, and you need to be willing and able to dig right into all the work. And in addition, you have to get decisions made. You need a person who will decide what position to take and move things along; otherwise the train will leave the station without L's contribution.

*Mr. Williamson*: As the third Legal Adviser [since 1969] with a Sullivan & Cromwell background, I obviously would look for somebody from Sullivan & Cromwell. (Laughter).

*Mr. Andrews*: I would agree that Abe has hit the nail on the head. You have to be a very, very fine lawyer. But you also have to be someone who can rely on the staff. I have to say that the finest law firm I've worked in over my career is L. So you need to have enough confidence in yourself to also rely on the advice of others. It's important to have someone who's comfortable with that.

*Mr. Matheson*: I agree with all the criteria that people have just mentioned. Most important is that the Secretary of State should choose somebody he has confidence in, and whom he will rely on – because he's going to have to do that.

*Ms. Slaughter*: I want to tell a story that Abe Chayes once told me about becoming Legal Adviser. He had never taken an international law course before being nominated; and he related the story about his Senate confirmation hearing. The Chair of the Committee asked Abe, "So, Mr. Chayes, how many judges are on the International Court of Justice?" And Abe was sitting there thinking, "Oh, my God – nine? No, that's our Supreme Court. Five? No." And he finally admitted that he didn't know. To which the senator replied, "Mr. Chayes, you are too ignorant to bother with." But he was confirmed. So clearly, the criteria are as complex as you all have said.

### Background and Training Indispensible for Being an Effective Legal Adviser

*Question*: You came from many different kinds of previous jobs. To what extent do you think your previous jobs impacted your work as Legal Adviser? In what ways did they limit you and in what ways provide advantages? To what extent did those jobs affect your views of public international law and therefore your performance at L?

*Ms. Slaughter*: I want to embroider on that for a bit while I give you a chance to think about it. I have to say that listening as you respond to these various questions, I have been so struck by the lawyerly nature of your analysis. You are answering as practicing lawyers – superb practicing lawyers – and many of us here, of course, are academics, and when we think about international law, we think about not only what international law is but what it should be, and we often think in very metaphysical terms. And so, to build on the question, I'd like to ask to what extent your background in lawyering, rather than in international law as a formal discipline, really shapes your approach to the job.

*Mr. Harper*: The beauty of the question is that I don't *know* what I didn't know that hurt me. But what I do know is that I felt for three years as if I was continually a student, and I welcomed something that I think all law firms would do well to arrange for. That is, that when there was a problem, or something came up that I didn't understand, or even if I did understand but still had questions about it, I would simply gather all the people that had a purchase on the subject matter, and we would talk it through – whether it took two hours or two days. I had Deputy Legal Adviser Mike Matheson, seated here next to me on the panel, who was continually being interrupted in his substantive work because I would come to him and say, "Mike, I just don't *understand*!" In that way it was a wonderful time – and so I also think that a person with a permanent sense of curiosity is needed for the job. Probably I would have been more efficient if I had had a different kind of background – but I must say that when I had to go and advise the Secretary of State, the fact that I was the person who knew the law was not the reason I was there. I was there to offer my best judgment.

*Mr. Robinson*: I felt that my background in the Department of State was a big advantage in knowing my way around the bureaucracy, and avoiding some very serious errors. When I started out, I went right from college into the Foreign Service, and at that time working for the Department of State was perceived as a very good and admirable thing to do. When I was at L, I remember one year we had two thousand applications for seven openings and hired more former Supreme Court clerks than any law firm in the country.

*Mr. Matheson*: I'd just like to say that in a practical sense, the Legal Adviser is primarily a problem solver. His job is to help the officials in the State Department solve the practical problems that they have. He operates in the context of international relations, so background knowledge of international law would be nice. But what he needs primarily to be able to do is to assess priorities and practicalities and use his own personal skills in reaching solutions to problems that are facing him and his clients. So I think probably we should not overemphasize the role of theoretical international law in the Legal Adviser's job. There are other skills and abilities, which are probably of more practical use to him in the day-to-day work.

## The Legal Adviser's Client

*Question*: On the panel there are three gentlemen from Republican administrations, three from Democratic administrations, and one who served both. The question is: who really is your client? Is it the Secretary of State? Is it the President? Is it the American people? Is it international law writ large? Should it include the academic community? Should it include some of the sense of obligation and duty that were discussed earlier? Or is it your own conscience?

*Mr. Sofaer*: It's a great question. The way the office works, it's broken down into subparts and each of the parts of the office has clients. The regional bureaus, the other bureaus – each is a client – and each of the lawyers in the office serves those clients and uses international law as well as domestic law in that service. All of the lawyers in the office give legal advice across the board. They have a huge impact on the development of policy – and it's very important that you not leave without having a sense of the way the work flows. All of the people in the State Department are our clients, and I say *our* clients because much of the work done in the office is done by the lawyers in the office. Very few issues actually have to reach the Legal Adviser, and many of those that do reach the Legal Adviser reach him just so that he can sign off on them. So it's very important to appreciate all of those good lawyers.

But this issue of who is the client arose very dramatically during the Iran-Contra episode. I was working to try to stop the lies and the stonewalling that were going on in the Reagan Administration about Iran-Contra. The State Department professionals were appalled that I was working with the White House lawyers and getting myself involved with the White House. They were petrified that, as one of them put it, "You'll end up in the gutter" – and they actually got Secretary Shultz to be very concerned about what I was up to. They told him, "He's going to get us somehow pulled into this stonewalling thing" – when in fact I was trying to do exactly the opposite. And Shultz was led at a meeting to ask me point blank the question you just asked. He said, "Who do you represent, Sofaer? Are you my lawyer? Whose lawyer are you?"

And I said, "I am the lawyer of the President of the United States. He's my client and through him, the people of the United States and the Congress of the United States. I'm a U.S. Government lawyer – and if you, Secretary Shultz, have any concern about the legality of any thing that you are doing, you'd better get separate counsel." He said he did not have to get separate counsel.

*Mr. Robinson*: I think it's a very fundamental question – and of course, if you're going to survive as Legal Adviser, the Secretary of State had better also be your client – internally, again, within the department. You work in the government at large, however, and this is again why I think it's so important that the lawyers have an opportunity to be involved in each issue from the start. The Legal Adviser's office for many years was viewed in the government at large as the moral conscience of American foreign policy. That may be a grandiose view of one's role, but it was impressed on me that the Legal Adviser has got to see to the observation of all of the international agreements, the treaties, the customary international law – and so, the client is certainly the President. I would agree with Abe that if there is a conflict between the President and the Secretary of State – and that does indeed occur (and having been the

Legal Adviser to Alexander Haig, I can assure you that it occurred with some frequency, but to his credit he fought for everything that he thought was right) – you'd better then cast your lot with the President. But then you've also got a duty to the Senate, which confirmed you. You've got a duty to the public. It's an extremely difficult question to answer and one that Legal Advisers should lose sleep over – and I think that probably every single one of us did on occasion.

*Mr. Harper*: Well, the question is essentially metaphysical. On a work-a-day basis, plainly the Secretary of State is the client. In the event of a fundamental disagreement between the Secretary and Legal Adviser, then of course the Legal Adviser's allegiance must go to the President. In the event of a fundamental disagreement with the President, then there is always of course the possibility of resignation on the one hand, but on the other there is the notion that there may be obligations to the Senate as the representative of the sovereign – because, of course, in our system the sovereign is "the People."

*Mr. Williamson*: I really beg to differ. I think your client is the State Department, and the person ultimately with the decision is the Secretary of State. Perhaps through the Secretary you serve the President, but I emphasize that *through the Secretary* – that's the metaphysical answer. Of course, there are lots of practical issues also.

*Mr. Matheson*: I don't think it's useful to think of this in terms of lawyer–client relationships. I think that lawyers in public service are public officials, and they have responsibilities parallel to those other public officials have. An intelligence officer has a duty to give the best reading of the facts in a situation that he can, regardless of what his clients (if you want to call them that) want to hear. It's the same for a lawyer. He has a duty to give honest legal advice and not to change it based upon what the client may expect or desire. So I would say that in that sense, a government lawyer has a duty to the entire body of the public even though he obviously has direct working relationships with a hierarchy in his own agency.

*Mr. Harper*: But let's add a footnote as a part of my further defense on the metaphysics of the issue. Herbert Wechsler was very troubled by the fact that he knew, having worked in the War Department and then the Justice Department, that there had been misrepresentation at a fundamental level in the Japanese relocation cases. And for many, many years his view was that he could not speak because of the duty of confidentiality in the attorney–client privilege. But there came a time when he believed that the claims of history and justice required that he come forward – and that's what I have in mind. At some point, depending on how serious the case is, one's obligations may run in fact to the sovereign.

*Mr. Hansell*: I think that Mike Matheson has it right. To me, a number of different strains run through this question: who is the employer, to whom do you owe a duty, of loyalty – but in the end, if there are disagreements up and down the line, the public interest is in the mind of the lawyer, and this applies to all lawyers that serve the public, not just at the State Department and not just the Legal Adviser. Clearly the ultimate decision has to be what's in the best interest of the public. It's important to keep in mind, as has already been said, that in 99.9 percent of the daily tasks, it's the Secretary of State or other officers of the Department for whom the Legal Adviser works; but ultimately it's the body of the public.

*Mr. Andrews*: I don't want to keep the metaphysical argument going, but it's one of the few times I do agree with Ed, so I thought I'd say that I really always did understand my responsibilities were to the Secretary of the State and through her to the President. And for issues such as Conrad mentions, those are the kinds of issues where resignation is the right path. If you have privilege and confidentiality problems, then you obviously do what Mr. Wechsler did; but I think that if you feel a duty to resign, then it arises from the obligation to the people.

### The Effect of Legal Advice in Non–Use-of-Force Cases

*Question*: One thing, whether you're a realist or a neo-Kantian, which we all recognize is that international law does operate quite a bit differently from domestic law. But to focus on use-of-force cases so heavily may skew the impression that people outside the government might have about the way international law does in fact affect the behavior of the

U.S. government. It may be a little misleading to focus so much on the use-of-force cases where the countervailing considerations – national security, politics, and other such considerations – may tip the balance against international law. Are there examples where international law did restrain policymakers, even in ways that were difficult for the policymakers to accept?

*Mr. Matheson*: I agree that the use-of-force cases are rather unusual situations where typically Presidents make decisions on the basis of what they consider to be overwhelming national security needs. And I agree on the other hand, that Presidents and other foreign policy decision makers are perfectly willing to accept that they are more constrained in other areas by international law norms. This is certainly true in economic affairs and other situations where there are treaty obligations, such as environmental obligations. So there really is a spectrum in which perhaps only on the extreme end of the spectrum does international law always win the day, but even on other parts of the spectrum, international law is a definite constraint on policymakers.

*Mr. Harper*: I would endorse that; and I would add that one kind of case in which things were always very delicate, and probably still continue to be, has to do with our power to extradite someone for trial in the United States when that person could face capital punishment. The necessary task of obtaining the right level of assurance from the state of the United States that's going to prosecute, that the accused will in fact not face the death penalty, is often a very difficult one. It's an obligation that flows of course directly to the federal government – but as a practical matter, the State Department and the Justice Department work very hard to make sure that the assurances in fact are given and that they're meaningful.

## The Evolution of the Office of the Legal Adviser

*Question*: How has the office of the Legal Adviser changed over the time you served and have watched others serve? What do you think has changed in the last couple of decades?

*Mr. Matheson*: I walked in the door of the Legal Adviser's office in 1967 and over the intervening thirty-seven years, I think the Legal Adviser's office and therefore the role of the Legal Adviser has changed in some important ways. First of all, it has grown tremendously. In particular, there are certain areas of the office that hardly existed or didn't exist at all in 1967, which have now become quite large – areas such as the management office, the law enforcement office, and the international claims office. What this means for the Legal Adviser is that he has to invest more of his time and effort in managing this large enterprise. That change has pros and cons. On the one hand, it obviously imposes greater management tasks upon him; but on the other hand, he has at his disposal more resources and therefore greater flexibility in trying to deal with immediate problems that may arise. I think there's been a great expansion in the areas covered by international law and the areas that have become foreign relations problems for the clients of the Legal Adviser's office. On the positive side, that makes the job of the Legal Adviser more interesting; on the other hand, he now must either acquire a little bit of expertise in a lot more subjects or else engage in more delegation to his subordinates. There's been a great expansion in domestic law and litigation that is relevant to the Department of State, particularly in the management area. There has also been an expansion in other aspects of domestic regulation. This plays into the personal expertise of many Legal Advisers, who often come from large law firms and have had experience in domestic affairs. But it does impose a greater burden. Therefore, I think over all there has been an increase in the normal struggle between a focus on management skills and responsibilities on the one hand, and on the other hand, the desire of every Legal Adviser to be able to focus on the priorities of his Secretary of State and the other principal officers – there's always that tension. I suppose this is a problem that is common to all large federal agencies. But the basic role of the Legal Adviser, I think, is still the same: he gives legal advice before decisions are made; he gives the best possible legal defense for the decision once it has been made; he contributes to solving practical problems with his lawyering skills; and he needs to be able to use the personnel available to accomplish these objectives.

*Mr. Hansell*: I'd like to tell an anecdote, which I think is relevant to this question. Marshall Schulman, whom some of you may have known, a distinguished professor at Columbia now retired, was special assistant to Secretary of State Dean Rusk and was a senior Adviser to Cyrus Vance. I once asked him how he thought the job of Secretary of State had changed in the years between Rusk and Vance – and he thought that the workload of the Secretary had doubled in that time. A great many more countries and a great many more issues confronted the Department of State and therefore, the Secretary. I would guess that the workload of the Legal Adviser and the range of activities have at least doubled again in the time from the Vance era to the current era.

*Mr. Robinson*: I'll comment about the other agencies. In my time, in the first six months that I was in office, the single largest file that I had was the dispute with the Department of Justice over which department would represent the U.S. Government in the Iran–United States Claims Tribunal; it was an enormous battle, and it had to be decided by the President. I understand that all over the world in almost every state there is the same problem. In this case, the President chose the State Department; that made sense because international tribunals are one of the arrows in the quiver that the Secretary of State has with which to address major international disputes. If the Secretary of State is not in charge of the representation at the tribunals, he can't effectively use that alternative; so in practical terms it's very important. But my understanding is that in the twenty years since I was in office, the role of the Legal Adviser's office internally within the U.S. Government is less prominent than it was, and I think that's very unfortunate.

*Mr. Andrews*: I'd just like to add that I spent a great deal of time collaborating with my colleagues at other agencies, and I think that is something that is a bit different today. I spent a great deal of time with the Treasury Department, and certainly with the Department of Defense. We had very good relations with Defense in those days, and with the

CIA and the Department of Justice and also Office of Legal Counsel. There were a few turf fights but there was a lot more collaboration.

*Mr. Sofaer*: The fact of the matter is that American foreign policy has shifted from the State Department not entirely, but largely, to other agencies. As foreign policies become more specialized, we've seen the Treasury Department with the trade representation particularly; and even communications – they all have the lead in many international issues. So I think the biggest change in the Legal Adviser's work, is really the change in how American foreign policy is run today.

## Comparing the Role of the U.S. Legal Adviser to Legal Advisers in Other Countries

*Question*: How does the role of the Legal Adviser compare with Legal Advisers in other countries?

*Mr. Harper*: I suppose the first thing to remark is that the number of lawyers in our Legal Adviser's office of the State Department far exceeds the number of lawyers in anybody else's Legal Adviser's office in any foreign ministry. This means that when we have an issue we are able to throw the necessary resources at it in a way that I think is the envy of many of our colleagues around the world. But the way in which we select our Legal Advisers is viewed I think by many as curious, if not eccentric. Many of our counterparts are people who are diplomats by training as well as lawyers, and their stint as Legal Adviser is a temporary one so that they come to the whole undertaking with a sense of nuance that sometimes escapes more flat-footed intellects like mine. I hasten to add though that while that may be generally true, our closest competitor in a sense would be the United Kingdom, which does have large staff and does have tradition of promoting from within to the Legal Adviser's office. When I was Legal Adviser, Frank Berman, who had that job at the United Kingdom, was the dean of Legal Advisers around the world; it was very helpful to work with someone who had been in the saddle that long. My sense is that the degree to which the various Legal

Advisers have scope for being creative or useful to their principals is a highly individualistic one. Abe and others made the point to me, when I was anticipating being Legal Adviser and I talked to all the then-living Legal Advisers, that the most important relationship one has is with the Secretary of State. If that goes well, it's a wonderful job. If it doesn't go well, it's not so wonderful and one would see that pattern around the world in terms of the influence and the effectiveness of one's counterparts.

## Relevance of Established International Law to Today's Threats and Issues (New Wine in Old Bottles)

*Question*: To what extent do you agree with the claim that we live in a time of old rules and new threats and the old rules need to be revised?

*Mr. Williamson*: Well, there's no doubt that we're living with old rules and with new threats. Whether the old rules are adequate or not, I think you and I might have some disagreement. Let me start by going back just a little to something that Abe said about the relationship with the other agencies within the government, because I think this very much has an impact on what rules we're playing by. I think we see today, very much as a post–9/11 development, a much greater role by the Departments of Defense and Justice/FBI in areas that have traditionally been the State Department's concerns. With that comes the increased influence of the General Counsel or in the case of the Justice Department, the OLC. So, a lot of things have been turned around. The Justice Department or the FBI is not now solely a domestic legal law enforcement agency but has turned 180 degrees around to look at the preventive side of terrorism. A lot has changed as a result of that.

But in the context of your question, I take it that the "old rules/new threats" question generally focuses on the issue of "Now that we're no longer in a bipolar world, what is the rest of the world going to do about this unilateralist-inclined United States?" Quite frankly, I think that the rules that exist are pretty good – and by that I mean the UN Charter, the Security Council with the five permanent members, and certainly the veto power. The problem with devising new rules is that I think that they would be very, very difficult to devise. One of the things that I mentioned is this worry about U.S. unilateralism – and I really don't think that charge is warranted to the extent that it seems to be accepted in many places. Saying "unilateralism" in the international context is sort of like saying "partisan" in the domestic context; people are bipartisan when they agree with my views, and they're being partisan when they don't agree with my views. In the same way, "unilateralism" appears to be when the United States says, "Sorry, you're not right – and we're going to go ahead, and we've actually found some other people who would like to go along with us and take a particular course of action." So when people talk about needing new rules to deal with new issues, I guess that would be, for example, when it's perceived that the Security Council is paralyzed. But I'm just not very confident that a better set of rules can be developed.

Something else that I'd like to mention in this context is that, as one looks at the rules, I think the question of the representation in multilateral bodies is a key question. I think that there are some things that are definitely somewhat out of date. If, for example, the European Union has a common foreign policy, given that there are two European Union members with permanent Security Council seats, is there really a justification for having other members of the European Union sit on the Security Council?

*Mr. Hansell*: I think the question of rules and threats is a bit narrow in the sense that so many of the issues that we confront in the international arena are comparatively new issues – the trade agenda, the law enforcement agenda, and various other global issues have arisen that I, as the senior member of this group, really had very little involvement with during my tenure as Legal Adviser. The international agenda today is so much broader than it used to be, that clearly there's a need for defining ways to deal with new issues. It's not so much replacing old rules as creating rules to confront situations that were not part of our agenda two or three decades ago. Even in the context, of security threats there are, it seems to me, new issues. It's very hard to say that there are "old rules" and "new rules," because the circumstances are so different in terms of the numbers of players and the nature of the threats that we confront – so I find that a very narrow way of making comparisons between where we are and where we have been.

*Mr. Robinson*: Well, I would just like to say on this issue about the old rules and the new threats, it seems to me that there has been a very fundamental change in the world. The United States has gone from facing one very large elephant to facing a thousand snakes. Dealing with one large elephant, I would argue, is much easier than dealing with 1,000 snakes. Many of those snakes are now nonsovereign States and the UN Charter at least as I understand it, was not really constructed to manage a world of a thousand non-State snakes.

*Mr. Harper*: I was taking the question on a mental level. Lawyers, I think are trained to smuggle into old jars new wine and make it appear not only that nothing has changed but in fact that it's the same old wine. To me that's the beauty of the calling that we share, so the question of new rules is to some degree a subliminal one. I think I was most successful during my time in the State Department when I could make it appear that something quite revolutionary was actually a standard practice. I must say that in this regard I had a wonderful precedent presented to me virtually as I walked in the door and that was the work that Michael Matheson and others had done to construct the statute of the Yugoslavia war crimes tribunal. Now there was something masquerading as something old that was in fact revolutionary – and the genius of it was that we were able to convince the world that it was just what everyone had always understood should be the case. While we were operating under Chapter 7, and the Security Council had created the tribunal, nonetheless people talked about Nuremberg and Tokyo and the post–World War I war crimes efforts as if they were the lineal ancestry of the Yugoslavia war crimes tribunal – when in fact of course this tribunal was something that the world had never seen before. Now, having done it once, we've done it again, and it really is old!

*Mr. Sofaer*: If I may say so, the problem raised by this question really reflects the use-of-force issue. Mike Glennan has made a career out of this idea that he has now discovered a new world that requires new rules. Before responding, I want to remind you that it's more than just dealing with the snakes; it's also the upside of what we have in the world today. Our expectations are different. We want a better world – we're more interested in really bringing about results and making the whole world more like the civilized country that we live in. We want better human rights; we want women to be treated better, and that's a huge issue in the world today. And we need to use force occasionally in order to bring some of these things about, or to stop major genocides. Certainly President Clinton was believable when he apologized for Rwanda. We should have been in Rwanda; we should have done so much more and we should do more.

So does it take new rules to do all of this? I don't think so. I think the academic international law cult has convinced itself that there are very narrow rules related to the use of force. They argue that force should only be permitted when explicitly authorized by the Security Council or to repulse an actual attack in progress. My position takes a more flexible view toward the use of force and I truly do believe that this is old wine. Abe Chayes wrote an article called "The Common Lawyer Approach to International Law," which always made a lot of sense to me – I've always relied on it. And many of the people sitting here at this table have written articles that approach the use-of-force in a broader way that takes into account a range of factors. It doesn't try to force each situation into a particular narrow category. So if it takes calling them new rules to get you guys moved over to our side on this issue, fine. Go ahead – call them new rules – but please, come on and join the fight!

*Ms. Slaughter*: So I actually hear agreement on the part of Edwin Williamson and Conrad Harper and Abe Sofaer that we don't need new rules – except perhaps tactically, if this last remark reflects that – but what we are hearing are very different interpretations of the old rules. Conrad Harper says, "Well, the old rules are fine, the glory of our craft" – and there I think you put it extremely eloquently "is that we know how to change things incrementally and sometimes not so incrementally but through sort of a seamless process." Edwin Williamson says, "We've got traditional rules and we should simply stick to them." Abe Sofaer says that those traditional rules are not the way many people in this room have traditionally interpreted them – that if we actually looked at their text they are in fact far more expansive – but he says that if we need to *call* those new rules, we can.

Now what are we to make of this? One argument would be to say, "If there's that much disagreement on the existing rules, we should recognize that we're in a new era – it's not 1945 – we haven't had a major catastrophe, we're not hoping to avert a major catastrophe and we should not call a new UN conference but rather, actively think about how to evolve the rules." The other view is that new doctrines are needed. Conrad Harper, let me come back to you: do you think you can use the approach you were describing to get us to a place where we can better address a Rwanda if it comes again? We heard Gareth Evans this morning saying, "No, no you really need a new doctrine – the responsibility to protect." Would you do that more incrementally?

*Mr. Harper*: I think Rwanda was a failure of will, not a failure of law. But will is something hard to mandate. It requires many factors to be effective including, of course, a sense of the imminence of catastrophe that must be averted. But I don't think that it's necessary to pursue wholesale change for retail results. I have yet to be persuaded that we are in an era of wholesale change. Now let me come to the figure that is already before us of a thousand snakes. It seems to me that the issues that terrorism presents are terrifically difficult, but I don't see them necessarily as issues that require a reformulation of major parts of international legal fabric.

## International Law and the Use of Force

*Mr. Robinson*: In my day we were very concerned about having a humanitarian intervention exception for Article 2(4) mainly because of the Brezhnev Doctrine in the Grenada case. We were very, very careful. That was a very unusual situation, because there the Legal Adviser and one other in the office knew about that rescue mission in advance, and the Legal Adviser's office had the time and the opportunity to get ready. That was a contrast with the mining of the Nicaraguan harbors where I'm sorry to say we knew absolutely nothing in advance. This is a fundamental problem about the use of force inside the U.S. Government. If the lawyers are able to be in on the take off, we can either avoid the crash landing or at least help it be much softer. But when it comes to use of force, I would argue, over the years, there's been a lot of skepticism about including the lawyers – for example, in planning covert operations. As far as I know, in a covert operation international law still applies, so if someone's going to undertake some secret operation involving the use of force, it's better to have the legal argument in place before undertaking it.

*Ms. Slaughter*: So you've just stated that how you *did* help was to make a use of force less embarrassing or more politically palatable. I think many people would say that they hope the role of the Legal Adviser's office is to say "This use of force is illegal" and help to block it. And indeed you suggest that many people in the government think that you *would* try to block it.

*Mr. Matheson*: I don't think it's realistic to think Presidents are often going to refrain from the use of force on what they consider to be essential security grounds because of the views of the Legal Adviser. On the other hand, I think there are important things that Legal Advisers *can* do with respect to the use of force. One is to see to it that the modalities used are as consistent with international law as possible. For example, the actions we took in Nicaragua, which were gratuitously in violation of international law need not necessarily have been so. Another aspect is that when the decision is made to use force, it's important what argument is made to justify that decision. There are some ways of justifying which will open up entirely new open-ended doctrines. There are others that are more consistent with past practices; the Legal Adviser can have a considerable amount of influence on what arguments are made, which in turn greatly influences what precedential effect that use of force might have.

*Mr. Harper*: Actually, sometimes it's a good idea not to use force. I can recall one occasion when a group of us lawyers from several departments (that is to say, the OLC incumbent, the representative of General Counsel's office at Defense, the CIA General Counsel, and L) were considering a proposed action, which I won't specify, and one member of the group had the view that this action was probably not legally sound. I say "probably" because he couldn't clearly demonstrate under accepted principles of international law that it was unsound, and he had a very skeptical audience – he had to convince the rest of the lawyers in this group, who didn't see how in the world we could go back to our principals and say that the proposed action "probably wasn't a good idea." But over the next several weeks, he actually managed to persuade *all* of us that the tendency of international law was in support of his position, not that of our principals. And having been persuaded, we all went back to our principals and convinced them – and the action was never taken. I thought that was wonderful! Every now and then, lawyers in fact ought to be praised for avoiding conflict rather than enhancing it.

*Mr. Sofaer*: I'm sure each one of us at one point or another has advised our clients not to use force in a situation and our advice was taken. Certainly it happened for me at least twice, and once at the very highest level imaginable. But it's popular to say something like, "Force is not always the thing to do." The reason we're driven to talk about using force in this world today is that *not* using force is a bigger problem today than *using* force, and we're realizing that. We just have to deal with it.

But of course it is important for the Legal Adviser to tell the clients, and I'm sure every one of us has done it: "Don't do this; this is NOT a good idea." And in fact, when they don't ask us it's almost always a disaster. I think you could do a chart and show that when the Legal Adviser was not consulted about some major use of force or some major foreign issue, it would often turn out to be an Iran-Contra or some other mistake of that scale. They don't talk to us then because they don't want to be told "no" and because they know the action is so absurd that they won't even ask!

*Mr. Hansell*: Well, use of force is not, generally speaking, entirely a question of rules or laws. Obviously there are legal issues, but also there are issues beyond legal considerations. We did have one Secretary of State who resigned over an issue of use of force, not because he thought it was unlawful but because he thought it was a mistake – for reasons that I think were vindicated. I think it was Oliver Wendell Holmes who said, "The life of the law is experience." We are creatures of our experience and we learn by our mistakes. I think the judgments and rules on use of force are *sui generis*. There's no other issue that concerns a government in the way that use of force does. The considerations that are involved – well I think that Abe is right, that probably if the lawyers are not consulted, the judgments tend to be mistaken; but I can't say to you that I think that they are *legal* judgments that are contributed by the lawyers so much as they are judgments of experience, judgments of wisdom.

*Mr. Andrews*: I just want to add that I think that Kosovo is a perfect example of that. There was never a definitive legal opinion on why we acted in Kosovo, but I think many in the room who criticized the action also at the same time would say that it was the right thing to do. And really it was the only choice we had – and I worked with a Secretary of State who was willing to use force in circumstances like that.

I think we did try to put new wine into the old bottles with the rationale for the 1999 NATO intervention, and I think that Ruth

Wedgewood, who wrote an article on this, probably said it the best.[2] We used a menu of factors that led us to take action in Kosovo – and any one of them singly, of course, would not stand the light of day – but collectively they seemed to make great sense: so that's the wine.

*Mr. Harper*: You can always tell when the law is under strain because what ought to be elegant becomes a little messy – and Kosovo, I think, was such an instance. The result was something that many would feel was correct but how you got there wasn't exactly a straight line. And I'm sympathetic with that. What I think happens over time when that occurs is that we tend to look at problems in the future in a slightly different way. So while there's not much precedent *before* it, as a *setting* of a precedent, Kosovo, I think, is illustrative of the beginning of a new fermentation.

*Mr. Williamson*: I beg to differ with these ideas. Maybe I was too legalistic in my approach to the job, but that may have resulted from my interview with Secretary Baker for the position. He asked if I was going to be satisfied with just doing legal issues and not doing foreign policy issues, and I assured him that I would – so I joked that my deal with Baker was that I wouldn't practice foreign policy if he wouldn't practice law. Unfortunately, only the first half of that was binding. But if we do not need a clearly articulated legal position on the use of force in Kosovo, then are we lawyers really around for anything? I didn't kid myself – I really thought I was hired to be a lawyer and not a foreign policy person. But another thing that I will deal with is the world's reaction, in particular the media's reaction. And I think that the rules on that are different depending on who the players are. We've been preached at through Republican administrations about the sanctity of the War Powers Resolution, how it had to be taken seriously and so forth. But the sixty-day clock ran out in Kosovo – and there was not a peep, as far as I could tell, from anyone. Not from the *New York Times* editorial page, not from the *American Journal of International Law*.

*Mr. Robinson*: I don't want to leave the impression that I meant that we would just simply go along with any decision. My entire point was that if the lawyers are engaged from the get-go, then the lawyers will have an opportunity not only to state what the law says and what the law does not say, but also to help form the decision. Even if the decision makers are insistent that they are going to go to war over this, that, or the other, and they're going to have a use of force no matter what – if the lawyers have been in from the very start, they can help. They can help especially, I would argue, with the fallout from the use of force – in the Congress, in the press, or wherever it is. If the lawyers were not there at the start, and simply have to deal after the fact with a train wreck, then the lawyers' job is much, much more difficult.

# 15 Foreign Legal Advisers' Roundtable

**A**YEAR AFTER THE FORMER STATE DEPARTMENT LEGAL Advisers gathered for the historic discussions that are captured in previous chapters, the authors assembled a panel of former Legal Advisers from several different countries to revisit some of the issues that were discussed among the U.S. Legal Advisers from a comparative perspective. The panel was held at the annual meeting of the American Society of International Law, and was chaired by one of the authors (Michael Scharf).

The panel consisted of Conrad Harper, former Legal Adviser of the U.S. Department of State; Sir Frank Berman, former Legal Adviser to the Foreign and Commonwealth Office in the United Kingdom; Ambassador Leonid Skotnikov,[1] former Director of the Legal Department of the Ministry of Foreign Affairs of Russia; Madame Xue Hanqin,[2] former Director-General of the Law and Treaty Department of the Ministry of Foreign Affairs of China and currently Ambassador of the People's Republic of China to the Kingdom of the Netherlands; P. S. Rao, former Legal Adviser of the Government of India and currently a member of the International Law Commission; and Ambassador Seifeselassie Lemma,[3] former Legal Adviser of the Ethiopian Foreign Ministry and currently the Ethiopian Representative to the United Nations.

## The Role of International Law

*Professor Scharf*: From the creation of the International Criminal Tribunal for the Former Yugoslavia to the 2003 invasion of Iraq, international law–related issues have dominated the news in recent years. The purpose of this Foreign Legal Advisers' Roundtable is to attempt to determine international law's importance to policymakers in the world today. From the perspective of high-level government officials, is international law a tool, an obstacle, or merely irrelevant? Let me begin by asking Sir Frank Berman to describe the process for selection and the role of the Legal Adviser in the United Kingdom.

*Sir Frank*: I should preface my remarks by saying that probably no two countries have the same pattern and experience concerning the Foreign Ministry's Legal Adviser. The Legal Adviser in the United Kingdom is the head of the office, made up of people who all exhibit similar characteristics. All members of the office are professional lawyers who serve their entire careers in the diplomatic service. The United Kingdom only recruits lawyers who are professionally qualified and admitted as a barrister, a Scottish Advocate, or a Solicitor. Selection is done through an open competition, similar to that used with respect to filling all public service posts in the United Kingdom. Because of this open competition and the fact that working in the Foreign and Commonwealth Office is a highly sought after position, extremely high entry-level requirements are imposed on applicants. As a corollary, I have always felt that direct, real-world experience was a major asset. The Foreign and Commonwealth Office usually hires people in their late twenties or a little older who have already obtained that invaluable experience.

The Legal Adviser in the United Kingdom is considered a senior foreign office position. Selection for Legal Adviser is via an in-house appointment process, which involves a high-level selection board, usually composed of the applicant's peers along with someone representing the interest of the Foreign Secretary. The final selection of the Legal Adviser is left to the Foreign Secretary, usually after consultation with the Prime

Minister. Unfortunately, there has yet to be a female UK Legal Adviser, although when I retired in 2000, the office was about 50 percent female and that percentage has since increased, making me confident that it won't be long until the first woman is appointed UK Legal Adviser.

## The Role of the Foreign Ministry Legal Adviser

*Professor Scharf*: As a follow-up, what is the relationship between the Foreign Ministry Legal Adviser and the other Legal Advisers within your governments? Let me start with Sir Frank Berman because I have read that the UK Attorney General issued a legal opinion on the legality of the 2003 invasion of Iraq, and I am curious as to the role the UK Foreign Ministry Legal Adviser would play in preparing such an opinion.

*Sir Frank*: The expertise on international law is concentrated in the Foreign Office. However, the Legal Adviser to the government on all questions is the Attorney General. The Attorney General in the United Kingdom is quite different from the Attorney General in the United States. His role is to provide ministerial-level advice on all areas of the law, including international law. If there is a serious issue concerning international law, then the issue will pass through the Attorney General before it is reported to the Prime Minister. This requires cross consultation between departmental legal staffs in the British Government. Usually this occurs with much cooperation instead of conflict. Very often, a question that goes before the Attorney General for his opinion will have been reviewed by the legal staffs of more than one department, including in particular the Foreign Office Legal Adviser, whose views on international legal questions carry a great deal of weight, because the Attorney General does not typically have much international law exposure or experience of his own.

*Mr. Rao*: My country, India, follows much of the same traditions as the United Kingdom. The biggest difference in India is that the Attorney General does not play as much of a central role, as is the case in the United Kingdom's system. Instead, India's Attorney General is involved in matters only when they are specifically referred to him by a department, which typically includes constitutional law implementation or domestic law implementation of an international obligation. When there are conflicts of opinion on an issue between the Legal Adviser Secretary (the head of ministry of law and justice and in charge of all domestic law legislation and implementation) and the Legal Adviser of the Foreign Office, it usually goes to the Attorney General for his resolution. In general, the Legal Adviser of the Foreign Office stands supreme and independent when an issue concerns international law advice.

*Ambassador Skotnikov*: In Russia, there is no open selection process. Instead, the Legal Adviser is usually succeeded by a Deputy Legal Adviser, and therefore it is a rather exclusive process. Moreover, officers of the legal department act in a dual capacity as diplomats as well as lawyers. Similar to India, the Foreign Ministry tries to be the supreme authority in international law in Russia.

*Ambassador Seifeselassie Lemma*: The Legal Adviser's role in Ethiopia is very different from what my colleagues have just described. This is mainly due to the fact that Ethiopia is a very poor country. Ethiopia's GDP is about $54.89 billion, as compared to the United States ($11.75 trillion), China ($7.262 trillion), India ($3.319 trillion), the United Kingdom ($1.782 trillion), and Russia ($1.408 trillion). This financial discrepancy creates a quality and quantity shortage of international lawyers in my country. Whereas in the United States, international lawyers can be found in many different agencies and departments, practically all of Ethiopia's international lawyers are found in the Foreign Ministry, and they are thus responsible for all international law issues concerning the country. The department advises the entire government, including the prime minister, even though it is primarily accountable to the Foreign Minister. Despite these resource limitations, the department deals with a wide range of international issues including drafting bilateral treaties and performing functions with respect to regional treaties like the African Union.

*Madame Xue*: Lawyers who work for China's legal department are diplomats first. The Legal Adviser is not a political appointee. Similar to Russia, the Legal Adviser is usually succeeded by a Deputy Legal Adviser. However, this is not always the case. Sometimes a senior diplomat may be selected if he or she has a recognized legal background. China's Foreign Ministry Legal Department has more than seventy lawyers, and it is responsible for many matters, including treaty issues, public and private international law, boundary matters, the law of the sea, and environmental law. Moreover, all procedural rules at the state and governmental department level must be reviewed by the legal department. Therefore, the work load is typically very heavy. To alleviate burnout, each staff member is given the opportunity to serve abroad at a Chinese embassy or mission on a rotating basis. Generally, China's Foreign Ministry Legal Department plays a vital role in giving opinions of international law. The Department is very well respected by the National People's Congress as well as the Provincial governments.

*Mr. Harper*: I find it noteworthy how similar the different countries' departments are. Like that of the United Kingdom, the Legal Adviser's Office in the United States is staffed by lawyers who are career civil servants, with the striking exception of the Legal Adviser himself, who is a political appointee, subject to the approval of the Senate. Concerning the finality of advice, the State Department Legal Adviser is the primary U.S. organ for determination of what international law is and how it applies to U.S. actions. The Legal Adviser must advise both the Secretary of State as well as the President. Often, however, varying departments throughout the government must collaborate to address an important issue of international law, which can be quite challenging given their divergent institutional perspectives.

## The Legal Adviser's Client

*Professor Scharf*: Who did you, as Legal Advisers, perceive your client to be: is it the Foreign Minister, the Attorney General, the President, or

Prime Minister, the people of your respective countries, or international law writ large?

*Sir Frank*: That is a very difficult question to answer, but I would say that the Legal Adviser ultimately serves the country at large. As stated earlier, all of the lawyers in the office must be professionally qualified as a condition for selection. This is no mere formality. To the contrary, the United Kingdom holds to the principle and practice that its lawyers operating within the government are at the same time professionals operating as part of their own legal profession; they must abide by the same rules of professional conduct as in any other legal profession. In this regard, let me recall a famous remark by former UK Legal Adviser and distinguished ICJ judge, Sir Gerald Fitzmorris. Fitzmorris was confronted with the question: "Surely it is the purpose of the government lawyer to give impartial advice, and how can you give impartial advice when you are in the position that a government lawyer is in?" Sir Fitzmorris responded that this was not in fact the purpose. Instead, he stated that the purpose was to give accurate and sympathetic advice. Consistent with this, I believe that the Legal Adviser must advise one's client with a particular knowledge of that client's needs and objectives, thus advising one's client on a sympathetic and knowledgeable basis. This in return makes it far more likely that the client will heed your advice because the client knows that you understand their needs and objectives. However, the Legal Adviser still owes an allegiance to the law and to his own professional conscience. Therefore, the Legal Adviser must always remember to advise on the law as it is and not on the law as some policymaker hopes that it might be or hopes that he might be able to persuade another to say that it is.

*Madame Xue*: There is not exactly a client–lawyer relationship in China, because foreign ministry Legal Advisers do not work as lawyers per se. Instead, they work as diplomats in the Foreign Service. While the Legal Adviser must still give sound legal analysis and opinion as a lawyer, she must also see the broader context of the law and how one's country's stance on a particular issue relates to other countries' positions on that same issue. Therefore, China's Legal Adviser should not simply give the client the legal conclusions he wants to hear.

*Mr. Rao*: I agree with Madame Xue that it is not exactly a client-lawyer relationship, though it can sometimes turn into one. I would say that that 99 percent of the time, policymakers recognize that there is a system of international law and that they must operate within that system. However, it's like a horoscope where policymakers still need to go see the equivalent of an astrologer for legal advice. This is in large part because international law's parameters are not always self-evident or clear. In routine matters, the Legal Adviser's role is similar to a priest's in a marriage in that both are around to perform formalities to ensure that everything occurs properly. These routine matters are typically handled by junior colleagues under the supervision of the Legal Adviser. In contrast, during times of crisis, the Legal Adviser's role is much more difficult because the client wants to know how close the issue is or how far they are on the wrong side of the law. In these instances, the Legal Adviser is more closely involved with the high-level discussion where opinions are rendered. Typically the Legal Adviser's opinions are followed, although there are notable exceptions.

*Mr. Harper*: I find Sir Frank's formulation a bit curious. I believe that a Legal Adviser must come to the best legal conclusion whether or not it is sympathetic to the objective of what the policymaker wants. Also, in order to be effective, it is paramount for the Legal Adviser to be very clear when he or she is speaking as a lawyer and when speaking as a policy adviser. To confuse the two roles is to doom one's credibility as a lawyer.

## The Ability of International Law to Constrain Policy Choices

*Professor Scharf*: Permit me to change the focus somewhat and ask each of you, whether there were times when international law restrained your respective policymakers even in ways that were difficult for the policymakers to accept.

*Ambassador Skotnikov*: As a general point I would say that policy-makers should be restrained by international law for their own good and that they should take further steps to remain restrained by it. For example, now that Russia is a party to the European Convention on Human Rights, Russia is obligated to act in compliance with the judgments of the Human Rights Court in Strasburg. We must do this for our own good. The Legal Adviser's role is to be a guide for policymakers and to lead them down the right path without jeopardizing national interest, and because national interest and international law are two very difficult concepts, the role of Legal Adviser is that much more challenging.

*Mr. Harper*: I can provide a specific example of such a situation. While I was Legal Adviser during the spring of 1994, the United States agreed to supply the Peruvian Air Force with real-time intelligence, which ultimately resulted in the Peruvian Air Force mistakenly shooting down a civilian aircraft. My office along with colleagues in the Department of Defense had to inform the policymakers that this policy could not sustain itself under the Chicago Convention, and the practice was thereafter reluctantly discontinued.

*Mr. Rao*: I don't recall any situations where the government was on the brink of committing a violation that forced my Office to step in and stop it from occurring. Yet, there were many times when treaties did not work well for India. In those instances, temptations to renounce unfavorable treaties were high, and I had to step in and point out that certain procedures of renouncement had to be strictly adhered to. This advice was sobering enough to keep the policymakers from backing out of any treaties during my tenure. A government can save itself by taking advice prior to taking action, as it is much better to get the legal opinion first instead of acting and then finding out if it was in violation of international law. In addition, the High Court of Bombay plays a major role in this area.

*Mr. Harper*: When there is a judicial body that can take an adverse position, it becomes much easier to inform a client of the results of potential actions, making the advice much more credible.

*Madame Xue*: I want to add that Legal Advisers do not blindly follow the policymakers by providing legal reasoning for the policymakers' decisions. Instead, on a daily basis, Legal Advisers' opinions are sought after since their opinions are based on sound legal footing.

## Lawyers as Clients

*Professor Scharf*: Do any of the panelists feel that Legal Advisers are more effective when their clients are lawyers. I note that 80 percent of the U.S. Secretaries of State, beginning with Thomas Jefferson, were lawyers.

*Madame Xue*: Just because a Legal Adviser's client is a lawyer does not mean that the client knows international law. International law is a very exclusive field.

*Sir Frank*: I think this question wrongly presupposes that policymakers first decide on a course of action and then go to the Legal Adviser and ask if it is permitted under international law. In a properly functioning Foreign Ministry, this would not be the case. Instead, the Legal Adviser is involved from the beginning of the process and apprises the policymakers of the legal aspects every step of the way.

*Ambassador Lemma*: I agree with Sir Berman. In Ethiopia, the Legal Adviser is involved during the entire policy-making process. Typically, the process works in two stages: First, the government wants to genuinely know what the law is. Then, if the government finds the law to be inexpedient, it seeks sympathetic legal advice from the Legal Adviser on how best to justify the action.

*Professor Scharf*: Let me respond to this rosy portrayal by pointing out that in published surveys of foreign ministry Legal Advisers from around the world, one of their main complaints has been that their clients predict in advance that they won't like the conclusions of the legal advice so they do not ask for it, which leaves the Legal Advisers out of the picture until after the fact. Have any of the panelists encountered this phenomenon?

*Mr. Harper*: I have to acknowledge that there were several times during my tenure when I was surprised to hear about policies and actions that had been implemented by various other bureaus of the State Department or other government agencies, and that it was often necessary for me and my staff to try our best to deal with the problems presented after the fact.

*Sir Frank*: Probably the most notorious incident where the UK Legal Adviser was deliberately cut out of the loop was the 1956 Suez invasion. But I would say that the lessons of that experience have generally been learned for the future.[4] It is considered a cardinal sin within the UK Foreign Office to put up a policy submission that did not clearly recite that the Legal Adviser or his staff had been consulted, or that did not include an analysis of the legal questions that were relevant to the decision. If the submission did not contain this, then any legitimate senior official or minister would send it back for a complete analysis to know what the law stated.

*Mr. Rao*: I was never cut off when a difficult issue was raised. But there were instances where the policymakers disagreed with the legal analysis or argued that prominent foreign governments had come to a different legal conclusion concerning the situation. When this occurred, I told them that they need to be on the side of the law instead of bending the law. Where the law is clear, I told them that it is clear. When it is not clear, I told them what the options are and I told them to watch out.

*Madame Xue*: International law is an important aspect in every country's foreign policy and diplomacy. Therefore, no country can afford to go against international law and declare that they are ignoring international law. Thus, every government tries to interpret its foreign policy within the framework of international law. Legal Advisers have a distinct advantage in knowing the country's consistent practice of international law, foreign counterparts' legal practice, and how the pertinent laws were formed or negotiated. Legal Advisers are able to use all of this knowledge in influencing proper policy-making decisions.

## The Future of International Law

*Professor Scharf*: What event during your respective tenures as Legal Advisers gave you the greatest cause for either optimism or pessimism concerning the future of international law and its relevance to the maintenance of world order?

*Mr. Harper*: I would point to the establishment of the several international war crimes tribunals, including the Yugoslavia Tribunal, which was created during my tenure. With substantial assistance from the United States, the Security Council has finally resurrected a principle of accountability that had been permitted to lie dormant for too long. I hope that the world's children will see a notion of accountability as enforced through international criminal tribunals as a key aspect of civilized life.

*Ambassador Skotnikov*: I would point to the application of international law to the dissolution of the Soviet Union in December 1991. This was an acute crisis. I am pleased to note, though, that never before was international law-related legal advice in such a demand, and the transition was accomplished in an orderly way. I credit not only the legal advice but also the political leadership that sought the legal advice on virtually every issue, from Russia's assumption of the Soviet Union's Security Council seat to the continuation of the Soviet Union's arms control treaties. Finally, I'd like to stress that international law is more than simply a tool; it is part of a very powerful process that has real ramifications. We might not pay for today's violations of international law, but our children will.

## Resigning in Protest

*Question from Ben Ferencz*: I was a prosecutor at Nuremberg sixty years ago. The greatest contribution of the Nuremburg tribunal was the declaration that aggressive war is an international crime. Until recently, the UK Deputy Legal Adviser was Elizabeth Wilmshurst, who was very knowledgeable in the subject of aggression and who fought valiantly to limit the extent of that crime as defined in the Rome Statute establishing the International Criminal Court. When the 2003 Iraq war broke out, she opined in a confidential memorandum that the invasion of Iraq was illegal. The UK Attorney General opined the opposite. As such, she felt compelled to and ultimately did resign, and her memorandum was subsequently made public by the UK Government. I'd like to ask the former Legal Advisers on the panel how they would have reacted had one of their deputies done the same.

*Sir Frank*: I believed her actions were the right and honorable course.

*Mr. Harper*: To be an effective Legal Adviser or Deputy Legal Adviser, one must recognize that the exit door must always be open. When there is a very important matter and the government refuses to follow advice that you consider to be essential, you are supposed to resign.

### Offering Legal Advice, Even When Not Asked

*Question from Davis Robinson*: Concerning the use of force in the United States, in most instances the Legal Adviser's Office was only in for the crash and not for the takeoff. I would like to know whether each of the Legal Advisers on the panel felt that they were able to self start and offer a formal legal opinion even where such advice has not been solicited by the policymakers.

All but Madame Xue answered yes to the question.

# 16 Lawyering the Treatment of Detainees in the War on Terrorism

**A**FTER THE EVENTS OF SEPTEMBER 11, 2001 AND THE invasion of Afghanistan, it became necessary for the United States to identify the international legal rules related to the detention, treatment, interrogation, and prosecution of suspected terrorists. Accordingly, the Bush Administration turned to its lawyers to identify this legal framework and to assess its binding character. The following review of the post-9/11 actions of the U.S. Government is intended to provide additional insight into the black box of whether and how international law operates to frame and in some instances constrain the development of U.S. policy on core matters relating to national security.

There are a number of legal issues that arose from the war on terror, including the legal basis for the invasion of Afghanistan, targeted killings, extraordinary rendition, surveillance of U.S. citizens, the use of the Guantanamo naval base as a detention center, the operation of CIA detention facilities, and the operation of military tribunals. This chapter will in particular focus on questions relating to the treatment and interrogation of detainees because the release of the so-called Torture Memos and subsequent publications by key insiders detail the legal back and forth between the Department of State, Department of Defense, Department of Justice, and the White House over the legality of certain coercive measures applied to detainees and provide a rich text for further illuminating the role of international law. Because there is a concrete paper trail of the legal positions of the relevant actors, the release of the Torture Memos has provided a rare glimpse into the black box that so often obfuscates the understanding of the role of international law. This chapter synthesizes the released information into an accessible and concise account of the decision making within the U.S. Government and is not an attempt to provide a comprehensive narration of the detainee issue.

Given the intense debate surrounding the legal foundation for the treatment and interrogation of detainees, we have chosen to base this chapter almost entirely upon the findings of the bipartisan Senate Armed Service Committee report,[1] following extensive hearings into the matter in the summer and fall of 2008[2]; the personal recollections of Jack Goldsmith[3] and John Yoo[4]; the commentary of two of the Legal Advisers interviewed for this project – William Taft and John Bellinger; and in limited instances other first-person accounts recorded by scholars.

## Legal War Council – *Sans* L

The story begins soon after the terrorist attacks of September 11, 2001 and the U.S. invasion of Afghanistan. Rather than vet questions related to the interpretation of international law through the legal departments of all the relevant agencies, much of the legal work related to the war on terrorism was done by a self-styled "war council," composed of White House Counsel Alberto Gonzales, the Vice President's Counsel David Addington, the Pentagon's Chief Counsel Jim Haynes, and the Deputy head of the Department of Justice's Office of Legal Counsel (OLC), John Yoo. David Addington was reportedly the dominant force among the group, and one high-level Bush Administration insider confided, "if you favored international law, you were in danger of being called 'soft on terrorism' by Addington."[5]

Notably absent from the group were the State Department Legal Adviser, William Taft, and National Security Council (NSC) Chief

Counsel, John Bellinger (who would three years later replace Taft as State Department Legal Adviser). John Yoo has been quite open in explaining why the "war council" cut L out of the decision-making process concerning treatment of detainees: "The State Department and OLC often disagreed about international law. State believed that international law had a binding effect on the President, indeed on the United States, both internationally and domestically," whereas Yoo and the other members of the war council did not hold to that view.[6] William Taft observed that L was likely excluded due to the fear that "in light of some of the positions we had taken, that we would not agree with some of the conclusions other lawyers in the Bush Administration expected to reach and that we might 'leak' information about the work to the press."[7]

## The Geneva Conventions

The four Geneva Conventions and their Additional Protocols establish the core obligations of States during an armed conflict.[8] They are widely considered to be the rulebook governing the lawful conduct of warfare. Every U.S. military officer is extensively schooled in the substance and application of this body of law.

The Geneva Conventions require States to provide certain rights and protections to noncombatants, wounded soldiers, and prisoners of war.[9] In particular, the Conventions, through Common Article 3, set forth the rights of persons "taking no active part" in an armed conflict (e.g., civilians and combatants who have been taken into custody), including freedom from torture and inhumane treatment, limits on interrogation, and access to judicial process.[10]

When seeking to develop a legal framework for the detention and treatment of suspected terrorists, John Yoo believed "the candid approach would be to admit that our old laws and policies did not address this new enemy [Al-Qaeda]."[11] Acting according to this perspective, Yoo drafted a series of legal memoranda, which concluded that under international law the protections of the Geneva Conventions did not apply to Afghanistan, to the Taliban, or to members of Al-Qaeda. These conclusions were supported by White House Counsel Albert Gonzales and submitted to the President for his approval.

On January 9, 2002, Yoo authored a key OLC memorandum, providing legal arguments to support Bush Administration officials' assertions that the Geneva Conventions did not apply to Al-Qaeda and Taliban detainees from the war in Afghanistan.[12] On January 22, 2002, Yoo authored a second memorandum responding to White House Counsel Alberto Gonzalez's request for the Department of Justice's views concerning the effect of international treaties and federal law on prisoners held by U.S. forces in Afghanistan.[13] The OLC memorandum advised that the President had "sufficient grounds to find that these treaties do not protect members" of Al-Qaeda or the Taliban militia. Importantly the memorandum also concluded that "customary international law, as a matter of domestic law, does not bind the President, or restrict the actions of the U.S. military, because it does not constitute either federal law made in pursuance of the Constitution or a treaty recognized under the Supremacy Clause."[14]

Repeating the arguments contained in Yoo's memoranda, on January 25, 2002, Gonzales sent a memorandum to President Bush, which opined that the President should declare the Taliban and Al-Qaeda outside the coverage of the Geneva Conventions.[15] This, Gonzales pointed out, would keep American interrogators from being exposed to the War Crimes Act, a 1996 law that makes it a federal crime to cause a grave breach of the Geneva Conventions or a violation of Common Article 3, which prohibits torture or other inhumane treatment.[16] Gonzales's memorandum also argued that the new paradigm of the "war" against terrorism "places a high premium on factors such as the ability to quickly obtain information from captured terrorists and their sponsors," and thus the Geneva Conventions' strict limitations on questioning of enemy prisoners were "obsolete" and even "quaint."[17]

When he learned of the Gonzales memorandum, Secretary of State Colin Powell quickly prepared his own memorandum for the White House, stating that the advantages of applying the Geneva Conventions to the Afghan detainees far outweighed those of their rejection.[18] Powell explained that declaring the Conventions inapplicable would "reverse over a century of U.S. policy and practice in supporting the Geneva Conventions and undermine the protections of the laws of war for our troops." He added that it would "undermine public support among critical allies," and that they may be less inclined to turn over suspected terrorists.

Secretary Powell's memorandum was accompanied by a legal memorandum from State Department Legal Adviser William Taft, which concluded that the Geneva Conventions did apply to the conflict with the Taliban, as well as to Al-Qaeda, because they were part of the conflict with the Taliban.[19] The Taft memorandum found that the United States was bound by customary international law and that such law required that detainees be treated humanely and were entitled to many of the rights contained in the Conventions.[20] Finally, the Taft memorandum also opined that it is important for the United States to confirm "that even in a new sort of conflict the United States bases its conduct on its international treaty obligations and the rule of law, not just its policy preferences."[21]

On February 7, 2002, the President signed an Executive memorandum accepting the legal conclusion of the Department of Justice that the Geneva Conventions did not apply to the conflict with Al-Qaeda as it was not a High Contracting party to the conventions. The memorandum provided that although legal authority existed to suspend the Conventions, such as those between the United States and Afghanistan, he would not do so at that time, and that the Geneva Conventions would apply to the conflict with the Taliban. The memorandum further concluded that common Article 3 of the Geneva Conventions did not apply to Al-Qaeda and Taliban detainees as "the relevant conflicts were international in scope, and common Article 3 applies only to 'armed conflict not of an international character.'" With respect to Taliban detainees the memorandum concluded they "were unlawful combatants and, therefore, did not qualify as prisoners of war under Article 4" of the Conventions.[22] And, because the Geneva Conventions did not apply to the conflict with Al-Qaeda, "Al-Qaeda detainees also do not qualify as prisoners of war."[23]

The Presidential memorandum did, however, provide that "As a matter of policy, the United States Armed Forces shall continue to treat detainees humanely and, to the extent appropriate and consistent with military necessity, in a manner consistent with the principles of Geneva."[24]

As recounted by William Taft, in the months following the President's decision, the Legal Adviser's Office drafted a lengthy memorandum, "which concluded that because our policy was to treat the Al-Qaeda and Taliban detainees consistent with the requirements of the Geneva Conventions, the question of whether they were entitled to this as a matter of law was moot."[25] According to Taft, the L memorandum expressed the continuing view that" customary international law required that the detainees in any event be treated humanely and had certain of the rights set out in the Conventions."[26]

L was under the impression that because it was U.S. policy to treat the detainees consistent with the protections provided in the Geneva Conventions, they were in fact being accorded those protections. As explained by William Taft, "it developed, however, that at the same time we were working on our memorandum, the Department of Justice lawyers were working separately with the lawyers at the Department of Defense to authorize certain departures from the Conventions' terms in the treatment of the detainees, particularly with regard to methods of interrogation."[27] According to Taft, "I and my staff were not invited to review this work and we were, indeed, unaware that it was being done."[28]

By shifting the obligation to adhere to the Geneva Conventions from a legal obligation to a policy determination, the stage was set for the circumvention of the protections provided in the Conventions. As noted by the Legal Advisers during the narratives above, international law is intended to be durable, whereas policy determinations can easily and quickly change.

As will be discussed immediately below, the protections offered by the Geneva Conventions were in fact quickly diluted through a series of additional legal memoranda prepared by the OLC. Once the U.S. Government had determined that the Geneva Conventions were not legally binding in relation to the Al-Qaeda and Taliban detainees, it laid the foundation for the creation of a law-free zone at Guantanamo Bay; it removed the safeguard against inhumane treatment, leaving only the outermost standards relating to torture in place; it evaded limits on imprisonment – opening the possibility for indefinite detention; it eliminated standard military procedures, such as Article 5 hearings to determine the combatant/noncombatant status of detainees; and it removed limits on due process, paving the way for military commissions that would not be required to meet even minimal standards.

## Presidential Power, Necessity, and the Limits of Torture

Once the prohibitions on interrogations afforded by the Geneva Conventions were deemed inapplicable, the Bush Administration was faced with the question of to what extent U.S. military and intelligence personnel could employ coercive measures to extract information from detainees without violating the United Nations Convention against Torture (Torture Convention).

The Torture Convention sets forth states' obligations to protect persons against State-sponsored torture.[29] The Convention defines state-sponsored torture as actions undertaken by State personnel or agents that inflict severe physical or mental pain or suffering for the purpose of obtaining information. The Convention calls on States to implement effective measures to prevent acts of torture, to prosecute nationals who commit acts of torture, and to provide effective redress to individuals subjected to illegal acts of torture. The Convention also prohibits States from turning a person over to another State where he or she is likely to be subjected to torture. The United States is a party to the Torture Convention and implements the Convention through a domestic statute making torture a federal crime.[30]

On August 1, 2002, the OLC issued two crucial memoranda, drafted by Yoo, and signed by Assistant Attorney General Jay Bybee, dealing with the torture issue. The first, addressed to White House Chief Counsel Gonzales, opined that the obligations under the Torture Convention did not apply to conduct outside of the territory of the United States, and that the Torture Convention prohibited only the most extreme forms of intentionally inflicted harm, namely those causing the most severe kind of physical pain tantamount to death or organ failure or psychological forms of pressure that cause permanent or prolonged mental harm. The memoranda further noted that this narrow ban applies only when interrogators specifically intend such harms but not when they are seeking information to defend the nation from attack.[31] Importantly, the memorandum also declared that under the doctrine of "necessity," the President could supersede national and international laws prohibiting torture.[32] This has come to be referred to as the "ticking time bomb exception." The memorandum also found that for it to be a war crime, torture must be committed against someone protected by the Geneva Conventions, and the United States had established that Al-Qaeda and the Taliban did not have this protection.

The second August 1 OLC memo, which responded to a request from the CIA, addressed the legality of specific interrogation tactics to be used against Abu Zubaydah, a high-level Al-Qaeda operative who the CIA believed was withholding information regarding terrorist networks in the United States and Saudi Arabia. The CIA was convinced that Zubaydah knew of plans to conduct attacks against U.S. interests, but that he had become accustomed to less-aggressive interrogation techniques and would not disclose the necessary information unless extraordinary techniques were employed.[33] The memoranda reviewed ten types of proposed interrogation techniques including walling, insects placed in a confinement box, cramped confinement, stress positions, sleep deprivation, and water boarding.[34] The memorandum reasoned that none of the proposed techniques came within the threshold of "severe pain or suffering" or mental pain. In particular it found that "the water board is simply a controlled acute episode, lacking the connotation of a protracted period of time generally given to suffering." Based on its conclusion that mental harm only comes from prolonged duration (months or years), the memorandum opined that water boarding should not be prohibited.[35] Abu Zubaydah was subsequently water boarded eighty-three times in August 2002.[36]

Two months later, on October 11, 2002, the Commander of Guantanamo Bay, Major General Michael Dunlavey, sent a memorandum to the Pentagon requesting that the U.S. military be granted similar authority to use aggressive interrogation techniques that were originally designed to simulate abusive tactics used by our enemies against our own soldiers, including tactics used by the Communist Chinese to elicit false confessions from U.S. military personnel. These included "stress positions," "exploitation of detainee fears," "removal of clothing," "hooding," "deprivation of light and sound," "deprivation of sleep," and "water boarding." Dunlavey's memorandum stated that the existing techniques permitted by the Army Field Manual 34–52 had been exhausted, and that some detainees (in particular, Mohammed al Qahtani, a Saudi Arabian believed to be the twentieth 9/11 hijacker) had more information that was vital to U.S. national security.

At this point the professional military lawyers began to raise serious concerns about the treatment being accorded detainees, and in particular concerning the proposed methods of interrogation. In response to General Dunlavey's requests, the Chairman of the Joint Chiefs of Staff General Richard Myers solicited the views of the several branches of the military. All stated their opposition to the proposed extraordinary interrogation techniques. The senior lawyer for the Air Force cited "serious concerns regarding the legality of many of the proposed techniques." The Chief of the Army's International and Operational Law Division wrote that the techniques "cross the line of 'humane' treatment" and would "likely be considered maltreatment" under the Uniform Code of Military Justice and "may violate the torture statute." The senior lawyer of the Marine Corps stated that the requested techniques "arguably violate federal law, and would expose our service members to possible prosecution."[37]

At this time, the State Department Legal Adviser remained shut out of the process. It is worth speculating whether if L had joined the campaign on the side of the professional military lawyers, this combined effort might have been sufficient to steer U.S. policy back within the framework of international law.

Despite the concerns raised by the senior lawyers of the military services, on November 27, 2002, Jim Haynes, the Pentagon's Chief lawyer (and a member of the "war council"), sent a one-page memorandum to Secretary of Defense Rumsfeld, recommending that he approve the techniques requested by Guantanamo Bay. A few days later, on December 2, 2002, Secretary Rumsfeld signed off on Haynes' recommendation."[38] By December 30, 2002, the interrogators at Guantanamo Bay were employing the extraordinary interrogation techniques (including hooding, removal of clothing, stress positions, twenty-hour interrogations, and use of dogs) on Mohammed al Qahtani and several other detainees.[39] In January 2003, these same techniques were being used at the U.S. detention center at Bagram Airfield in Afghanistan, and eventually migrated to the Abu Ghraib detention facility in Iraq.[40]

During this period, Navy General Counsel Alberto Mora intensively engaged with Haynes concerning his reservations about the interrogation techniques that had been approved for Guantanamo Bay, opining that they constituted at a minimum, cruel and inhumane treatment and "could rise to the level of torture, and probably will cause significant harm to our national legal, political, military and diplomatic interests."[41] He prepared a memorandum to that effect, which he threatened to sign unless he heard definitively that the use of the techniques had been suspended.

In part as a result of Mora's concerns/threats, Secretary of Defense Rumsfeld signed a memorandum rescinding authority for the techniques on January 15, 2003. That same day, Rumsfeld directed the establishment of a "Working Group" to review the interrogation techniques and requested another legal opinion from OLC in light of the objections that had been raised.[42] Importantly, the working group did not include the State Department Legal Adviser.

On March 14, 2003, John Yoo provided an OLC memorandum to the Working Group that repeated much of what the first Bybee memorandum had said six months earlier about the definition of torture.[43] In addition, it advised that interrogators could not be prosecuted by the Justice Department for using interrogation methods that would otherwise violate the law because federal criminal laws of general applicability do not apply to properly authorized interrogations of enemy combatants undertaken by military personnel in the course of armed conflict. The basis for this finding was that "such criminal statutes, if they were misconstrued to apply to the interrogation of enemy combatants, would conflict with the Constitution's grant of the Commander in Chief power solely to the President"[44]

Yoo's March 14 memorandum also asserted that based on the U.S. reservation to the Convention against Torture, "the United States' obligation extends only to conduct that is 'cruel and unusual' within the meaning of the Eighth Amendment or otherwise 'shocks the conscience' under the Due Process Clauses of the Fifth and Fourteenth Amendments."[45] In response to L's earlier assertions concerning customary international law, the memorandum argued that customary international law could not impose a standard that differs from U.S. obligations under the Convention against Torture; and those obligations must be narrowly interpreted through U.S. domestic law. The memorandum went further to assert that, "[i]n any event, our previous opinions make clear that customary international law is not federal law and that the President is free to override it at his discretion."[46] The memorandum concluded with a reaffirmation and possible expansion of the ticking time bomb exception by noting that necessity or self-defense could provide defenses to a prosecution based on allegations that an interrogation method might violate any of the various criminal prohibitions.[47]

Armed with the new OLC memo, Secretary of Defense Rumsfeld, on April 16, 2003, authorized the use of twenty-four specific interrogation techniques for use at Guantanamo Bay. In addition, the Secretary's memorandum stated that "if, in your view, you require additional interrogation techniques for a particular detainee, you should provide me, via the Chairman of the Joint Chiefs of Staff, a written request describing the proposed technique, recommended safeguards, and the rationale for applying it with an identified detainee." Rumsfeld subsequently approved specific requests for hooding, sensory deprivation, and "sleep adjustment."[48]

According to the December 2008 Senate Armed Services Committee Report,[49] "senior officials in the United States government solicited information on how to use aggressive techniques, redefined the law to create the appearance of their legality, and authorized their use against detainees."[50] The Committee found that the Secretary of Defense's authorization of aggressive interrogation tactics were a direct cause of detainee abuse at Guantanamo Bay and contributed to the use of abusive tactics in Afghanistan and Iraq.[51] Specifically with respect to the memoranda written by the OLC, the Report states: "Those OLC opinions distorted the meaning and intent of anti-torture laws, rationalized the abuse of detainees in U.S. custody and influenced Department of Defense determinations as to what interrogation techniques were legal for use during interrogations conducted by U.S. military personnel."[52]

By interpreting away the obligations of the Torture Convention, the U.S. Government opened itself up to the possibility that its military and intelligence personnel might cross the line, and that abuses would migrate from the highly monitored Guantanamo interrogation center to detention facilities in Afghanistan and Iraq.

According to William Taft, it is "highly regrettable that the Legal Adviser's Office was not involved in the legal work following the decisions in February 2002," as had L been involved, "several conclusions that were not consistent with our treaty obligations under the Convention against Torture and our obligations under customary international law would not have been reached."[53] Mr. Taft notes that subsequently, "when we worked with the Department of Justice on the revision of the memorandum on the Torture Convention that had been withdrawn earlier in the year, we were able to reach agreement on a very respectable opinion."[54]

## Realigning U.S. Interrogation Policy and International Law

In late 2003 and 2004, U.S. policy began to haltingly realign with international law. This realignment was driven by greater public awareness of the conditions of detention of suspected terrorists, personnel change at the OLC, the intervention of Congress and the Supreme Court, and the reengagement of L.

In October 2003, Jack Goldsmith became head of the Department of Justice's Office of Legal Counsel. Early in his tenure, Goldsmith withdrew the controversial August 1, 2002 and March 14, 2003 OLC opinions that described what constituted prohibited acts of torture and whether the federal torture statute would apply to U.S. military interrogations of "unlawful enemy combatants."[55]

Goldsmith explained that he rescinded the torture memoranda not because he thought they had reached the wrong conclusions, but rather because he thought the memoranda "rested on cursory and one-sided legal arguments," and were "legally flawed, tendentious in substance and tone, and overbroad and thus largely unnecessary."[56] Goldsmith subsequently confirmed that he believed extraordinary interrogation techniques can be legally justified in so-called ticking time bomb situations "in which the President believed that exceeding the law was necessary in an emergency, leaving the torture law intact in the vast majority of instances."[57]

Goldsmith, however, did not rescind the second August 1, 2002 OLC memorandum, issued to the CIA, which concluded that specific proposed techniques including water boarding were compatible with international law.[58] Goldsmith left the memorandum to the CIA in place in order to provide CIA personnel with what Goldsmith describes as a "golden shield"[59] that would protect them against prosecutions under the Federal War Crimes Act (implementing U.S. obligations under the Geneva Conventions) and the Federal Anti-Torture Act (implementing U.S. obligations under the Torture Convention).[60] The effect was, however, to permit the continued and expanded use of water boarding and other abusive techniques by CIA interrogators. Goldsmith also drafted a March 19, 2004 memorandum, which opined that it was legal for the United States to seize noncitizens from Iraq or other territory over which it exercises de facto control and transfer them for purposes of interrogation in other countries. This memorandum provided legal cover for the CIA's controversial policy of "rendition."[61]

In 2005, the U.S. Congress passed the Detainee Treatment Act (popularly known as the McCain amendment),[62] which provided that detainees held in U.S. military custody were entitled to the protections of the Geneva Conventions. Although the McCain amendment ended extraordinary interrogation by members of the U.S. armed forces, it did not apply to CIA personnel, and as a result the interrogations of high-level Al-Qaeda operatives were moved under the control of the CIA.

During this time, the State Department Legal Adviser, which had been frozen out of the initial legal/policy decisions, began to play an increasingly important role in seeking to "clarify and adopt a more robust legal framework for the detention, treatment, and prosecution of captured terrorists."[63] The Legal Adviser led an effort to persuade the Bush Administration that Common Article 3 of the Geneva Conventions should be applied to detainees. Although it was initially unsuccessful in this endeavor, the Supreme Court, as discussed below, did eventually rule that Common Article 3 was applicable, radically transforming the legal landscape and Bush Administration detainee policies. Further, L was effective in working with the Secretary of State to persuade the President that most Al-Qaeda detainees should be moved from CIA custody to the military base at Guantanamo Bay, thereby bringing them within the coverage of the Detainee Treatment Act. The Secretary of State was also able to convince the Bush Administration that the detainees at Guantanamo should be granted access to the International Committee of the Red Cross (ICRC), and the ICRC subsequently issued several reports that put pressure on the Bush Administration to make other reforms in its detention policies.[64]

The Legal Adviser was also called on to fulfill the role of rebuilding relationships with America's allies on the question of the application of international law in the war on terror.[65] In this regard, L initiated a series of bilateral and multilateral meetings and conferences designed to attempt to harmonize the approaches of America and its allies to developing an effective legal framework for combating terrorism. L was also tasked with facilitating interaction between the ICRC and the White House, State Department, and the CIA.[66]

The Legal Adviser also became engaged in the preparation of a domestic legislative framework for detention, which, however, was not adopted by the Bush Administration. L also provided assistance with the drafting of the Military Commission Act, which, although subject to criticism, was widely viewed as a substantial improvement over the initial 2001 Presidential Order creating the Military Commissions.[67]

## Supreme Court Engages

Meanwhile, in 2004, 2006, and 2008, the U.S. Supreme Court issued a trio of decisions on the detainee issue that began to swing the pendulum back in line with international legal standards and away from unfettered Presidential power in the war on terrorism. In 2004, the Court decided the case of *Rasul v. Bush*, rejecting by a 6–3 majority the President's contention that Guantanamo Bay was outside of the jurisdiction of U.S. courts, and ruling that detainees there must be provided access to legal assistance and given judicial review of the legality of their detention.[68] The Bush Administration sought to implement the *Rasul* decision by establishing a Combatant Status Review Tribunal at Guantanamo Bay to determine on a case-by-case basis the status of the Guantanamo Bay detainees.[69] The Combatant Status Review Tribunal process did not, however, provide the detainees assistance of counsel or any means to find or present evidence to challenge the Government's case, and was later overturned by the Supreme Court.

Next, in the 2006 case of *Hamdan v. Rumsfeld*, the Supreme Court held by a 5–3 majority that the military tribunals established by Executive Order to prosecute accused Al-Qaeda terrorists were unlawful because their procedures "violate both the Uniform Code of Military Justice and the four Geneva Conventions of 1949."[70] The Supreme Court confirmed that Common Article 3 of the Geneva Conventions applied to all Guantanamo detainees, whether they were Taliban or Al-Qaeda. "Common Article 3," wrote the Court, "affords some minimal protection, falling short of full protection under the Conventions, to individuals who are involved in a conflict in the territory of a signatory." The Court reached this conclusion by looking at the official commentaries to the Geneva Convention, which confirmed its wide scope. The Court invoked the *U.S. Army's Law of War Handbook*, which described Common Article 3 as "a minimum yardstick of protection in all conflicts, not just internal armed conflicts." The Court also relied on decisions of the International Court of Justice and the International Criminal Tribunal for the former Yugoslavia.[71]

Shortly thereafter, at the urging of President George W. Bush, the U.S. Congress responded by enacting the Military Commissions Act of 2006, which provided a legislative basis for Military Commissions to try unlawful enemy combatants at Guantanamo Bay and stripped the federal courts of jurisdiction to hear suits by enemy combatants relating to any aspect of their transfer, detention, treatment, trial, or conditions of confinement.[72] Two years later, in the case of *Boumediene v. Bush*, the Supreme Court declared parts of the Military Commissions Act unconstitutional, determined that the Combatant Status Review Tribunals were "inadequate," and ruled that the 270 foreign detainees held for years at Guantanamo Bay have the right to appeal to U.S. civilian courts to challenge their indefinite imprisonment without charges.

Justice Anthony Kennedy, writing for the 5–4 majority, acknowledged the terrorism threat the United States faces, but he declared: "The laws and Constitution are designed to survive, and remain in force, in extraordinary times."[73]

On January 14, 2009, Susan Crawford, the Bush Administration–appointed Convening Authority of the U.S. Military Commissions and a former Chief Judge of the U.S. Court of Appeals for the Armed Forces, announced the dropping of charges against Mohamed al Qahtani, the detainee for whom the enhanced interrogation policy was originally designed. Without equivocation, Crawford declared, "We tortured al Qahtani. His treatment met the legal definition of torture. And that's why I did not refer the case for prosecution."[74]

## The Obama Administration – Fighting the War on Terror within the Broad Framework of International Law

In the aftermath of the leaked publication of the Torture Memos and abuse photos from Abu Ghraib, the debate over the legal framework for the conduct of the war on terror had become so intense that it was regularly addressed on the campaign trail. During Barack Obama's campaign, Greg Craig, then candidate Obama's Foreign Policy Adviser and now President Obama's White House counsel, made clear during public presentations that the United States' international legal obligations would set the foundation for the Obama Administration's policy decisions.[75] Among other things, Craig stated that Obama would close the Guantanamo Bay detention facility and restore habeas corpus for those detainees, put into place a faster and fairer process to assess the status of detainees, use either military court martial or the federal courts to try detainees, enforce the prohibition on torture, and end the practice of secret detentions and the practice of extraordinary renditions.[76]

Just two days into his presidency, on January 22, 2009, President Obama took an important step toward further realigning U.S. policies with international law by signing Executive Orders requiring the closure of the Guantanamo Bay facility within twelve months,[77] the dismantling

of the CIA's network of secret prisons around the globe, and the prohibition on the CIA's use of coercive interrogation methods that devi-
ate from the requirements of the Army Field Manual.[78] The Executive Order on Interrogations specifically prohibits U.S. Government
personnel or agents from relying on the Bush Administration OLC
Memoranda in interpreting federal criminal laws, the Convention against
Torture, or the requirements of Common Article 3 of the Geneva
Conventions.

Subsequent to these early actions, which brought U.S. policy back
within the bounds of international and domestic law, the Obama
Administration indicated that it would likely continue several of the
controversial counterterrorism methods of the Bush Administration,
including employment of extensive surveillance authority, administrative detention for suspected terrorists, the use of military commissions,
the denial of habeas corpus to detainees in Afghanistan, the invocation
of the "state secrets" privilege to terminate lawsuits,[79] and refusing to
rule out the ticking time bomb justification for some forms of extraordinary interrogation in the future[80] – so long as a sound legal basis can be
found for these actions and these actions are carried out in accordance
with the law.

The actions of the Obama Administration not only reveal that the
framework of international law is durable – in that U.S. policy has
returned to within the commonly accepted bounds of legality – but also
that it is supple enough to enable a state to take necessary actions to
protect its national security.

## What Does the U.S. Government's Evolved Response
## to the Treatment of Detainees Tell Us about
## the Nature of International Law?

The review of the efforts of the U.S. Government to craft a response to
the 9/11 terrorist attacks and to the conduct of the war on terror within
the framework of international law reinforces a number of the insights
reflected in the narratives of the Legal Advisers.

First, it indicates the growing trend, identified by the Legal Advisers, of the increasing number of actors with either a responsibility or an ability to provide counsel to the President on matters of international law. It also confirmed the Legal Adviser's concern that L might be shut out of the process, and the consequences that would follow.

Second, it reflects the active engagement of the Legislative branch in establishing legal regimes, in part based on international law, to govern aspects of the war on terror, and the engagement of the Judicial branch to interpret the application of the U.S. Constitution, and in some cases international law, as applied to the President's approach to the war on terror. As recounted by John Bellinger, after the Supreme Court ruled that the detainees must be treated in accord with the Geneva Conventions and customary international law, L was brought back into the process and ended up playing a significant role in formulating new policies and procedures related to treatment of detainees.[81]

Third, the positions taken by the State Department Legal Adviser and his counterparts in the military services demonstrated that important bureaucratic players perceived the Geneva Conventions, the Torture Convention, and customary international law as applicable and binding. Like the Office of the State Department Legal Adviser,[82] the Legal Offices of the various military services were staffed by careerists who had internalized and absorbed a strong belief in the constraints and value of international law. General Richard Myers, the Chairman of the Joint Chiefs of Staff under George W. Bush explained the nature of this culture of compliance in the following terms: "We train our people to obey the Geneva Conventions, it's not even a matter of whether it is reciprocated – it's a matter of who we are."[83]

Importantly, these career lawyers were concerned about the repercussions of noncompliance with international law. They repeatedly warned about reciprocity costs and the prospects of prosecution for violating the international prohibition against torture. Of primary concern was the perceived affect on bilateral relations and long-term multilateral or systemic reciprocity.

Fourth, over time influential actors within the Executive and Legislative branches stressed the important role that reputation as a law-abiding state should play in reshaping detainee policy. The bipartisan Commission that investigated the September 11 attacks concluded in 2005 that "the U.S. policy on treating detainees is undermining the war on terrorism by tarnishing America's reputation as a moral leader."[84] The 2008 Senate Armed Services Committee Report similarly observed, "the fact that America is seen in a negative light by so many complicates our ability to attract allies to our side, strengthens the hand of our enemies, and reduces our ability to collect intelligence that can save lives."[85] Such systemic reciprocity and reputational concerns are often at the heart of the compliance pull of international law.

Upon assuming office, President Barack Obama took extraordinary steps to shore up the United States' reputation as a nation known for its commitment to the rule of law in the context of the war on terrorism. In his first speech to the United Nations on September 23, 2009, Obama acknowledged, "I took office at a time when many around the world had come to view America with skepticism and distrust." To loud applause he said, "On my first day in office, I prohibited – without exception or equivocation – the use of torture by the United States of America. I ordered the prison at Guantanamo Bay closed, and we are doing the hard work of forging a framework to combat extremism within the rule of law. Every nation must know: America will live its values, and we will lead by example." And he concluded his speech by saying: "The world must stand together to demonstrate that international law is not an empty promise, and that treaties will be enforced."[86] A month later, the Norwegian Nobel Committee announced their selection of President Obama for the 2009 Nobel Peace Prize, stressing Obama's commitment to international law and diplomacy: "For 108 years, the Norwegian Nobel Committee has sought to stimulate precisely that international policy and those attitudes for which Obama is now the world's leading spokesman."[87]

# 17 Conclusion

T
HIS BOOK BEGAN WITH FIVE QUESTIONS ABOUT THE NATURE
of international law and the role of State Department and
Foreign Ministry Legal Advisers. The following answers
emerged from our structured conversations with these Legal Advisers.

## Did the Legal Advisers Perceive International Law to Be Binding Law?

Since the dawn of the Cold War, there has been a rich tradition of skepticism about the "legality" of international law on both ends of the political spectrum. John Bolton, the U.S. Ambassador to the United Nations during the Bush Administration, once declared: "International law is not law; it is a series of political and moral arrangements that stand or fall on their own merits, and anything else is simply theology and superstition masquerading as law."[1] None of the Legal Advisers engaged for this project would agree with that extreme position. Importantly, neither the United States nor any other government has ever taken the position that international law is not binding on it.

The Legal Advisers commonly perceived international law as real law that is binding on their governments and that operates as a constraint on policymakers, even where important national security interests are at stake. In Chapter 7, Abe Sofaer illustrated the constraints presented by international law in his discussion of the seizure of the Italian cruise liner

*Achille Lauro* by PLO operatives. The terrorists were put on a plane in Egypt for safe haven in Tunis, and the United States sought to thwart their escape. According to Sofaer:

> The President authorized that the plane be ordered to land, but he did not authorize the use of force in the event that it did not comply. The plane agreed to land as directed, but the only place we could find for such a landing was a NATO base in Italy. While the aircraft was on its way there, my staff and I reviewed the accord under which we operated the base. It clearly precluded any non-NATO operation without Italy's consent. Therefore, when the Italians surrounded the plane as soon as it landed, we had no legal alternative to turning over the terrorists.

Moreover, even where international law seemed in the short term to hinder foreign policy goals, the Legal Advisers agreed that their governments' longer-term interests in protecting their citizens abroad and in effectively conducting foreign policy counsel for policies that uphold the integrity and stability of international law. In the foreword to this book, current U.S. Legal Adviser Harold Koh remarked that:

> In most cases, following international law *is* in America's interest. Like individuals who obey domestic law, nations who obey international law find that it is both the right and the smart thing to do. No law is a straitjacket, but as Americans have learned since September 11, if we don't obey international law, we squander our moral authority and shrink our capacity to lead. When we break international law, we weaken its power to protect our own citizens.

At the same time, the Legal Advisers acknowledged that their clients were often leery of the relevance of international law, and, with few exceptions, there were no extant domestic or international institutions with authority to opine on the legality of a particular foreign policy decision. In Chapter 6, Davis Robinson emphasized that this is particularly true of customary international law:

A further task of the Office of the Legal Adviser is to uphold the dictates of customary international law, a demanding chore because of the ongoing debate in the United States Government and in the international community as to exactly what is encompassed in that rather amorphous body of law and, furthermore, as to whether customary international law is binding upon the President of the United States as a matter of domestic Constitutional law (i.e., whether the President could potentially be subject to impeachment if the tenets of customary international law are violated).

This does not mean, however, that the Legal Advisers did not perceive that there were serious consequences that flow from violating bilateral treaties, multilateral conventions, or rules of customary international law. The Legal Advisers all recognized (and advised policymakers) that violations can engender international condemnation, strain relations with allies, and interfere with the ability of their government to obtain international support for important policy initiatives, in particular, in fighting international terrorism, suppressing narcotics trafficking, controlling weapons of mass destruction, and achieving fair and free trade. The international community's reaction to the U.S. Government's refusal to apply the Geneva Conventions and Torture Convention to Guantanamo detainees is certainly a stark example of these consequences. Moreover, the Legal Advisers recognized that when a State elects to ignore or reinterpret an existing international rule according to its own short-term interests, it runs the risk of being unable to invoke the rule in the future, to its ultimate detriment.

Under the international law principle of reciprocity one State can use another State's arguments to justify its actions when roles are reversed. Although some scholars focus solely on bilateral reciprocity, the Legal Advisers suggested that multilateral (or systemic) reciprocity is also of concern. If a State ignores or interprets away a rule of international law, the precedent may be used by other States in the international community, both with respect to their relations with that State and with each other, thereby weakening the general rule of law and rendering the international system less stable. For instance, when asked why Article 51 of the UN Charter was not invoked as the sole justification for intervening in Grenada, Davis Robinson explained in Chapter 6 that:

> We did not want to make that argument for fear of undercutting Article 2(4) of the United Nations Charter. The so-called Brezhnev Doctrine of the Soviet Union was in vogue with the Russians at that time, and we were very concerned that, if we relied solely upon the potential harm to U.S. nationals, we would have undercut the restrictions of Article 2(4) and might be seen as somehow endorsing or replicating the Brezhnev Doctrine.

The potential impact of multilateral reciprocity was also something recognized by lawyers within the Bush Administration who opposed the conclusions of the Torture Memoranda. In particular, Secretary of State Colin Powell expressed concern that the nonapplication of the Geneva Conventions to detainees would "undermine the protections of the laws of war for our troops."[2]

### Are International Legal Rules Ever Clear Enough to Constrain Policy Preferences?

Although there was a consensus among the Legal Advisers that international law is binding law, there was also broad agreement that international legal rules are often quite vague, and consequently there is ample room for the interplay between law and politics. International law thus often sets the framework within which political decisions are made to achieve the strategic interests of States.

As the legal to and fro of the lawyering on the Torture Memos demonstrates, the international legal framework may not always dictate one singular conclusion, but instead provides boundaries inside of which policy decisions are taken. As explained in Chapter 15 by Ambassador Leonid Skotnikov, former Director of the Legal Department of the Ministry of Foreign Affairs of Russia, "the Legal Adviser's role is to be a guide for policymakers and to lead them down the right path without jeopardizing national interest, and because national interest and international law are two very different concepts, the role of the Legal Adviser is that much more challenging."

The Legal Advisers all stressed that the vagueness of many areas of international law provided States with a great deal of latitude in foreign affairs. This was seen to be equally true with respect to treaty provisions and unwritten customary international law. They also recognized, however, that vagueness could not be relied on as a basis for simply disregarding international law. As Ambassador Skotnikov remarked in Chapter 15: "International law is more than simply a tool; it is part of a very powerful process that has real ramifications. We might not pay for today's violations of international law, but our children will."

Most of the Legal Advisers acknowledged that where international law is unsettled or legitimately open to differing interpretations, they would naturally favor the interpretation most consonant with the course of action advocated by policymakers. Moreover, the Legal Advisers suggested that to maintain their clout within the government it was important for them to be seen as trying to find a solution for every difficulty rather than a difficulty for every solution. As Harold Koh recognized in the Foreword to this book, the creative solutions developed by international lawyers to these difficulties promote the role of international lawyers in the policy-making process. Koh remarked that "properly deployed, [international lawyers] can identify otherwise invisible legal constraints and fathom available legal channels through which policy decisions can flow. By so doing, they help shape policy decisions, which in turn shape legal instruments, which in time become internalized into bureaucratic decision-making processes." As an example of such creativity, in Chapter 11 David Andrews described the catalogue of justifications L crafted for the 1999 NATO intervention to halt ethnic cleansing in Kosovo as "putting new wine into old bottles."

The Legal Advisers were cognizant of the fact that their State's interpretation of international law on any given issue would have ramifications for that policy determination, as well as future interactions with other States. As explained in Chapter 15 by Madame Xue Hanqin, Director-General of the Law and Treaty Department of the Ministry of Foreign Affairs of China, "[w]hile the Legal Adviser must still give sound legal analysis and opinion as a lawyer, she must also see the broader context of the law and how one's country's stance on a particular issue relates to other countries' positions on the same issue."

### Does the Legal Adviser Have a Duty to Oppose Proposed Actions that Conflict with International Law?

Two common perceptions exist in the legal community as to the job of the Legal Adviser in providing legal opinions to the State. One school of thought is that it is not the Legal Adviser's job to render "impartial" advice, any more than a corporate lawyer is expected to do so. A government wants its international lawyer to promote rather than judge the aims of the administration.[3] A competing school maintains that the Legal Adviser has a special or higher professional responsibility to provide a disinterested assessment, because his advice is not normally tested in courts of law or by other outside checks.[4]

Perhaps surprisingly, all of the Legal Advisers leaned toward the latter view. Davis Robinson observed: "The Legal Adviser's office for many years was viewed in the government at large as the moral conscience of American foreign policy. That may be a grandiose view of one's role, but it was impressed upon me that the Legal Adviser has got to see to the observation of all of the international agreements, the treaties, [and] the customary international law." In the Foreword to this book, Harold Koh further reaffirmed this sentiment, remarking that:

> Ideally, the Legal Adviser should act not just as a counselor, but also as a conscience to the U.S. Government with respect to international law. As counselor, the Legal Adviser should always accurately advise his client as to what domestic and international law says.[5] But as the government's conscience on international law, wherever possible,

the Legal Adviser should search for options that promote the sound
development of international law and warn his clients not to follow
an option that is awful, even if it may be lawful.[6]

Former Legal Adviser William Taft observed in Chapter 12 that it
may have been this reputation of the Legal Adviser that contributed to
the ill-fated decision of administration officials to exclude L from legal
determinations regarding detainee treatment and interrogation techniques.

As Michael Matheson, who served in L for nearly thirty years, including as Acting Legal Adviser during the Bush and Clinton Administrations, explained in Chapter 14:

> I think that lawyers in public service are public officials and they have
> responsibilities parallel to those other public officials have. An intel-
> ligence officer has a duty to give the best reading of the facts in a
> situation that he can, regardless of what his clients (if you want to call
> them that) want to hear. It's the same for a lawyer. He has a duty to
> give honest legal advice and not to change it based on what the client
> may expect or desire. So I would say that in that sense, a govern-
> ment lawyer has a duty to the entire body of the public even though
> he obviously has direct working relationships with a hierarchy in his
> own agency.

Former Legal Adviser to the Foreign and Commonwealth Office
in the United Kingdom Sir Frank Berman echoed this sentiment in
Chapter 15, explaining that "the Legal Adviser must always remember
to advise on the law as it is and not on the law as some policymaker
hopes it might be or hopes that he might be able to persuade another to
say that it is."

When consulted at an early stage, the Legal Advisers saw their initial
responsibility as providing a candid opinion of what the legal situation
is, as well as spelling out the possible consequences for violating international law in the particular area and advocating policy choices that
would not violate international law. The Legal Advisers also recognized

the dual role of the office in both presenting accurate legal analysis of the state's international law obligations and then defending policy-makers' decisions to the best of their ability. As explained in Chapter 15 by Ambassador Seifeselassie Lemma, former Legal Adviser of the Ethiopian Foreign Ministry, there are two distinct stages to the counsel provided by the Legal Adviser: "First, the government wants to genuinely know what the law is. Then, if the government finds the law to be inexpedient, it seeks sympathetic legal advice from the Legal Adviser on how best to justify the action." And, as Michael Matheson explained, "The Legal Adviser gives legal advice before decisions are made; he gives the best possible legal defense for the decision once it has been made; and he contributes to solving practical problems with his lawyering skills." Even as national advocates, however, the Legal Advisers indicated that they sought to shape their arguments with an eye to interpreting rules in the manner most beneficial to the long-term and broad national interest.

## How Influential Is the Advice of the Legal Adviser?

There are naturally times in each of the Legal Advisers' tenure where they advised against a course of action that they perceived to be in violation of international law. The clarity of a given international legal standard affected the degree to which each Legal Adviser was inclined to take such a position or how strongly to advocate it. The factors the Legal Advisers said they took into account in deciding whether to opine that a proposed course of action would violate international law include the extent to which the relevant rules of international law are unambiguous, well established, and broadly accepted; and the extent to which an international or domestic forum exists that can pronounce judgment on the correctness of the administration's interpretation of the law in question. The Legal Advisers recognized, moreover, that the ability to claim that an act is not in violation of international law is limited by the opinions of both the domestic and international legal communities, as reflected in the public statements of governments, nongovernmental organizations (NGOs), international organizations, and scholars.

Generally speaking, policymakers tended to accord substantial weight to the Legal Adviser's legal opinions. The Legal Advisers mentioned several instances, including some cases involving questions of use of force, where policymakers reluctantly heeded their legal advice despite policy preferences to the contrary. For example, in Chapter 5, Roberts Owen related the story of how in the middle of the Iranian hostage crisis, the policymakers decided not to use force against the Iranian Embassy in Washington, DC because "Secretary Vance was a good law-abiding lawyer and, based on L's advice, he concluded that Iran's wrongdoing wouldn't justify wrongdoing by the United States."

Abe Sofaer recalled in Chapter 7 how he successfully convinced the policymakers not to attack Libya after it was disclosed that Libya had provided confiscated Tunisian passports to the terrorists that attacked airline passengers at the Rome and Vienna airports in 1985 because the United States had not yet publicly articulated its position that States that support terrorists would be subject to attack, and because it "had not fully exhausted non-forcible options." Conrad Harper, in turn, recounted in Chapter 15: "While I was Legal Adviser during the spring of 1994, the United States agreed to supply the Peruvian Air Force with real-time intelligence, which ultimately resulted in the Peruvian Air Force mistakenly shooting down a civilian aircraft. My office informed the policymakers that this policy could not sustain itself under the Chicago Convention, and the practice was thereafter reluctantly discontinued."

In a particularly telling episode related by John Bellinger in Chapter 13, L convinced the White House to issue a Presidential Memorandum to implement the International Court of Justice's decision in the *Avena/Medellin* case, exhorting state courts to give effect to the ICJ's judgment that a new trial was necessary because the Texas authorities had not apprised the Mexican defendant of his right to consult a consular officer at the time of arrest as required by the Vienna Convention on Consular Relations. According to Bellinger, "the significance of

President Bush's decision cannot be overstated, given that the President was the former Governor of Texas and a supporter of the death penalty and that Mr. Medellin had been convicted of an especially grisly crime in Texas – the rape and murder of two teenage girls. Ordering review of his conviction and sentence in order to comply with a decision by an international tribunal in The Hague was not a popular decision in Texas."

At other times, L was influential in shaping the modalities and articulating the rationale for use of force so that it would be accepted by the international community. As Michael Matheson explains in Chapter 14:

> I don't think it's realistic to think Presidents are often going to refrain from the use of force on what they consider to be essential security grounds because of the views of the State Department Legal Adviser. On the other hand, I think there are important things which Legal Advisers *can* do with respect to the use of force. One is to see to it that the modalities used are as consistent with international law as possible. For example, the actions we took in Nicaragua which were gratuitously in violation of international law need not necessarily have been so. Another aspect is that when the decision is made to use force, it's important what argument is made to justify that decision. There are some ways of justifying which will open up entirely new open-ended doctrines. There are others which are more consistent with past practices; the Legal Adviser can have a considerable amount of influence on what arguments are made, which in turn greatly influences what precedential effect that use of force might have.

Davis Robinson in Chapter 6 described the 1983 "rescue mission" in Grenada as an example of this. "In our legal justification, we consciously avoided arguments that might imply any weakening in the legal restraints that apply to the use of force. For example, we did not claim that we were exercising an inherent right of self-defense under the United Nations Charter. Furthermore, we did not assert any broad doctrine of humanitarian intervention."

At the same time, the Legal Advisers recognized that their voice was not the government's leading voice on *all* matters of international law.

As Abe Sofaer observed in Chapter 7, "The fact of the matter is that American foreign policy has shifted from the State Department to other agencies. As foreign policies become more specialized, other agencies have the lead in many international issues." The complications that can result from the diffusion of legal counsel are well illustrated in the Torture Memorandum lawyering example in Chapter 16.

Where a significant international law-related issue came within the special purview of these other legal offices, the State Department lawyers are ordinarily expected to work with their counterparts (and vice versa) through a "clearance process" in an attempt to ensure that a single legal position would emerge. Where this proved not to be possible, divergent legal opinions are presented to the President and Cabinet within the text of a decision memo. To maximize their legal influence, State Department Legal Advisers found that they had to be much more than gifted lawyers and administrators; they also had to be skillful and sometimes aggressive bureaucrats, unafraid to tackle the internecine turf battles that were inherent in the interagency process. Often the most important battle was simply to ensure that L had a proverbial "seat at the table."

The Legal Advisers pointed out that the internal clearance procedure did not always operate in this proscribed manner, and on a handful of notable occasions L was intentionally kept out of the decision-making process, even on matters that turned entirely on interpretation of international law. This tended to happen when State Department officials from other bureaus or government officials from other departments or agencies foresaw that L would likely oppose a proposed course of action. As Davis Robinson stated in Chapter 6: "Some policymakers will on occasion assume the following attitude: 'Oh, let's not involve L. First, they are likely to say no. Second, they will take forever – they are so slow. And, if you're not careful, once they get involved, they will run away with your store." The Legal Advisers mentioned the following cases in which L was cut out of the decision making process: the 1980s mining of Nicaraguan harbors and armed support for the "contras," the 1990 kidnapping of Dr. Alvarez-Machain from Mexico, and, as recounted in the lawyering example in Chapter 16, the adoption of the initial policies related to treatment of "unlawful enemy combatants" detained in the aftermath of the attacks on 9/11.

The same policymakers that cut L out of the decision-making process, however, display no hesitancy in seeking L's assistance in crafting after-the-fact legal justifications for the decisions and actions taken. No matter his own opinion on the matter, the Legal Adviser is then asked to become advocate for the U.S. position. As Stephen Schwebel, a former Deputy Legal Adviser who later served as President of the International Court of Justice, once remarked: "The Legal Adviser is always called in to pick up the pieces even if he was not influentially involved in the initial decision."[7] In relation to the mining of Nicaragua's harbors, former Legal Adviser Davis Robinson stated in Chapter 6: "As it turned out, all that the lawyers could contribute was assistance in after-the-fact containment of a train wreck. I remember one Secretary of State under whom I served stating, 'I have only one rigid rule and that is, don't ever let me be blindsided.' I can only have wished that this sensible rule had applied to L as well."

During the roundtable discussion with foreign Legal Advisers (Chapter 15), former UK Legal Adviser Sir Frank Berman offered a comparative perspective on this problem:

> Probably the most notorious incident where the UK Legal Adviser was deliberately cut out of the loop was the 1956 Suez invasion.[8] But I would say that the lessons of that experience have generally been learned for the future. It is considered a cardinal sin within the UK Foreign Office to put up a policy submission that did not clearly recite that the Legal Adviser or his staff had been consulted, or which did not include an analysis of the legal questions which were relevant to the decision. If the submission did not contain this, then any legitimate senior official or minister would send it back for a complete analysis to know what the law stated.

During the Carnegie meeting, the former U.S. State Department Legal Advisers concluded that the United States would do well to adopt a similar iron-clad procedural requirement. As Davis Robinson summed up in Chapter 6: "The main lesson that I drew from my days in L is that, if the U.S. Government is to realize the full benefit of the potential contribution of its international lawyers, the lawyers need to participate from the beginning of a take-off in policy and not just in a crash landing whenever things go wrong." Similarly, in discussing, the detainee policies after 9/11 and the Torture Memoranda, William Taft recounted in Chapter 12, "I am convinced, however, that if we had been involved and our views considered, several conclusions that were not consistent with our treaty obligations under the Convention against Torture and our obligations under customary international law would not have been reached."

Interestingly, none of the Legal Advisers said they ever seriously considered resigning from office when their legal advice was not heeded or when they were cut out of the loop, though all agreed that resignation might be necessary in an extreme case. In particular, in Chapter 15 the Legal Advisers discussed the case of UK Deputy Legal Adviser Elizabeth Wilmshurst, who resigned when the Government of the United Kingdom decided to disregard her legal memorandum opining that the proposed 2003 invasion of Iraq was not lawful.[9] Conrad Harper remarked, "To be an effective Legal Adviser or Deputy Legal Adviser, one must recognize that the exit door must always be open. When there is a very important matter and the government refuses to follow advice that you consider to be essential, you are suppose to resign." In this regard, in Chapter 5 Roberts Owen related the story of Secretary of State Cyrus Vance's resignation to protest the Iranian hostage rescue mission that was launched over his opposition.

## Do the Legal Advisers View International Law as Helpful or as a Hindrance?

No matter whether a particular Legal Adviser leaned more toward constructivism or political realism, they all embraced international law as a tool for achieving their governments' foreign policy goals. For, as Professor Louis Henkin has written, "realists who do not recognize the uses and the force of law are not realistic."[10] At the same time, constructivists who would approach international law as a straight jacket that precludes innovative interpretation are not constructive.

The Legal Advisers shared a number of instances where creative interpretation and use of international law furthered foreign policy aims and avoided the necessity of using force. These include L's lead role in establishing the Iran–United States Claims Tribunal, which was part of the deal for the release of U.S. hostages, and the Iraqi Compensation Commission and Boundary Dispute Commission, which were part of the ceasefire agreement in the aftermath of the 1991 Gulf War.

In this regard, in Chapter 11, David Andrews detailed the role L played in negotiating the several international agreements and Security Council Resolutions that made it possible to try the two Libyan officials charged with blowing up Pan Am 103 before a special Scottish Court sitting in The Netherlands. This creative solution severed a thirty-year cycle of violence between the United States and Libya and facilitated the transformation of Libya from a terrorist-supporting State to a partner in the war against terrorism.

Similarly, in Chapter 15, Ambassador Skotnikov underscored the role of innovative interpretation of international law in facilitating the peaceful dissolution of the Soviet Union in 1991:

> This was an acute crisis. I am pleased to note, though, that never before was international law-related legal advice in such demand, and the transition was accomplished in an orderly way. I credit not only the legal advice but also the political leadership that sought the legal advice on virtually every issue, from Russia's assumption of the Soviet Union's Security Council seat to the continuation of the Soviet Union's arms control treaties.

Michael Matheson, in turn, recounted in Chapter 10 L's pivotal role in the creation of the International Criminal Tribunal for the former

Yugoslavia, the first international war crimes tribunal since Nuremberg. It was L that came up with the idea of having the Security Council create the tribunal under its Chapter VII powers rather than seek to negotiate a treaty (as the Europeans had proposed), which would take a great deal more time and might yield unpredictable results. The Security Council had never before been used to establish a judicial body, but L succeeded in convincing the other members of the Council that such action was legitimate and would yield a better result than the treaty route. The launch of the Yugoslavia War Crimes Tribunal in 1993 led to the Security Council's creation of the Rwanda Tribunal a year later and ultimately paved the way to the establishment of a permanent International Criminal Court four years after that.

N THE FINAL ANALYSIS, THIS PROJECT HAS RECONFIRMED that international law is "real law" because it plays a real role in shaping the conduct of States even in times of crises implicating essential national security concerns. International law matters because government lawyers and policymakers use it and are influenced by it. Thus, rather than ask "Did the relevant actors feel compelled to obey international law?" a more useful question is: "How did international law affect their behavior?"[11] In this regard, the observations of the Legal Advisers and the qualitative insights set forth in this book tell us much about how international law is actually used for legitimating political actions, for rallying support, for imposing restraints, and for persuading policymakers to choose a particular course consonant with international law to achieve their desired goals.

# Glossary of Terms

**Abu Ghraib** After the 2003 invasion of Iraq, reports surfaced of U.S. abuse of detainees at the Abu Ghraib detention facility near Baghdad.

**Afghanistan, 2001 invasion** Following the September 11, 2001 terrorist attacks, the United States invaded Afghanistan using the rationale of self-defense because the Taliban government was aiding and sheltering the Al-Qaeda perpetrators of the 9/11 attacks.

**AJIL (*American Journal of International Law*)** Quarterly journal published by the American Society of International Law, founded in 1906.

**Algiers Accords** Agreement concluded January 19, 1981 to resolve the crisis, which began with the November 4, 1979 seizure of the U.S. Embassy in Teheran and the taking of 52 American hostages. It included the unfreezing of Iranian assets in the United States and the establishment of the Iran–United States Claims Tribunal in The Hague for processing claims arising from these events.

**Alien Tort Statute** The Alien Tort Claims Act of 1789 (28 U.S.C §1350) grants jurisdiction to U.S. Federal Courts over "any civil action by an alien for a tort only, committed in violation of the law of nations or a treaty of the United States." Little used for its first two centuries, it has recently been relied on by litigants seeking redress in human-rights abuse cases.

**Alstoetter Case** Nuremberg-era case tried by a U.S. military commission in which Nazi justice ministry officials and judges were convicted for their role in using the German justice system as a weapon against Jews and other perceived enemies of the regime.

**Alvarez-Machain Case** This case arose from the 1985 torture and murder of an American DEA agent in Mexico. Dr. Humberto Alvarez-Machain was suspected of participating in the crime. Unable to extradite him, the DEA arranged to have Dr. Alvarez-Machain kidnapped and brought into the United States. At trial, charges against Alvarez-Machain were dismissed for lack of evidence; Alvarez-Machain later sued his abductors under the Alien Tort Claims Act.

**Anti-Ballistic Missile Treaty** After several years of discussions culminating in the Strategic Arms Limitation Talks (SALT I, 1969–1972), on May 26, 1972 U.S. President Richard Nixon and USSR Secretary Brezhnev signed an Interim Agreement limiting strategic offensive weapons and the Anti-Ballistic Missile Treaty limiting the extent of and regulating the oversight of strategic defensive systems. Additional discussions and interpretations have continued.

**Article 3 of the Geneva Convention and Additional Protocol II** "Common Article 3" is a provision included in each of the four Geneva Conventions of 1949 (see below); it addresses the protection of victims of noninternational armed conflicts.

**Article 51** Article 51 of the Charter of the United Nations provides that "Nothing in the present Charter shall impair the inherent right of individual or collective self-defense if an armed attack occurs against a Member of the United Nations, until the Security Council has taken the measures necessary to maintain international peace and security...."

**Black sites** Covert CIA operated detention/interrogation facilities in the aftermath of the 9/11 terrorist attacks.

***Boumediene v. Bush*** 2008 Supreme Court Case that declared parts of the Military Commissions Act unconstitutional, determined that the Combat Status Review Tribunals were inadequate, and ruled that the foreign detainees at Guantanamo Bay have the right to appeal to U.S. federal courts to challenge their indefinite detention without charges.

**Brezhnev Doctrine** Declared in 1968, this policy stated that the USSR would combat "anti-socialist forces" within its sphere of influence (such as reforms of the Czechoslovakian "Prague Spring" movement), with the justification of defending the strengthening socialist community, the greatest "achievement of the international working class."

**Bryan-Suarez Treaty** This is a 1914 dispute-resolution treaty between Chile and the United States. Under it, the two countries agreed to submit to an international commission the question of how much Chile should provide in *ex gratia* payments in the Letelier/Moffitt assassination case.

**CAAC-747** Airplane owned by the Civil Aviation Administration of China.

**Camp David I and Camp David II** I: In meetings from September 5 to 17, 1978, President Sadat of Egypt, Prime Minister Begin of Israel, and President Carter of the United States agreed on a "framework for peace" based on UN Resolutions 242 and 338 and Article 33 of the UN Charter.

II: In meetings from July 11 to 24, 2000, President Clinton of the United States, Prime Minister Barak of Israel, and Chairman Arafat of the

Palestinian National Assembly, with others, tried to negotiate a final settlement of the Palestine–Israel conflict. Negotiations ended without a settlement because not all issues could be resolved.

**Case Act** Law requiring the President to inform the Congress of all Executive Agreements. There is a special procedure for notification of confidential agreements.

**Charter of the Organization of American States** Signed in 1948 and in effect since 1951, this document has been ratified by all thirty-five independent nations of the Americas. Its purposes are for the member nations "to achieve an order of peace and justice, to promote their solidarity, to strengthen their collaboration, and to defend their sovereignty, their territorial integrity, and their independence."

**Compliance theory** International Relations theories that attempt to answer the question of whether international law is "real" law. Historically, they included an Austinian positivistic realist strand; a Hobbesian utilitarian, rationalistic strand; a Kantian liberal strand; and a Bentham process-based strand. More recently, the dominant approaches to compliance scholarship include an "instrumentalist" strand; a "liberal internationalist" strand; a "constructivist" strand; and an "institutionalist" approach.

**Contra movement** Armed opponents of Nicaragua's leftist Sandinista government following the 1979 overthrow of the forth-three-year rule by the Somoza family. "Contra" (from Spanish *contrarevolucionario*) was a term often used to cover a range of groups with little inherent unity.

**Convention on Certain Conventional Weapons (CCW)** Concluded in 1980 and entered into force 1983. This convention is based on the principles of protecting the civilian population from the effects of hostilities and the prohibition of weapons and methods of warfare that cause superfluous injury or unnecessary suffering. The convention itself provides a framework for protocols that address specific conventional weapons. The four protocols that are in force prohibit: nondetectable fragments; mines, booby-traps, and other devices; incendiary weapons; and blinding laser weapons. A fifth protocol on explosive remnants of war was negotiated and adopted on November 28, 2003.

**Conventions on Diplomatic and Consular Relations** The Vienna Convention, based on a draft prepared by the UN International Law Commission, codifies the established practices governing diplomatic relations. The Convention covers establishment of diplomatic relations and missions, use of flag and emblem, appointment of staff, privileges and immunities, inviolability of premises, persona non grata, and termination of diplomatic function among many other subjects. The almost universal acceptance of this instrument reflects the importance of its subject matter to the international community. The Vienna Convention on Consular Relations also sets out the accepted rules of diplomatic and consular privileges and immunities to which states adhere in their pursuit of friendly international relations and the maintenance of international peace and security. Article 5 delineates consular functions, including protection of nationals, development of commercial, cultural, and scientific relations, and issuing of passports and visas, among many others.

**Cuban Missile Crisis** The Cuban Missile Crisis was a tense confrontation between the Soviet Union and the United States over the Soviet deployment of nuclear missiles in Cuba. The crisis began on October 16, 1962 and lasted for thirteen days. It is regarded by many as the moment when the Cold War was closest to becoming nuclear war.

**Customary International Law** Rules created by the constant and uniform practice of States and other subjects of international law in their legal relations, in circumstances, which give rise to a legitimate expectation of similar conduct in the future. Where such a rule exists, for any State to be bound by the rule it is not necessary to show that State's consent to the rule or belief in the rule's obligatory character.

**Darfur, Sudan** Darfur, a region in The Sudan, was the site of war crimes, ethnic cleansing, and possibly genocide committed by government troops and government-backed rebel groups from 2004 to the present. In 2009, the International Criminal Court issued an international arrest warrant for the President of The Sudan.

**Dayton Accords** An agreement reached in November 1995 at Wright-Patterson Air Force Base among representatives for Bosnia, Croatia, and Serbia, containing measures to end hostilities in the former Yugoslavia. It was signed in Paris, France, on December 14, 1995, by the presidents of the three warring nations.

***Dellums v. Bush*** 752 F. Supp. 1141 (1990). On December 13, 1990, Judge Harold H. Greene of the U.S. District Court for the District of Columbia denied the motion for summary judgment by plaintiffs (fifty-three Congressmen and one Senator) requesting an injunction to prevent the President from initiating an offensive attack against Iraq without explicit Congressional authorization.

**Entebbe rescue** (July 3–4, 1976), rescue by an Israeli commando squad of 103 hostages from a French jet airliner en route from Israel to France that, after stopping at Athens, had been hijacked on June 27 by Palestinian terrorists and flown to Entebbe, Uganda. At Entebbe, the hijackers had freed those of the 258 passengers who did not appear to be Israeli and held the rest hostage for the release of 53 fellow terrorists.

**Ethnic cleansing** Euphemistic term used in lieu of genocide in an effort to avoid political pressure to intervene during mass atrocities in Bosnia and Rwanda.

***Ex gratia* payment** A payment not legally required.

**Executive agreement** An international agreement entered into by the President, outside of the treaty ratification process. To be implemented, it requires a simple majority vote of the House and Senate. Many agreements require subsequent implementing bills passed by both chambers before they can take force. Congress can express its opposition to any particular executive agreement by withholding the necessary implementing legislation.

The President's authority to negotiate executive agreements flows from two sources: the power granted him in the Constitution as chief executive, and/or specific powers delegated to him by earlier act of Congress.

**Farsi** Farsi is the most widely spoken member of the Iranian branch of the Indo-Iranian languages, a subfamily of the Indo-European languages. It is the language of Iran (formerly Persia) and is also widely spoken in Afghanistan.

***Fatwa*** A legal pronouncement in Islam, issued by a religious law specialist on a specific issue. Usually a fatwa is issued at the request of an individual or a judge to settle a question where Islamic jurisprudence is unclear. A scholar capable of issuing a fatwa is known as a Mufti.

Because there is no central Islamic priesthood, there is also no unanimously accepted method to determine who can issue a fatwa and who cannot, leading some Islamic scholars to complain that too many people feel qualified to issue *fatwas.*

**Foreign Sovereign Immunities Act of 1976** 28 U.S.C. §§1330, 1332, 1391(f) 1441(d), 1602–1611. Under this Act, issues of personal jurisdiction, subject matter jurisdiction, and immunity from suit are intertwined. A court must determine whether the foreign state defendant is immune from suit in order to determine whether the court has personal and subject matter jurisdiction. The court may find that the defendant is immune, or that there is an exception to immunity.

**Gaza** The Gaza Strip is a narrow strip of land just northeast of the Sinai Peninsula. At the end of the 1948 Arab–Israeli War it was occupied by the Egyptians, under which it remained until it was claimed by Israel during the Six-Day War of 1967. The Gaza Strip is unusual in being a densely settled area not recognized as a *de jure* part of any sovereign country.

Together with parts of the West Bank, it is mostly run by the Palestinian Authority. Substantial portions of the Gaza Strip (mainly the sites of areas populated by Israeli citizens) are controlled by Israel. The Palestinian Authority is not permitted conventional military forces; there are, however, a Public Security Force and a civil Police Force.

West Bank and Gaza Strip are Israeli-occupied with current status subject to the Israeli–Palestinian Interim Agreement (of September 28 1995); permanent status to be determined through further negotiation.

**Geneva Conventions of 1949** The Geneva Conventions of 1949 and their two Additional Protocols of 1977 form the basis of the modern laws of warfare (also known as international humanitarian law). The first Geneva Convention protects wounded and sick soldiers on land during war. The Second Geneva Convention protects wounded, sick, and shipwrecked military personnel at sea during war. The Third Geneva Convention applies to prisoners of war. The Fourth Geneva Convention affords protection to civilians, including in occupied territory.

**Genocide Convention** Convention on the Prevention and Punishment of the Crime of Genocide. This convention was unanimously adopted by the UN General Assembly in 1948 in the aftermath of the Holocaust. It defines the crime of genocide.

**Goldstone Commission** Richard J. Goldstone (b. 1938) is a South African judge and international war crimes prosecutor. Before taking a seat on the Constitutional Court of South Africa, Goldstone served as chairperson of the Standing Commission of Inquiry Regarding Public Violence and Intimidation – later known as the Goldstone Commission in South Africa. The Commission played a critical role in defusing the political violence that erupted when apartheid in South Africa began eroding in the late 1980s as the country moved toward its first democratic elections.

**Grenada "rescue mission"** In 1877 Grenada became a Crown Colony, and in 1967 it became an associate state within the British Commonwealth before gaining independence in 1974. In 1979, an attempt was made to set up a socialist/communist state in Grenada. Four years later, at the request of the Governor General, the United States, Jamaica, and the Eastern Caribbean States intervened militarily. Launching their now famous "rescue mission," the allied forces restored order, and in December 1984 a general election reestablished democratic government.

**Guantanamo Bay detention facility** After the 2001 invasion of Afghanistan, some nine hundred captured members of the Taliban and Al-Qaeda were transferred to and detained at the U.S. detention facility at Guantanamo Bay, Cuba.

**Gulf of Maine maritime boundary delimitation case** On October 12, 1984, the International Court of Justice decided "[t]hat the course of the single maritime boundary that divides the continental shelf and the exclusive fisheries zones of Canada and the United States of America in the Area referred to in the Special Agreement concluded by those two States on 29 March 1979 shall be defined by [specified] geodetic lines. . . . "

***Hamdan v. Rumsfeld*** 2006 Supreme Court case that held that the Military Tribunals established by President Bush violated the Uniform Code of Military Justice and the Geneva Conventions.

**Helsinki Accords** The Helsinki Accords is the Final Act of the Conference on Security and Cooperation in Europe held in Helsinki in 1975 between the United States, Canada, the Soviet Union, and the countries of Europe, including Turkey but not Albania. The civil rights portion of the agreement provided the basis for the work of Helsinki Watch, an independent NGO created to monitor compliance to the Helsinki Accords (which later evolved into several organizations, including Human Rights Watch). Although the provisions of the Accords applied to all signatories, the focus of attention was on their application to the Soviet Union and its satellites, Bulgaria, Czechoslovakia, East Germany, Hungary, Poland, and Romania.

**ICJ opinion on Article 51 of the Charter** The International Court of Justice has issued opinions in the Nicaragua Case and in the Congo Case suggesting that only an attack by one State against another State (to be contrasted from attacks by nonstate groups) would give rise to the inherent self-defensive right to enter the State from which an attack emitted.

**Injunctive order (injunction)** A court order commanding or preventing an action. To get an injunction, the complainant must show that there is no plain, adequate, and complete remedy at law and that an irreparable injury will result unless the relief is granted.

**Intelligence Oversight Act** The Intelligence Oversight Act of 1980 provided that the heads of intelligence agencies would keep the oversight committees "fully and currently informed" of their activities including "any significant anticipated intelligence activity." Detailed ground rules were established for reporting covert actions to the Congress, in return for the number of Congressional committees receiving notice of covert actions being limited to the two oversight committees.

**Intermediate-Range Nuclear Forces Treaty (INF)** The INF Treaty eliminated all nuclear-armed ground-launched ballistic and cruise missiles with ranges between 500 and 5,500 kilometers (about 300 to 3,400 miles) and their infrastructure. The INF Treaty is the first nuclear arms control agreement to actually reduce nuclear arms, rather than establish ceilings that could not be exceeded. Altogether it resulted in the elimination by May 1991 of 846 longer-and shorter-range U.S. INF missile systems and 1846 Soviet INF missile systems, including the modernized U.S. Pershing II and Soviet SS-20 missiles.

The INF Treaty was signed by President Reagan and Soviet General Secretary Gorbachev at a Washington Summit on December 8, 1987 and entered into force on June 1, 1988.

**International Court of Justice (ICJ)** The International Court of Justice, which sits at The Hague in the Netherlands, acts as a world court. It decides in accordance with international law disputes of a legal nature submitted to it by States, whilst in addition certain international organs and agencies are entitled to call upon it for Advisory opinions. It was set up in 1945 under the Charter of the United Nations to be the principal judicial organ of the Organization, and its basic instrument, the Statute of the Court, forms an integral part of the Charter.

**International Criminal Court** In 2002, the Rome Treaty establishing an International Criminal Court entered into force. It now has 110 parties. During the George W. Bush Administration, the United States actively opposed this Court. That policy changed in 2005 when the United States abstained on a Security Council Resolution referring the Darfur situation to the International Criminal Court.

**International Criminal Tribunal for Rwanda (ICTR)** Recognizing that serious violations of humanitarian law were committed in Rwanda, and acting under Chapter VII of the United Nations Charter, the Security Council created the International Criminal Tribunal for Rwanda (ICTR) by Resolution 955 of November 8, 1994. The purpose of this measure is to contribute to the process of national reconciliation in Rwanda and to the maintenance of peace in the region. The International Criminal Tribunal for Rwanda was established for the prosecution of persons responsible for genocide and other serious violations of international humanitarian law committed in the territory of Rwanda between January 1, 1994 and December 31, 1994. It may also deal with the prosecution of Rwandan citizens responsible for genocide and other such violations of international law committed in the territory of neighboring States during the same period.

**International Criminal Tribunal for the former Yugoslavia (ICTY)** The International Criminal Tribunal for the former Yugoslavia (ICTY) was established by Security Council Resolution 827. This resolution was passed on May 25, 1993 in the face of the serious violations of international humanitarian law committed in the territory of the former Yugoslavia since 1991, and as a response to the threat to international peace and security posed by those serious violations.

The ICTY is located in The Hague, The Netherlands.

In harmony with the purpose of its founding resolution, the ICTY's mission is fourfold:

- to bring to justice persons allegedly responsible for serious violations of international humanitarian law,
- to render justice to the victims,
- to deter further crimes, and
- to contribute to the restoration of peace by promoting reconciliation in the former Yugoslavia.

**International law of expropriation** There is debate over whether there exists an external, international standard of treatment to which foreign investors are entitled. There are at least two competing points of view:

the Hull rule ("prompt, adequate, and effective" compensation), often advocated by capital exporting countries and partial compensation, preferred by capital importing states.

**International Maritime Organization** United Nations Agency concerned with the safety of shipping and cleaner oceans. In 1948 an international conference in Geneva adopted a convention formally establishing IMO (the original name was the Inter-Governmental Maritime Consultative Organization, or IMCO, but the name was changed in 1982 to IMO). The IMO Convention entered into force in 1958 and the new Organization met for the first time the following year.

**Iran-Contra Affair** In the Iran-Contra Affair, U.S. President Ronald Reagan's Administration secretly sold arms to Iran, which was engaged in a bloody war with its neighbor Iraq from 1980 to 1988 (see Iran–Iraq War), and diverted the proceeds to the Contra rebels fighting to overthrow the leftist and democratically elected Sandinista government of Nicaragua. Those sales thus had a dual goal: appeasing Iran, which had influence with militant groups that held several American hostages in Lebanon and supported bombings in Western European countries, and funding a guerrilla war aimed at aborting Nicaraguan independence from U.S. hegemony.

Both transactions were contrary to acts of Congress, which prohibited the funding of the Contras and the sale of weapons to Iran. In addition, both activities violated UN sanctions.

**Iran–United States Claims Tribunal** In 1981, the United States and Iran entered into the Algiers Accords, which brought an end to the Embassy hostage crisis and created the Tribunal to resolve existing disputes between the two countries and their nationals. The Tribunal sits in The Hague, The Netherlands and is comprised of nine arbitrators:

three appointed by Iran, three by the United States, and three by the party-appointed members acting jointly or, in absence of agreement by an appointing authority.

Under the Accords, the United States released the vast majority of Iran's "frozen" assets and transferred them directly to Iran or to various accounts to pay outstanding claims. Almost all of the approximately 4,700 private U.S. claims filed against the Government of Iran at the Tribunal have been resolved and have resulted in more than $2.5 billion in awards to U.S. nationals and companies. The period for filing new private claims against Iran expired on January 19, 1982.

The two governments have also filed claims against each other. The vast majority of these intergovernmental claims were filed by Iran against the United States. While some parts of those claims have been resolved, a number of major cases remain to be adjudicated at the Tribunal.

**KGB** Russia's Committee for State Security (Komitet Gosudarstvennoi Bezopasnosti) The basic organizational structure of the KGB was created in 1954, when the reorganization of the police apparatus was carried out. In the late 1980s, the KGB remained a highly centralized institution, with controls implemented by the Politburo through the KGB headquarters in Moscow.

**Khomeini, Ayatollah Ruhollah** Ayatollah Seyyed Ruhollah Khomeini (May 17, 1900 – June 3, 1989) was an Iranian Shia cleric and the political and spiritual leader of the 1979 revolution that overthrew Mohammad Reza Pahlavi, the then Shah of Iran. He is considered to be the founder of the modern Shiite State and ruled Iran from the Shah's overthrow to his death in 1989.

**Kosovo** A region within the former Yugoslavian republic of Serbia that has a substantial proportion of Yugoslavia's ethnic Albanian population.

**Kosovo Liberation Army (KLA)** An organization striving for autonomy for Kosovo from Serbia; after the 1995 Dayton Accords omitted such a provision, the KLA increased attacks on Serbs within Kosovo and was labeled a terrorist organization.

**Kurds** A non-Arab Middle Eastern minority population that inhabits the region known as Kurdistan, an extensive plateau and mountain area in South West Asia including parts of Eastern Turkey, North East Iraq, and North West Iran and smaller sections of North East Syria and Armenia.

**Lawfare** A term coined by Major General Charles Dunlap meaning "the strategy of using or misusing law as a substitute for traditional military means to achieve an operational objective."

**Land-for-Peace Formulation of Security Council Resolution 242** United Nations Security Council Resolution 242 (S/RES/242) was adopted unanimously by the UN Security Council on November 22, 1967 in the aftermath of the Six Day War. It calls for the "withdrawal of Israeli armed forces from territories occupied in the recent conflict" in exchange for an end to the Arab–Israeli conflict. The "territories" here refer to the West Bank, East Jerusalem, the Gaza Strip, the Sinai Peninsula, and the Golan Heights. It is one of the most commonly referenced UN resolutions in Middle Eastern politics.

**Law of the Sea Convention (1982)** This international agreement establishes a legal order for the oceans. It contains provisions on territorial sea and innocent passage, international navigation, archipelagic states, exclusive economic zone (EEZ), continental shelf, high seas, regime of islands, enclosed seas, right of access of land-locked states, protection, and preservation of the marine environment, marine scientific research, marine technology, and settlement of disputes.

**Maritime Terrorism Convention** Convention for the Suppression of Unlawful Acts against the Safety of Maritime Navigation, with related Protocol, March 10, 1988.

**Merits phase of the case** The phase of a case dealing with the elements or grounds of a claim or defense – the substantive considerations to be taken into account in deciding the case – as opposed to extraneous or technical points, especially of procedure.

**Mexican case (of March 31, 2004)** Before the International Court of Justice, *Avena and Other Mexican Nationals (Mexico v. United States of America)*: The Court finds that the United States of America has breached its obligations to Mr. Avena and fifty other Mexican nationals and to Mexico under the Vienna Convention on Consular Relations. (Announced March 31, 2004.)

**Middle East War (of 1973)** Also known as the Yom Kippur War, this conflict was fought from October 6 to October 22–24, 1973, between Israel and a coalition of Egypt and Syria who were attempting to regain territory lost to Israel in 1967.

**Mining of the Harbors case (Nicaragua)** Before International Court of Justice: Military and Paramilitary Activities in and against Nicaragua (*Nicaragua v. United States of America*) (1984–1991).

**Montreal Convention** The Montreal Convention applies to acts of aviation sabotage such as bombings aboard aircraft in flight. It was concluded at the International Conference on Air Law held at Montreal, September 8–23, 1971, under the auspices of the International Civil Aviation Organization (ICAO). This Convention is supplemented by the Protocol for the Suppression of Unlawful Acts of Violence at Airports Serving International Civil Aviation, done at Montreal on February 24, 1988.

**National Emergencies Act** 50 U.S.C §§1601, 1621, 1622, 1631, 1641, 1651: dealing with the declaration of national emergency.

*nolo contendere* Latin, "I do not wish to contend," a plea of no contest. (Often shortened to *nolo*.)

**North Atlantic Treaty Organization (NATO)** An alliance of twenty-six countries from North America and Europe, the North Atlantic Treaty Organization (NATO) was established in 1949. NATO members agree to treat an armed attack on one or more members as an attack on all members, who will then take action to restore and maintain security.

**NATO intervention, 1999** In 1999, without first obtaining Security Council authorization, NATO launched a seventy-eight-day bombing campaign against Serbia in order to halt ethnic cleansing against Kosovar Albanians in the Serb province of Kosovo.

**NPT** The Non Proliferation Treaty is a landmark international treaty whose objective is to prevent the spread of nuclear weapons and weapons technology, to promote cooperation in the peaceful uses of nuclear energy, and to further the goal of achieving nuclear disarmament and general and complete disarmament. The Treaty represents the only binding commitment in a multilateral treaty to the goal of disarmament by the nuclear-weapon States.

**Nuremberg and Tokyo tribunals** The Nuremberg Trials is the general name for two sets of trials of Nazis involved in World War II and the Holocaust. The trials were held in the German city of Nuremberg from 1945 to 1949 at the Nuremberg Palace of Justice (the only court in Germany large enough to host the event that had not been destroyed by Allied bombing). The first and most famous of these trials was the Trial of the Major War Criminals Before the International Military Tribunal or IMT, which tried twenty-four of the most important captured (or still believed to be alive) leaders of Nazi Germany. It was held from November 20, 1945 to October 1, 1946. The second set of trials was of lesser war criminals under Control Council Law No. 10, including the famous Doctors' Trial.

Japanese defendants accused of war crimes were tried by the International Military Tribunal for the Far East, which was established by a charter issued by U.S. Army General Douglas MacArthur. The so-called Tokyo Charter closely followed the Nürnberg Charter. The trials were conducted in English and Japanese and lasted nearly two years. Of the twenty-five Japanese defendants (all of whom were convicted), seven were sentenced to hang, sixteen were given life imprisonment, and two were sentenced to lesser terms. Except for those who died early of natural causes in prison, none of the imprisoned Japanese war criminals served a life sentence. Instead, by 1958 the remaining prisoners had been either pardoned or paroled.

From their outset, the war crimes trials were dismissed by critics merely as "victor's justice," because only individuals from defeated countries were prosecuted and because the defendants were charged with acts that allegedly had not been criminal when committed.

**Occupied territories** Substantial portions of the Gaza Strip, (mainly the sites of areas populated by Israeli citizens) are controlled by Israel. See "Gaza," above.

**OLC** Office of Legal Counsel at the U.S. Department of Justice

**One-China recognition** The One-China policy is the principle that there is one China and both mainland China and Taiwan are part of that China. The acknowledgement of this policy relates to the political status of Taiwan has been the dilemma in relations between the People's Republic of China (PRC) and Republic of China (ROC). Its acknowledgment is required for all countries seeking diplomatic relations with the PRC, although other definitions of the policy exist.

One interpretation, which was adopted during the Cold War, is that either the PRC or the ROC is the sole rightful government of all China and that the other government is illegitimate. Although much of the Western bloc maintained relations with the ROC until the 1970s as a bastion of capitalism under this policy, much of the Eastern bloc maintained relations with the PRC. Whereas the ROC considered itself the remaining holdout of a democratic government of a country overrun by Communist "rebels," the PRC claimed to have succeeded the ROC in the Communist revolution. Although the ROC no longer portrays itself as the sole legitimate government of China, the position of the PRC has remained unchanged.

Another interpretation is that there exists only one geographical region of China, which was split into two Chinese states by the Chinese Civil War. This is largely the position of current supporters of Chinese reunification in Taiwan who believe that this "one China" should eventually reunite under a single government.

**Operation Desert Shield/Operation Desert Storm** The Gulf War was a conflict between Iraq and a coalition force of thirty-four nations led by the United States. The war started with the Iraqi invasion of Kuwait in August 1990. The result of the war was a decisive victory for the coalition forces, which drove Iraqi forces out of Kuwait with minimal coalition deaths. The main battles were aerial and ground combat within Iraq, Kuwait and bordering areas of Saudi Arabia. The war did not expand outside of the immediate Iraq/Kuwait/Saudi border region, although Iraq fired missiles on Israeli cities.

Other common names for the conflict include: the Persian Gulf War, War in the Gulf, Iraq–Kuwait Conflict, UN–Iraq conflict, Operations Desert Shield, Desert Storm, Desert Sabre, 1990 Gulf War (for the Iraqi invasion of Kuwait), 1991 Gulf War (1990–1991), and Gulf War Sr. and First Gulf War (to distinguish it from the 2003 invasion of Iraq).

**"OPP" – "other physical principles"** One important issue in interpretation of the Limitation of Anti-Ballistic Missile Systems (ABM Treaty) was the extent to which systems based on "other physical principles" (e.g., lasers, particle beams) than those actually described in the treaty might still be developed, tested, and/or deployed.

**OPIC** The Overseas Private Investment Corporation (OPIC) was established as a development agency of the U.S. Government in 1971. OPIC helps U.S. businesses invest overseas, fosters economic development in new and emerging markets, complements the private sector in managing the risks associated with foreign direct investment, and supports U.S. foreign policy.

**Organization of Eastern Caribbean States** The Organization of Eastern Caribbean States (OECS) came into being on June 18, 1981, when seven Eastern Caribbean countries signed a treaty agreeing to cooperate with each other and promote unity and solidarity among the Members. The Treaty became known as the Treaty of Basseterre, so named in honor of the capital city of St. Kitts and Nevis where it was signed.

The OECS is now a nine-member grouping comprising Antigua and Barbuda, Commonwealth of Dominica, Grenada, Montserrat, St. Kitts and Nevis, St. Lucia, and St.Vincent and the Grenadines.

Anguilla and the British Virgin Islands are associate members of the OECS.

**Ortega government** Daniel Ortega Saavedra (b. November, 11 1945) was President of Nicaragua from 1985 to 1990, during the Sandinista government, and is currently the leader of the Sandinista party.

**Ottawa Convention** The Antipersonnel Mine Ban Convention (APMBC) imposes a total ban on antipersonnel landmines. The key obligations outlined by the APMBC include:

- "Never to use, develop, produce, stockpile or transfer antipersonnel landmines, or to assist any other party to conduct these activities;
- To destroy all stockpiled antipersonnel landmines within four years of the Convention's entry into force;
- To clear all laid landmines within ten years of the Convention's entry into force; and
- When it is within their means, to provide assistance to mine clearance, mine awareness, stockpile destruction, and victim assistance activities worldwide."

Article 7 (Transparency Measures) requires that states report information including the quantity, location and types of mines they possess and the status of de-mining programs.

**Palestine Liberation Organization (PLO)** The Palestine Liberation Organization (PLO) is a political and paramilitary organization of Palestinian Arabs dedicated to the establishment of an independent Palestinian state to consist of the area between the Jordan River and the Mediterranean Sea, with an intent to replace Israel. Yasser Arafat was the PLO chairman from 1969 until his death in 2004 when he was succeeded by Mahmoud Abbas (also known as Abu Mazen.) In recent years the official goal has been redefined to consist of only the West Bank and Gaza Strip, although substantial parts of the organization do not abide by the new definition.

Founded in 1963, the PLO has a nominal legislative body of three hundred members, the Palestinian National Council (PNC). Actual political power and decisions are controlled by the PLO Executive Committee, made up of fifteen people voted in by the PNC. PLO ideology can be found in its constitution, the Palestinian Covenant, which was created in 1964. This covenant was amended in 1968; this version is made up of thirty-three articles. The original intention of the PLO was to establish a state of Palestine, which was called for in the Palestinian National Charter. Many articles in the Charter were publicly abrogated in 1993, but a new official text has not been produced.

**Palestinian problem** The Palestine problem became an international issue toward the end of World War I with the disintegration of the Turkish Ottoman Empire. Palestine was among the several former Ottoman Arab territories, which were placed under the administration of Great Britain under the Mandates System adopted by the League of Nations pursuant to the League's Covenant (Article 22).

All but one of these Mandated Territories became fully independent States, as anticipated. The exception was Palestine where, instead of being limited to "the rendering of administrative assistance and advice" the Mandate had as a primary objective the implementation of the "Balfour Declaration" issued by the British Government in 1917, expressing support for "the establishment in Palestine of a national home for the Jewish people."

During the years of the Palestine Mandate, from 1922 to 1947, large-scale Jewish immigration from abroad, mainly from Eastern Europe took place, the numbers swelling in the 1930s with the notorious Nazi persecution of Jewish populations. Palestinian demands for independence and resistance to Jewish immigration led to a rebellion in 1937, followed by continuing terrorism and violence from both sides during and immediately after World War II. Great Britain tried to implement various formulas to bring independence to a land ravaged by violence. In 1947, Great Britain in frustration turned the problem over to the United Nations.

After looking at various alternatives, the United Nations proposed the partitioning of Palestine into two independent States, one Palestinian Arab and the other Jewish, with Jerusalem internationalized (Resolution 181 (II) of 1947). One of the two States envisaged in the partition plan proclaimed its independence as Israel and in the 1948 war expanded to occupy 77 percent of the territory of Palestine. Israel also occupied the larger part of Jerusalem. More than half the indigenous Palestinian population fled or were expelled. Jordan and Egypt occupied the other parts of the territory assigned by the partition resolution to the Palestinian Arab State, which did not come into being.

In the 1967 war, Israel occupied the remaining territory of Palestine, until then under Jordanian and Egyptian control (the West Bank and Gaza Strip). This included the remaining part of Jerusalem, which was subsequently annexed by Israel. The war brought about a second exodus of Palestinians, estimated at half a million. Security Council resolution 242 (1967) of November 22, 1967 called on Israel to withdraw from territories it had occupied in the 1967 conflict.

In 1974, the General Assembly reaffirmed the inalienable rights of the Palestinian people to self-determination, national independence, and sovereignty, and to return.

**Pan Am 103 Bombing** In 1988, Pan Am Flight 103 blew up over Lockerbie, Scotland, killing over three hundred people, many of them American passengers. Two years later, the United States and the United Kingdom issued indictments against two Libyan officials allegedly responsible for the bombing. After years of negotiation between the United States, the United Kingdom, Libya, The Netherlands, and the United Nations, in 1998 a trial was held before three Scottish judges sitting in Camp Zeist, The Netherlands. One defendant was convicted, the other was set free. In 2009, the convicted defendant was freed on humanitarian grounds due to terminal cancer.

**Panama Canal Treaty** The Panama Canal Treaties of 1977–1978 meant to rectify a long-term, contentious issue in United States–Latin American relations. In 1903, U.S. military force supported Panamanian revolutionaries in their quest for independence from Colombia, and ensured U.S. control, for a century, of a strip of land in the center of Panama for the Canal. By the 1960s, Panamanian calls for sovereignty over the Canal Zone had reached high pitch, and United States relations with the isthmian country deteriorated.

President James E. ("Jimmy") Carter saw returning the Panama Canal as key to improving U.S. relations in the hemisphere and the developing world. Although opponents of the Treaty returning the Canal to Panama by the year 2000 criticized Carter's efforts on the basis of "We Built it, We Paid for it, It's Ours," the Treaty narrowly passed the Senate in April 1978. Although U.S. relations with Panama were cordial in the early 1980s, by the mid-1980s, with the country under the leadership of General Manuel Antonio Noriega, relations again deteriorated.

**Peace treaty between Egypt and Israel** See **Camp David I**, above.

*perestroika* Perestroika is the Russian word (which passed into English) for the economic reforms introduced in June 1987 by the Soviet leader Mikhail Gorbachev. Its literal meaning is "restructuring," which refers to restructuring of the Soviet economy.

Gorbachev's new system bore the characteristics of neither central planning nor a market economy. Instead, the Soviet economy went from stagnation to deterioration. At the end of 1991, when the union officially dissolved, the national economy was in a virtual tailspin.

**Permanent Court of Arbitration (PCA)** The Permanent Court of Arbitration (PCA), also known as the Hague Tribunal, is an international organization based in The Hague in the Netherlands. It was established in 1899 as one of the acts of the first Hague Peace Conference. In 2004, 101 countries were party to the treaty. The Court deals in cases submitted to it by consent of the parties involved, and it handles cases between countries and between countries and private parties.

The PCA is housed at the Peace Palace in The Hague, along with the International Court of Justice.

**Pinochet regime** General Augusto José Ramón Pinochet Ugarte (b. November 25, 1915) was head of the military government that ruled

Chile from 1973 to 1990. He came to power in a violent coup that deposed Salvador Allende, the first Socialist to be elected President of Chile. The coup ended a period of strained relations between the United States – which had actively sought Allende's removal – and Chile.

On September 11, 1973, the military led by Pinochet stormed the presidential palace and seized power from President Allende, who was found dead soon after. A junta headed by Pinochet was established, which immediately suspended the constitution, dissolved Congress, imposed strict censorship, and banned all political parties. In addition, it embarked on a campaign of terror against leftist elements in the country. As a result, approximately 3,000 Chileans were executed or disappeared, more than 27,000 were imprisoned or tortured, and many were exiled and received abroad as political refugees.

In 1980, a new constitution was approved via a dubious referendum, which prescribed a single-candidate presidential plebiscite in 1988 and a return to civilian rule in 1990. Pinochet lost the 1988 plebiscite, which triggered multicandidate presidential elections in 1989 for his replacement. Pinochet transferred power to Patricio Aylwin, the new democratically elected president, in 1990 but retained his post as commander in chief of the Army until 1998, when he assumed what could have been a lifelong seat in the Chilean Senate. He was forced to abandon his senate seat in 2002 due to a Supreme Court ruling that he suffered from "vascular dementia" and therefore could not stand trial for human rights abuses, claims that had been formally filed against him by the hundreds, for more than a decade, but never acted upon. In May 2004 Chile's Supreme Court stripped him of his dementia status, and he was charged with several crimes in that year.

***Rasul v. Bush*** 2004 Supreme Court Case in which the Court rejected the President's contention that the Guantanamo Bay detention facility was outside the jurisdiction of U.S. Courts.

**Recognition/diplomatic relations** Recognition is official action by a country acknowledging, expressly or by implication, *de jure* or *de facto*, the legality of the existence of a government, a country, or a situation, such as a change of territorial sovereignty.

Diplomatic relations refers to the customary form of permanent contact and communication between sovereign countries.

Nonofficial diplomatic relations may be maintained without official recognition, as between the United States and the Republic of China (ROC, or Taiwan) under the Taiwan Relations Act.

**Red Crescent Society** The International Red Cross and Red Crescent Movement is the world's largest group of humanitarian nongovernmental organizations, often known simply as the Red Cross, after its original symbol. The Movement is composed of, but must be distinguished from:

- the International Committee of the Red Cross (ICRC), a committee of Swiss nationals based in Geneva, Switzerland, which leads the international movement and that has special responsibilities under international humanitarian law;
- the International Federation of Red Cross and Red Crescent Societies (IFRCS), which is the composed body of all national Red Cross and Red Crescent societies, which was established to coordinate international relief actions and promote humanitarian activities); and
- the 178 individual national Red Cross and Red Crescent societies.

The red cross (an inversion of the flag of Switzerland) was adopted as the symbol of the movement under the original Geneva Convention. However, in the 1870s, the Ottoman Empire refused to use the red cross and declared that, although it would still recognize the red cross when used by others, it would use the red crescent instead. In 1929, the red crescent, as then in use in Egypt and Turkey, and the red lion and sun, as used in Persia, were both formally recognized as alternative emblems, and this situation is reflected in Article 38 of the First Geneva Convention of August 12, 1949, which recognizes three emblems for the International Red Cross and Red Crescent Movement:

- the red cross,
- the red crescent, and
- the red lion and sun (not used since 1980, when following the Iranian Revolution, Iran began using the red crescent).

As of 2004, the movement accepts these symbols and refuses to recognize additional ones, requiring all organizations to accept either the red cross or the red crescent emblems.

**Remand** Action taken by an appeals court to send back (a case or claim) to the court or tribunal from which it came for some further action in keeping with the appeals court's decision.

**Resolution 687 (UN)** United Nations Security Council Resolution 687 was adopted at the 2981st meeting on April 3, 1991, to welcome the restoration of the independence of Kuwait. It was passed by twelve votes to one (Cuba) with two abstentions (Ecuador and Yemen).

**Restatement** One of several influential treatises, published by the American Law Institute, describing the law in a given area and guiding its development. Although the Restatements are frequently cited in cases and commentary, they are not binding on the courts.

**Rio Treaty** The parties to the Inter-American Treaty of Reciprocal Assistance agree that an armed attack on any American State is considered to be an armed attack against all American States, and the parties will assist in meeting the attack according to the right to individual or collective self-defense. In the event of a threat to the integrity of the territory or sovereignty or political independence of an American State, or

in the event of a threat that endangers the peace of America, the organ
of consultation will meet to agree on measures to be taken.

**Rule of Law** The supremacy of regular as opposed to arbitrary power.

**Sandinista Government in Nicaragua** The *Frente Sandinista de Libera-
ción Nacional* (Sandinista National Liberation Front), usually referred
to as simply the Sandinistas or FSLN, is a leftist political movement in
Nicaragua.

For many decades it was the main rebel group against successive governments of the Somoza family. After emerging victorious from a brief civil
war it formed the government of Nicaragua from 1979 until 1990, facing heavy opposition from the United States and allied countries. It lost
the February 25, 1990 elections and peacefully surrendered power. The
FSLN remains the country's leading political opposition to the current
governing Liberal Constitutionalist Party (PLC).

**Security Council** The United Nations Security Council is the most powerful organ of the United Nations. It is charged with maintaining peace
and security between nations. Whereas other organs of the UN only
make recommendations to member governments, the Security Council
has the power to make decisions that member governments must carry
out under the United Nations Charter. The decisions of the Council are
known as UN Security Council Resolutions. The Council has five so-
called permanent members. They were originally the five victorious powers of World War II:

- Republic of China
- France
- Soviet Union
- United Kingdom
- United States

The Republic of China was, in effect, expelled in 1971 and replaced with the People's Republic of China. After the USSR broke up and then formally dissolved itself in 1991, the Russian Federation was treated as its successor.

Ten other members are elected by the General Assembly for two-year terms starting on January 1, with five replaced each year. The members are chosen by regional groups and confirmed by the United Nations General Assembly. The African, Latin American, and Western European blocs choose two members each, and the Arab, Asian, and Eastern European blocs choose one member each. The final seat alternates between Asian and African selections.

**Seditious libel** Libel made with the intent of inciting sedition (an agreement, communication, or other preliminary activity aimed at inciting treason or some lesser commotion against public authority).

**Semiotics** Theory that the meaning of words and concepts are not static over time but are rather subject to changing meaning based on the understanding of changing interpretive communities.

**Shanghai Communiqué** In 1972, U.S. President Nixon visited China and signed the Shanghai Communiqué, which looked forward to the establishment of normal relations between the United States and the People's Republic of China – and led to the ending of official diplomatic relations with the Republic of China (Taiwan).

**Shiites** Shi'as (the adjective in Arabic is *shi'i*; English has traditionally used *Shiite*) make up the second largest sect of believers in Islam, constituting about 25 to 30 percent of all Muslims. (The largest sect, the Sunni Muslims, make up about 70 percent of all Muslims.)

Shi'a Muslims live in all parts of the world, but some countries have a higher concentration of Shi'a. Iran is almost entirely Shi'a, and of the

95 percent Muslim population of Iraq, about 70 percent are Shiʻa. Large Shiʻa populations are also found in Pakistan (25%), the Eastern Province of Saudi Arabia (19%), Bahrain (almost 80%), and Oman, with smaller groups in other parts of the Persian Gulf.

**Siberian pipeline sanctions** Following several Cold War-era developments including the earlier Soviet invasion of Afghanistan and the declaration of martial law in Poland, on July 2, 1982, the United States banned participation in the Siberian pipeline project by European subsidiaries of U.S. companies.

On November 7, 1982, the Reagan Administration withdrew the measures to avert adverse rulings in multiple pending legal cases in both U.S. and overseas courts and to ease tensions with our major trading partners.

**Standing** A party's right to make a legal claim or seek judicial enforcement of a duty or right. To have standing, a plaintiff must show (1) that the challenged conduct has caused the plaintiff actual injury, and (2) that the interest sought to be protected is within the zone of interests meant to be regulated by the court in question.

**Strategic Defense Initiative** The Strategic Defense Initiative (SDI) is a system proposed by U.S. President Ronald Reagan on March 23, 1983 to use space-based systems to protect the United States from attack by strategic nuclear missiles. It was first dubbed "Star Wars" by opponent Dr. Carol Rosin, a former spokesperson of Wernher von Braun who was instrumental in the development of ballistic missiles. Some critics used that term implying it is an impractical science fiction fantasy, but supporters have adopted the usage as well on the grounds that yesterday's science fiction is often tomorrow's engineering.

**Supremacy Clause** Article VI, section 1, clause 2 of the U.S. Constitution, which states that "This Constitution, and the Laws of the United

States which shall be made in Pursuance thereof; and all Treaties made, or which shall be made, under the Authority of the United States, shall be the supreme Law of the Land; and the Judges in every State shall be bound thereby, any Thing in the Constitution or Laws of any State to the Contrary notwithstanding.

**Taiwan** An island off the coast of China, where the Government of the Republic of China relocated after it ent was overthrown by the Communist Chinese in 1949.

**Taiwan Relations Act** The Taiwan Relations Act is an act of the U.S. Congress passed in 1979 after the establishment of relations with the People's Republic of China and the (pro forma) breaking of relations between the United States and the Republic of China on Taiwan by President Jimmy Carter.

The act authorizes quasidiplomatic relations with the ROC Government by establishing the American Institute in Taiwan and upholds all international obligations previously made between the ROC and United States prior to 1979.

The act stipulates that the United States will "consider any effort to determine the future of Taiwan by other than peaceful means, including by boycotts or embargoes, a threat to the peace and security of the Western Pacific area and of grave concern to the United States."

**Torture Convention** The United States ratified the 1984 Convention Against Torture and Other Cruel, Inhuman, or Degrading Treatment or Punishment in 1994. The Convention makes it an international crime to intentionally inflict "severe pain or suffering, whether physical or mental" for such purposes as obtaining information or a confession.

**Torture Memoranda** A series of memoranda authored by the Office of Legal Counsel (OLC), which opined that extraordinary rendition and water boarding (as well as other controversial interrogation techniques) were not a violation of international or domestic law.

**UN Landmines Protocol** Prior to Ottawa, the only international treaty that applied to landmines was the Convention on Prohibition or Restrictions on the Use of Certain Conventional Weapons (CCW), which had a section (protocol) on landmines. The Convention only applies to States, which have "ratified" its provisions. Since its adoption in 1980, only forty-nine countries have ratified the treaty, whereas a further sixteen have signed but not yet ratified the Convention.

The main provisions of the landmine protocol within the CCW include the directives that mines may only be used against military objectives; that records must be kept of the location of preplanned minefields; and that at the end of hostilities, the parties are to try to agree either among themselves or with other States or organizations to clear the minefields.

**United Nations Charter** The United Nations Charter is the constitution of the United Nations. It was signed at San Francisco on June 26, 1945, by the fifty original member countries. It entered into force on October 24, 1945, after being ratified by the five founding members – the Republic of China, France, the Soviet Union, the United Kingdom, and the United States – and a majority of the other signatories.

As a treaty, all signatories are bound by international law to obey the provisions of the Charter. Furthermore, it explicitly says that the Charter trumps all other treaty obligations. It was ratified by the United States on August 8, 1945, making that nation the first to join the new international organization.

**USS *Vincennes*** On July 3, 1988, the USS *Vincennes* shot down Iran Air Flight 655, a commercial airliner, killing all 290 passengers and crew members. After eight years of negotiations, the United States paid Iran $61.8 million in victim compensation.

**Vienna Convention on Consular Relations** See **Conventions on Diplomatic and Consular Relations**.

**War Powers Resolution** The War Powers Resolution (Public Law 93–148) limits the power of the President of the United States to wage war without the approval of the Congress. The Resolution is sometimes referred to as the War Powers Act, but that is an older law intended to define limits on trade with enemies during wartime.

The Senate and the House of Representatives achieved the two-thirds majority required to pass this joint resolution over President Nixon's veto on November 7, 1973.

Portions of the War Powers Resolution require the President to consult with Congress prior to the start of any hostilities as well as regularly until U.S. armed forces are no longer engaged in hostilities (Sec. 3); and to remove U.S. armed forces from hostilities if Congress has not declared war or passed a resolution authorizing the use of force within sixty days (Sec. 5(b)).

Every President to date has declared the War Powers Resolution to be unconstitutional, and the Supreme Court has struck down the "legislative veto" embodied in Section 5(c) of the Resolution in the case *INS v. Chadha* (1983). However, in every instance since the act was passed, the President has requested and received authorization for the use of force (although not a formal declaration of war) consistent with the provisions of the resolution. The reports to Congress required of the President have been drafted to state that they are "consistent with" the War Powers Resolution rather than "pursuant to" so as to take into account the Presidential position that the Resolution is unconstitutional.

The intended purpose of the act was to serve as a check on the power of the President to commit the United States to military action by exercising the constitutional authority of Congress to declare war under Article One. Many constitutional scholars have questioned the usefulness of the resolution, pointing out that Congress has tended to defer to the Executive when conducting war.

**Water boarding** An interrogation technique that simulates drowning that was authorized by OLC for use against terrorist detainees in 2002.

**West Bank** The West Bank is a territory in the Middle East constituting the area west of the Jordan River annexed by Jordan at the end of the 1948 Arab–Israeli War. The territory formed part of Jordan from 1948 to 1967, after which it was captured by Israel in the 1967 Six-Day War. It is currently controlled partly by Israel and partly by the Palestinian Authority; together with the Gaza Strip, it forms the Palestinian territories at the center of the Israeli–Palestinian conflict.

# Notes

**FOREWORD**

1. Or as former Legal Adviser Davis Robinson suggests in Chapter 16, "The Legal Adviser's office for many years was viewed in the government at large as the moral conscience of American foreign policy."
2. Pub. L. No. 71–715; 46 Stat. 1214 (Feb. 23, 1931). Before that time, legal advice was given to the State Department by the Counselor of the Department (a role that continues today without a defined legal component) and a Justice Department employee known as the Solicitor, a role played before that, dating back to 1848, by the Examiner of Claims, whose job was to handle international claims asserted against the United States.
3. Excellent discussions of the role of the Legal Adviser may be found in Report of The Joint Committee Established by the American Society of International Law and the American Branch of the International Law Association. *The Role of the Legal Adviser of the Department of State*, 85 Am. J. Int'l L. 358–373 (1991); and Richard B. Bilder, *The Office of the Legal Adviser: The State Department Lawyer and Foreign Affairs*, 56 Am. J. Int'l L. 633–684 (1963).
4. *See* Abram Chayes, The Cuban Missile Crisis: International Crises and the Role of Law (1974). The coursebook for that class was Abram Chayes et al., International Legal Process: Materials for an Introductory Course (1968–69). For a discussion of the history and influence of the International Legal Process school in international legal theory, and its relationship to the Transnational Legal Process approach I have supported, *see* Harold Hongju Koh, *Why Do Nations Obey International Law?* 106 Yale L.J. 2599, 2618–2627. For Abe Chayes' oral history recalling his own years as Legal Adviser, *see* Abram Chayes, *Living History Interview*, 7 Transnat'l L. & Contemp. Probs. 459 (1997). www.jfklibrary.org/Historical±Resources/Archives/Summaries/col_chayes_abram.htm.

5. David E. Rosenbaum, *Abram Chayes, John Kennedy Aide, Dies at 77*, N.Y. TIMES, Apr. 18, 2000, at B8.

6. As Mike Matheson explains in Chapter 14, The Legal Adviser "has a duty to give honest legal advice and not to change it based on what the client may expect or desire."

7. As Conrad Harper recalls in Chapter 14, "[W]hen I had to go and advise the Secretary of State, the fact that I was the person who knew the law was not the reason I was there. I was there to offer my best judgment." *See also* the comment of Abe Sofaer in Chapter 14, "[O]f course it is important for the Legal Adviser to tell the clients – and I'm sure every one of us has done it–'Don't do this; this is NOT a good idea.' And in fact, when they don't ask us it's almost always a disaster."

8. Remarks of President Barack Obama – As Prepared for Delivery; Address to Joint Session of Congress; Tuesday, February 24, 2009, available at www. whitehouse.gov/the_press_office/remarks-of-president-barack-obama-address-to-joint-session-of-congress/ (February 24, 2009).

9. Transcript of Hillary Clinton's Confirmation Hearing as Secretary of State, www.cfr.org/publication/18225/transcript_of_hillary_clintons_confirmation_hearing.html (January 13, 2009).

10. For a fuller explication of this form of this "new sovereignty," *see* ABRAM CHAYES & ANTONIA HANDLER CHAYES, THE NEW SOVEREIGNTY: COMPLIANCE WITH INTERNATIONAL REGULATORY AGREEMENTS(1995) (reviewed in Koh, *Why Do Nations Obey? supra* note 4).

11. *See generally*, Harold Hongju Koh, *The 1998 Frankel Lecture: Bringing International Law Home*, 35 HOUS. L. REV. 623 (1998); Harold Hongju Koh, *Transnational Legal Process*, 75 NEB. L. REV. 181 (1996).

12. Abram Chayes, *A Common Lawyer Looks at International Law*, 78 HARV. L. REV. 1396, 1413 (1965).

13. With respect to the Cuban Missile Crisis, for example, Abe Chayes later recalled:

> It was very important for both the validity of the [American political] decision, the subsequent justification, and the mobilization of support that the legal considerations were taken fully into account during the decision-making process. Somebody did not just make the decision and then call the lawyer in and ask the lawyer to cook up some sort of legal theory to defend it.

*See* Abram Chayes, *Living History Interview*, *supra* note 4, at 480. Contrast this with Davis Robinson's recollection in his chapter about the mining of the harbors of Nicaragua during the Reagan Administration, which was undertaken by the CIA without the opinion of the Legal Adviser's Office. He recalled:

I would argue strongly that if L had been involved in the take-off in the case of the mining of the harbors of Managua, we could have provided constructive legal advice.... The input of L would, I believe, have added a significant dimension to the decision-making process and also improved the implementation of the President's ultimate decision. However, as it transpired, instead of being ready for the fire storm that followed the public disclosure of the mining of the harbors, the Administration was legally caught off guard. Thus, all that the lawyers could contribute was assistance in after-the-fact containment of a train wreck.

See Chapter 6.

14. *See generally*, Antonio Cassese, *The Role of Legal Advisers in Ensuring that Foreign Policy Conforms to International Legal Standards*, 14 Mich. J. Int'l L. 139 (1992). Mike Matheson succinctly summarizes the basic role of the Legal Adviser in Chapter 14: "he gives legal advise before decisions are made; he gives the best possible legal defense for the decision once it has been made; he contributes to solving practical problems with his lawyering skills; and he needs to be able to use the personnel available to accomplish these objectives."

## INTRODUCTION

1. John Chipman Gray, The Nature and Sources of the Law 127 (1927).
2. Oona A. Hathaway & Ariel N. Levinbuk, *Rationalism and Revisionism in International Law*, 119 Harv. L. Rev. 1404, 1441 (2006).
3. For earlier efforts to explore the role of L and Legal Advisers, *see* Richard B. Bilder, *The Office of the Legal Adviser: The State Department Lawyer and Foreign Affairs*, 56 Am. J. Int'l L. 633 (1962); Joint Committee of the American Society of International Law & American Branch of the International Law Society, *The Role of the Legal Adviser of the Department of State*, 85 Am. J. Int'l L. 358; Antonio Cassese, *The Role of the Legal Advisers in Ensuring that Foreign Policy Conforms to International Legal Standards*, 14 Mich. J. Int'l L. 139 (1992); and John Warner, Law and the Lawyer in the State Department's Administration of Foreign Policy, 54 (1971).

## 1. THE COMPLIANCE DEBATE

1. Michael P. Scharf, *Earned Sovereignty: Juridical Underpinnings*, 31 Denver J. Int'l L. 373, 373 n.20. The Peace of Westphalia was composed of two separate agreements: (1) the Treaty of Osnabruck concluded between the Protestant Queen of Sweden and her allies on the one side, and the Holy Roman Habsburg Emperor and the German Princes on the other; and (2) the Treaty

of Munster concluded between the Catholic King of France and his allies on the
one side, and the Holy Roman Habsburg Emperor and the German Princes on
the other. The Conventional view of the Peace of Westphalia is that by recognizing the German Princes as sovereign, these treaties signaled the beginning of a new era. But in fact, the power to conclude alliances formally recognized at Westphalia was not unqualified, and was in fact a power that the
German Princes had already possessed for almost half a century. Furthermore,
although the treaties eroded some of the authority of the Habsburg Emperor,
the Empire remained a key actor according to the terms of the treaties. For
example, the Imperial Diet retained the powers of legislation, warfare, and tax-
ation, and it was through Imperial bodies, such as the Diet and the Courts,
that religious safeguards mandated by the Treaty were imposed on the German
Princes.

2. Harold Hongju Koh, *Why Do Nations Obey International Law?* **106** YALE L.J.
   2599 (1997).

3. JOHN AUSTIN, THE PROVINCE OF JURISPRUDENCE DETERMINED, 127, 201 (Weiden-
   feld & Nicolson 1954) (1832).

4. ARTHUR NUSSBAUM, A CONCISE HISTORY OF THE LAW OF NATIONS, 58–59, 112–125
   (1947) (discussing the contributions of Hobbes and other early positivists).

5. Immanuel Kant, *To Perpetual Peace: A Philosophical Sketch* (1795), in PERPET-
   UAL PEACE AND OTHER ESSAYS, 107 (Ted Humphrey, trans., 1983).

6. 2 JEREMY BENTHAM, THE WORKS OF JEREMY BENTHAM, 538, 540, 552–554 (John
   Bowring ed., Edinburgh & London, W. Tait 1843).

7. Harold Hongju Koh, *Why Do Nations Obey International Law?* **106** YALE L.J.
   2615 (1997).

8. Philippe Sands, Lawless World: International Law After 9/11 and Iraq, The
   Mishcon Lecture 2005, available at www.warmwell.com/philipsandsmischon05.
   html.

9. MARTTI KOSKENNIEMI, THE GENTLE CIVILIZER OF NATIONS: THE RISE AND FALL
   OF INTERNATIONAL LAW 1870–1960, 471 (2001).

10. GEORGE F. KENNAN, AMERICAN DIPLOMACY 1900–1950, 96 (1984).

11. Professor Koh distinguishes between the Harvard and Yale methods, observing
    that the Harvard approach focused on process as a policy constraint, whereas the
    New Haven approach was more value-oriented, focusing on process as policy
    justification. Koh, *supra*, at 2623.

12. ABRAM CHAYES, THE CUBAN MISSILE CRISIS: INTERNATIONAL CRISIS AND THE ROLE
    OF LAW, 7 (1974); *see generally*, ABRAM CHAYES ET AL., INTERNATIONAL LEGAL
    PROCESS (2 vols., 1968).

13. HENRY STEINER & DETLEV VAGTS, TRANSNATIONAL LEGAL PROBLEMS (1968) (now
    HENRY STEINER, DETLEV VAGTS, & HAROLD HONGJU KOH, TRANSNATIONAL LEGAL
    PROBLEMS (4th ed. 1994).

14. *See* INTERNATIONAL REGIMES (Stephen D. Krasner, ed., 1983); ROBERT O. KEO-HANE JR., INTERNATIONAL INSTITUTIONS AND STATE POWER: ESSAYS IN INTERNATIONAL RELATIONS THEORY (1989).

15. THOMAS M. FRANCK, THE POWER OF LEGITIMACY AMONG NATIONS (1990).

16. JOHN F. MURPHY, THE UNITED STATES AND THE RULE OF LAW IN INTERNATIONAL AFFAIRS (Cambridge University Press, 2004).

17. Robert O. Keohane Jr., *International Relations and International Law: Two Optics*, Sherrill Lecture, quoted in Koh, *supra*, at n. 171.

18. Duncan Snidal, *Coordination versus Prisoners' Dilemma: Implications for International Cooperation and Regimes*, **79** AM. POL. SCI. REV. 923 (1985).

19. Kenneth W. Abbott, *Modern International Relations Theory: A Prospectus for International Lawyers*, **14** YALE J. INT'L L. 335 (1989).

20. John Setear, *An Iterative Perspective on Treaties: A Synthesis of International Relations Theory and International Law*, **37** HARV. INT'L L.J. 139 (1996).

21. Anne-Marie Slaughter, *International Law in a World of Liberal States*, **6** EUR. J. INT'L L. 503 (1995).

22. THE CULTURE OF NATIONAL SECURITY: NORMS AND IDENTITY IN WORLD POLITICS (Peter J. Katzenstein ed., 1995); INTERNATIONAL RULES: APPROACHES FROM INTERNATIONAL LAW AND INTERNATIONAL RELATIONS 4–8 (Robert J. Beck et al. eds., 1996); FRIEDRICH V. KRATOCHWIL, RULES, NORMS, AND DECISIONS: ON THE CONDITIONS OF PRACTICAL AND LEGAL REASONING IN INTERNATIONAL RELATIONS AND DOMESTIC AFFAIRS (1989).

23. ABRAM CHAYES & ANTONIA HANDLER CHAYES, THE NEW SOVEREIGNTY: COMPLIANCE WITH INTERNATIONAL REGULATORY AGREEMENTS, 32–33 (1995).

24. Harold Hongju Koh, *Why Do Nations Obey International Law?* **106** YALE L.J. 2599, 2641 (1997).

25. Harold Hongju Koh, *Why Do Nations Obey International Law?* **106** YALE L.J. 2599, 2655 (1997).

26. Quoted in Samantha Power, *Boltonism*, THE NEW YORKER, March 21, 2005.

27. U.S. Department of Defense, *The National Defense Strategy of the United States of America 6* (2005), available at: www.defenselink.mil/news/Apr2005/d20050408strategy.pdf.

28. Pub. L. No. 109–366, 120 Stat. 2600 (Oct. 17, 2006).

29. George Washington University Law Professor Edward Swaine writes that U.S. elites may seize on Goldsmith/Posner's book to justify noncompliance with international law and may have done so already. Edward Swaine, *Restoring and (Risking) Interest in International Law*, **100** AM. J. INT'L L. 259 (2006). University of Maryland Law Professor David Gray has opined that Goldsmith/Posner's views "are sure to become standard currency in international law theory and practice." David Gray, *Rule-Skepticism, Strategy, and the Limits of International Law*, **46** VA. J. INT'L L. 563, 583 (2006).

30. JACK L. GOLDSMITH & ERIC A. POSNER, THE LIMITS OF INTERNATIONAL LAW (Oxford University Press, 2005).

31. JACK GOLDSMITH, THE TERROR PRESIDENCY: LAW AND JUDGMENT INSIDE THE BUSH ADMINISTRATION 21 (2007).

32. Eric Posner, *Do States Have a Moral Obligation to Obey International Law?* **55** STANFORD L. REV. 1901, 1918 (2003).

33. JACK L. GOLDSMITH & ERIC A. POSNER, THE LIMITS OF INTERNATIONAL LAW 43 (Oxford University Press, 2005).

34. Id., at 225.

35. *See also,* Alexander Thompson, *Applying Rational Choice Theory to International Law: The Promise and Pitfalls,* J. LEG. STUDIES, **31** (2002); Robert Keohane, *Rational Choice and International Law,* J. LEG. STUDIES, **31** (2002).

36. Goldsmith and Posner are particularly concerned about international law's propensity to shift decisional authority from local government and the federal executive to international institutions and activist federal judges.

37. JACK GOLDSMITH, THE TERROR PRESIDENCY: LAW AND JUDGMENT INSIDE THE BUSH ADMINISTRATION 69 (2007).

38. JACK GOLDSMITH, THE TERROR PRESIDENCY: LAW AND JUDGMENT INSIDE THE BUSH ADMINISTRATION 60 (2007).

39. JACK GOLDSMITH, THE TERROR PRESIDENCY: LAW AND JUDGMENT INSIDE THE BUSH ADMINISTRATION 80–81 (2007).

40. Professor Allen Buchanan of Duke University has argued that Goldsmith and Posner's "normative claims, if valid, would lend support to the view that it is wholly permissible for the U.S. Government to take a purely instrumental stance toward international law, and that its citizens do not have a moral obligation to try to prevent their government from doing so. Allen Buchanan, *Democracy and the Commitment to International Law,* **34** GA. J. INT'L & COMP. L. 306, 307 (2006). Similarly, Professor Oona Hathaway of Yale Law School has argued that there is a necessary connection between Goldsmith and Posner's underlying "revisionist" political agenda and their book's methodological approach and conclusions. Oona A. Hathaway & Ariel N. Levinbuk, *Rationalism and Revisionism in International Law,* **119** HARV. L. REV. 1404 (2006). And as Professor Margaret McGuinness of University of Missouri-Columbia observes: "The book cannot be viewed as separate from the authors' broader normative project – a project that seeks to minimize U.S. participation in international institutions and to limit the application of international law in the United States by expanding presidential power and limiting the role of the judiciary." Margaret E. McGuinness, *Exploring the Limits of International Human Rights Law,* **34** GA. J. INT'L & COMP. L. 393, 421 (2006).

41. *See* Peter Berkowitz, *Laws of Nation,* POLICY REVIEW (reviewing JACK GOLDSMITH & ERIC POSNER, THE LIMITS OF INTERNATIONAL LAW (2005)).

42. Goldsmith & Posner, at 195.
43. Peter J. Spiro, *A Negative Proof of International Law*, **34** Ga. J. Int'l & Comp. L. 445, 453 n.16 (2006) (citing Department of Justice statistics related to the clearance rate for homicide cases from 1976–2005).
44. Peter J. Spiro, *A Negative Proof of International Law*, **34** Ga. J. Int'l & Comp. L.445, 451 (2006).
45. Kenneth Anderson, *Remarks by an Idealist on the Realism of the Limits of International Law*, **34** Ga. J. Int'l & Comp. L. 253, 280–281 (2006).
46. Peter J. Spiro, *A Negative Proof of International Law*, **34** Ga. J. Int'l & Comp. L. 445, 454–462 (2006).
47. Professor Daniel Bodansky of the University of Georgia, and a former Attorney-Adviser in L argues that by defining reputation as one of a State's instrumentalist interests rather than considering it part of the compliance pull of international law, Goldsmith and Posner have rendered their theory non-falsifiable and lacking in predictive value. According to Bodansky, under Goldsmith and Posner's approach, "international law cannot be an exogenous influence on state behavior for the simple reason that it has already been made endogenous." Daniel Bodansky, *International Law in Black and White*, **34** Ga. J. Int'l & Comp. L. 285, 295 (2006).
48. Professor David M. Golove of New York University differs with the supposition that reputation is of little concern for a State, as this supposition arises out of Goldsmith and Posner's single-issue game approach using the prisoner's dilemma model. According to Professor Golove, the metaphorical games that States actually play are vastly more complex. "They repeatedly and intensively interact across a wide range of subject areas, and they do so indefinitely into the future." Viewing international interaction instead as a "super game" requires that significantly more value be placed on reputation than Goldsmith and Posner are willing to acknowledge. States obtain a benefit if they are perceived as reliable partners not just with the particular State on the particular issue in question in a given interaction, but also with third States on a range of issues long into the future. According to Golove, once a norm is named a customary international law rule or is codified in a treaty to which a State is a party, violation of that norm will have far more serious reputational costs. David M. Golove, *Leaving Customary International Law Where It Is: Goldsmith and Posner's The Limits of International Law* **34** Ga. J. Int'l & Comp. L. 333, 345 (2006). *See also* Paul Schiff Berman, *Seeing Beyond the Limits of International Law*, **84** Texas L. Rev. 1265, 1294 (2006). Goldsmith and Posner's response is to argue that State reputations are compartmentalized. For example, they assert that a State might have a good record complying with trade treaties and a bad record complying with environmental treaties, and that the State's trading partners will not hold its environmental shortcomings against it. *See* Goldsmith and Posner, at 102.

If this were true, answers Professor Golove, it would only mean that preserving the State's reputation as a law abiding State would be more significant with respect to that State's trade relations than in the environmental area; it would not mean that reputation is irrelevant. Nor does their self-evident assertion that "a reputation for compliance will not always be of paramount concern" mean that reputation should automatically be dismissed as inconsequential. If compliance reputation makes a difference in the margins, putting a thumb on the scale in favor of compliance, than it is neither irrelevant nor inconsequential. David M. Golove, *Leaving Customary International Law Where It Is: Goldsmith and Posner's The Limits of International Law*, **34** GA. J. INT'L & COMP. L. 333, 345 (2006).

49. Professor Andrew T. Guzman of California Berkeley's Boalt Hall School of Law argues Goldsmith and Posner's aim is to refute the constructivist theory of compliance, through the selective use of a handful of case studies, which are no more than anecdotal in nature, and their identification of the controlling State interests in each is almost entirely conjectural. According to Guzman, they offer no explanation for how they chose the particular historical events that they employ, nor do they cite to other scholars of history or political science who concur with their appraisals of those events. He argues that in fact "at least some of those case studies are consistent with competing claims." Andrew T. Guzman, *The Promise of International Law*, **92** VA. L. REV. 533, 540 (2006) (arguing that Goldsmith and Posner misrepresent the facts in their international trade case study); *see also* David Golove, *Leaving Customary International Law Where It Is: Goldsmith and Posner's The Limits of International Law*, **34** GA. J. INT'L & COMP. L. 333 (2006) (arguing that Goldsmith and Posner's account is "cherry-picked and fails to present a fair picture of the "Free Ships, Free Goods" example).

50. Oona A. Hathaway & Ariel N. Levinbuk, *Rationalism and Revisionism in International Law*, **119** HARV. L. REV. 1404 (2006).

51. David Golove, *Leaving Customary International Law Where It Is: Goldsmith and Posner's The Limits of International Law*, **34** GA. J. INT'L & COMP. L. 333 (2006).

## 2. A BRIEF HISTORY OF L

1. Richard B. Bilder, *The Office of the Legal Adviser: The State Department Lawyer and Foreign Affairs*, **57** AM. J. INT'L L. 633, 634 (1963).

2. The individuals who have served as State Department Legal Adviser are Green Hackworth, Charles Fahy, Ernest Gross, Adrian Fisher, Herman Phleger, Loftus Becker, Eric Hager, Abram Chayes, Monroe Leigh, Herb Hansell, Bob Owen, Davis Robinson, Abe Sofaer, Edwin Williamson, Conrad Harper, David Andrews, William Taft IV, John Bellinger III, and Harold Hongju Koh. We have included Michael Matheson in our dialogues, a long-serving Principal

Deputy Legal Adviser who served as Acting Legal Adviser on several occasions during transitions between Administrations.

3. *See* Abram Chayes, *Living History Interview*, 7 TRANSNAT'L L. & CONTEMP. PROBS. 459 (1997).

4. *See* Abram Chayes, *Living History Interview*, 7 TRANSNAT'L L. & CONTEMP. PROBS. 459 (1997).

5. RICHARD B. LILLICH, *Preface to* THE IRAN-UNITED STATES CLAIMS TRIBUNAL, 1981–1983 (1984).

6. JOHN WARNER OUTLAND, LAW AND THE LAWYER IN THE STATE DEPARTMENT'S ADMINISTRATION OF FOREIGN POLICY 54 (1971).

## 3. THE PATH TO L

1. For Abe Chayes' account of his time as Legal Adviser under President John F. Kennedy, *see* Abram Chayes, *Living History Interview*, 7 TRANSNAT'L L. & CONTEMP. PROBS. 459 (1997).

## 4. THE CARTER ADMINISTRATION – HERBERT J. HANSELL (1977–1979)

1. *Joint Communique on the Establishment of Diplomatic Relations Between the United States of America and the People's Republic of China, January 1, 1979*, DEPT. S. BULL., Jan. 1979, at 25, *reprinted in* **18** ILM 274 (1979).

2. *See U.S.-Taiwan-China Relations*, **93** AM. J. INT'L L. 894 (Sean D. Murphy, ed., 1999).

3. *Goldwater v. Carter*, 481 F.Supp. 949 (D.D.C. 1979).

4. *Goldwater v. Carter*, 617 F.2d 697 (D.D.Cir. 1979).

5. *Goldwater v. Carter*, 444 U.S. 996 (1979).

6. Exec. Order No. 12143, 44 Fed. Reg. 37191 (June 22, 1979).

7. Taiwan Relations Act, 22 U.S.C. § 3301 (1979).

8. Egyptian-Israeli Peace Treaty, Egypt-Isr., March 26, 1979. 32 U.S.T. 2146.

9. *See* EGYPT, MERKAZ HAYIM HERTSOG LE-HEKER HA-MIZRAH HA-TIKHON YEHA-DIPLOMATYAH, THE CAMP DAVID ACCORDS AND RELATED DOCUMENTS (Chaim Herzog Center for Middle East Studies & Diplomacy 1998).

10. S.C. Res. 242, U.N. Doc. S/RES/242 (Nov. 22, 1967).

11. *See* EPHRAIM DOWEK, ISRAELI-EGYPTIAN RELATIONS 1980–2000, 110–125 (Routledge 2001).

12. For additional information on the U.S. role in Panama, *see generally*, Anthony D'Amato, Tom J. Farer, & Ved P. Nanda, *Agora: U.S. Forces in Panama: Defenders, Aggressors or Human Rights Activists?* **84** AM. J. INT'L L. 494 (1990).

13. *See* J. MICHAEL HOGAN, THE PANAMA CANAL IN AMERICAN POLITICS: DOMESTIC ADVOCACY AND THE EVOLUTION OF POLICY (Southern Illinois University Press 1986).

14. Panama Canal Treaty, U.S.-Pan., Sept. 7, 1997, 33 U.S.T. 39.

15. The Treaty Concerning the Permanent Neutrality and Operation of the Panama Canal, U.S.-Pan., Sept. 7, 1977, 33 U.S.T. 1.

16. *See* David Skidmore, *Foreign Policy Interest Groups and Presidential Power: Jimmy Carter and the Battle over Ratification of the Panama Canal Treaties, in* JIMMY CARTER: FOREIGN POLICY AND POST-PRESIDENTIAL YEARS 297–328 (Herbert D. Rosenbaum and Alexej Ugrinsky eds., Greenwood Press 1994).

17. *Goldwater v. Carter, supra.*

18. *Edwards v. Carter*, 580 F.2d 1055 (D.C.Cir. 1978). *cert. denied*, 436 U.S. 907 (1978).

19. *Goldwater v. Carter, supra.*

20. *See* Guy M. Miller, Note, *Treaty Termination under the United States Constitution: Reassessing the Legacy of* Goldwater v. Carter, **27** N.Y.U. J. INT'L L. & POL. 859 (1995).

21. *Joint Communique on the Establishment of Diplomatic Relations between the United States of America and the People's Republic of China, supra* note 1.

22. 22 U.S.C. § 3301, *supra.*

23. *Id.*

24. Vienna Convention on the Law of Treaties, May 23, 1969, 155 U.N.T.S. 331.

25. *Joint Communique on the Establishment of Diplomatic Relations between the United States of America and the People's Republic of China, supra* note.

26. 22 U.S.C. § 3301, *supra.*

27. Egyptian-Israeli Peace Treaty.

## 5. THE CARTER ADMINISTRATION – ROBERTS B. OWEN (1979–1981)

1. A relatively complete history of the whole crisis appears in a volume compiled by the Council on Foreign Relations, AMERICAN HOSTAGES IN IRAN (Yale University Press 1985).

2. Vienna Conventions on Diplomatic and Consular Relations art. 40, Apr. 24, 1963, 21 U.S.T. 77, 596 U.N.T.S. 261.

3. Nicholas Cumming-Bruce, *Americans Still Captive in Tehran Embassy: British Mission Held 5 Hours by Students*, WASHINGTON POST, Nov. 6, 1979, at A1.

4. Case Concerning United States Diplomatic and Consular Staff in Tehran (*U.S. v. Iran*) Request for the Indication of Provisional Measures 1979 I.C.J. 7 (Dec. 15).

5. Warren Christopher, *Introduction, in* AMERICAN HOSTAGES IN IRAN 26–27 (Paul Kreisberg ed., Yale University Press 1985). It must be noted that, when the rescue operation was debated at the White House, Secretary Vance opposed the mission on the basic ground that the hostages were not in sufficient danger to justify the use of military force. He was the lone dissenter and was overruled by

the President, at which point, much to the distress of his colleagues and the President, Vance resigned. Thus the degree of danger then faced by our hostages was a matter of some debate, but it was clearly the President's prerogative to decide the issue as he did. *See* Gary Sick, *Military Options*, in AMERICAN HOSTAGES IN IRAN, at 281–282.

6. Gary Sick, *in* AMERICAN HOSTAGES IN IRAN, at 154–166.

7. Case Concerning United States Diplomatic and Consular Staff in Tehran (*U.S. v. Iran*), 1980 I.C.J. 3, 43 (May 24) ("The Court therefore feels bound to observe that an operation undertaken in those circumstances, from whatever motive, is of a kind calculated to undermine respect for the judicial process in international relations; and to recall that in paragraph 47, 1B, of its Order of December 15, 1979 the Court had indicated that no action was to be taken by either party which might aggravate the tension between the two countries.")

8. Case Concerning United States Diplomatic and Consular Staff In Tehran (*U.S. v. Iran*), 1979 I.C.J. 3, 19 § 1 (b) (Dec 15) ("pursuant to the foregoing international legal obligations, the Government of Iran is under a particular legal obligation immediately to secure the release of all United States nationals currently being detained within the premises of the United States Embassy in Tehran.")

9. Oscar Schachter *in* AMERICAN HOSTAGES IN IRAN, at 339–345.

10. Commonly known as the "Algiers Accords." Declaration of the Government of the Democratic and Popular Republic of Algeria (19 Jan. 1981), reprinted in 1 IRAN-U.S. CL. TRIB. REP. 3–8; Declaration of the Government of the Democratic and Popular Republic of Algeria Concerning the Settlement of Claims By the Government of the United States of America and the Government of the Islamic Republic of Iran (19 Jan. 1981), reprinted in 1 IRAN-U.S. CL. TRIB. REP. 9–12.

11. The International Court of Justice found that the United States violated international law by supporting Contra guerrillas in their war against the Nicaraguan government and by mining Nicaragua's harbors. Military and Paramilitary Activities in and against Nicaragua (*Nicaragua v. U.S.*) Merits 1986 I.C.J. 392 (June 27).

## 6. THE REAGAN ADMINISTRATION – DAVIS R. ROBINSON (1981–1985)

1. *See generally*, U.S. Department of State, Iran–United States Claims Tribunal, http://www.state.gov/s/l/3199.htm (last visited April 2, 2009).

2. For additional information on Davis Robinson's views concerning adjudicating the Gulf of Maine Case, *see* David A. Colson, Bruce C. Rashkow, & Davis Rowland Robinson, *Some Perspective on Adjudicating Before the World Court: The Gulf of Maine Case*, **79** AM. J. INT'L L. 578 (1985).

3. *See generally*, U.S. Department of State, Office of the Legal Adviser, www.state.gov/s/l/ (last visited April 2, 2009) (official Web site).

4. PARRY AND GRANT ENCYCLOPAEDIC DICTIONARY OF INTERNATIONAL LAW 109 (John P. Grant & J. Craig Barker eds., Oceana Publications 2003) (1986) (customary international law has two elements: "a concordant practice of a number of states acquiesced in by others; and a conception that the practice is required by or consistent with the prevailing law [*opinio juris*]").

5. *See generally*, Saikrishna Prakash, *International Law and the State of the Constitution: The Twenty-Fifth Annual National Student Federalist Society Symposium on Law and Public Policy – 2006: The Constitutional Status of Customary International Law*, **30** HARV. J.L. & PUB. POL'Y 65 (2006).

6. For additional information on the debate surrounding the duties of the President to uphold customary international law, *see generally*, Jonathan I. Charney, Anthony D'Amato, Michael J. Glennon, Louis Henkin, Frederic L. Kirgis Jr., & Jordan J. Paust, *Agora: May the President Violate Customary International Law?* **81** AM. J. INT'L L. 371 (1987).

7. Intelligence Oversight Act, H.R. 5954, 109th Cong. (2d Sess. 2006).

8. For additional information on the role of law in Grenada, *see* Abram Chayes et al., *International Lawlessness in Grenada*, **78** AM. J. INT'L L. 172 (1984).

9. *See generally*, Ronald H. Cole, Operation Urgent Fury: The Planning and Execution of Joint Operations in Grenada 12 October – 2 November 1983 (Joint History Office of the Office of the Chairman of the Joint Chiefs of Staff, Washington, DC 1997), available at www.dtic.mil/doctrine/jel/history/urgfury.pdf.

10. UN Charter art. 2, para. 4.

11. UN Charter art. 51.

12. Inter-American Treaty of Reciprocal Assistance Sept. 2, 1947, 62 Stat. 1631, T.I.A.S. No. 1838.

13. O.A.S. Charter, art. 28.

14. UN Charter, art. 2.

15. *See generally*, BOB WOODWARD, VEIL: THE SECRET WARS OF THE CIA, 1981–1987 (Simon & Schuster 2005).

16. *See* CHARLES N. BROWER & JASON D. BRUESCHKE, THE IRAN–UNITED STATES CLAIMS TRIBUNAL (Kluwer Law International 1998).

17. Delimitation of Maritime in Gulf of Maine Area (U.S. / Can.), 1984 I.C.J. 246 (Oct. 12).

18. Military and Paramilitary Activities (*Nicar. v. U.S.*), 1986 I.C.J. 14 (June 27).

19. *See generally*, Fred L. Morrison, *Legal Issues in the Nicaragua Opinion*, **81** AM. J. INT'L L. 160 (1987).

20. Avena and Other Mexican Nationals (*Mex. v. U.S.*), 2004 I.C.J. 12 (Mar. 30).

21. *See generally*, MATTHEW OUIMET, THE RISE AND FALL OF THE BREZHNEV DOCTRINE IN SOVIET FOREIGN POLICY (University of North Carolina Press, Chapel Hill & London 2003).

22. For additional information on Leonid Skotnikov's views on the legal use of force, *see* Leonid Skotnikov, *Legal Limits on the Use of Force*, **11** INTERNATIONAL AFFAIRS (2003).

## 7. THE REAGAN AND BUSH ADMINISTRATIONS – ABRAHAM D. SOFAER (1985–1990)

1. *See* U.S. Department of State, Letter and Statement Concerning Termination of Acceptance of I.C.J. Compulsory Jurisdiction (Oct. 7, 1985), **24** ILM 1742, 1742–1745 (1985).
2. *See* U.S. Department of State, Statement on U.S.–Italy submission of the Raytheon/Machlett dispute to the I.C.J., **24** ILM 1745; Case Concerning Elettronica Sicula S.p.A. (ELSI) (*U.S. v. Italy*), 1989 I.C.J. 15 (July 20).
3. *See* Heathrow Airport User Charges (*U.S. v. U.K.*), **102** ILR 215–582 (Perm. Ct. Arb. 1992–93).
4. *See* Applicability of Article VI, Section 22, of the Convention on the Privileges and Immunities of the United Nations, Advisory Opinion, 1989 I.C.J. 177 (Dec. 15).
5. *See* Abraham D. Sofaer, *Adjudication in the International Court of Justice: Progress through Realism*, **44** REC. ASS'N B. CITY N.Y. 462 (1989). The idea consisted of the five permanent members submitting collectively to the mandatory jurisdiction of the ICJ in a uniform manner by treaty for the adjudication of a list of issues that could be expanded over time. Other States would have been allowed to join this submission. In addition, states that wished to expand the grounds of their submission could do so, and procedures were set in place to enable parties in all cases to utilize panels of fewer than all the judges of the court. Substantial progress was made in negotiating agreement to this treaty, but the effort was abandoned after I left office, due to objections from British Foreign Ministry attorneys.
6. 39 Stat. 1645 (Jan. 22, 1916) "Treaty between the United States and Chile for the Advancement of General Peace." Art. IV.
7. *See* Jeane J. Kirkpatrick & Allan Gerson, *The Reagan Doctrine, Human Rights, and International Law*, *in* RIGHT V. MIGHT: INTERNATIONAL LAW AND THE USE OF FORCE 19–36, (Council on Foreign Relations, 1989).
8. For additional information on Abram Chayes' views concerning the ABM Treaty, *see* Abram Chayes & Antonia Handler Chayes, *Testing and Development of 'Exotic' Systems under the ABM Treaty: The Great Reinterpretation Caper*, **99** HARV. L. REV. 1956 (1986).
9. For additional information on Abraham Sofaer's views concerning the ABM Treaty, *see* Abraham D. Sofaer, *The ABM Treaty and the Strategic Defense Initiative*, **99** HARV. L. REV. 1972 (1986).

10. *See* Paul H. Nitze, From Hiroshima to Glasnost: At the Center of Decision 445–447 (1989).

11. *See* Abraham D. Sofaer, *The ABM Treaty: Legal Analysis in the Political Cauldron*, **10** Washington Q. 59, 61–62, (Autumn 1987).

12. George P. Shultz, Turmoil and Triumph: My Years as Secretary of State 748–750 (1993).

13. Abraham D. Sofaer, *Terrorism and the Law*, **64** Foreign Affairs 901, 905 (Summer 1986).

14. *Harvard Research in International Law*, **29** Am. J. Int'l L. (Supp. 1935).

15. Convention for the Suppression of Unlawful Acts against the Safety of Maritime Navigation, with Related Protocol, Mar. 10, 1988, S. Treaty Doc. No. 101–1 (1989), **27** ILM 668, 669–690 (1988).

16. 22 Weekly Comp. Pres. Doc. 22–23 (Jan. 7, 1986).

17. Libya ultimately accepted responsibility for the LaBelle disco bombing. On October 4, 2004, the Libyan Government paid the first installment of a $35 million settlement to the non-U.S. victims' families.

18. For additional information on Abraham Sofaer's views concerning the Iran-Contra Affair, *see* Abraham D. Sofaer, *Iran-Contra: Ethical Conduct and Public Policy*, **40** Hous. L. Rev. 1081 (2003). For additional information on the Iran-Contra Affair, *see generally, Symposium, Legal and Policy Issues in the Iran-Contra Affair: Intelligence Oversight in a Democracy*, **11** Hous. J. Int'l L. 83 (1988).

19. For additional information on David Andrews' views concerning the Lockerbie Trial, *see* David Andrews, *A Thorn on the Tulip – A Scottish Trial in the Netherlands: The Story behind the Lockerbie Trial*, **36** Case W. Res. J. Int'l L. 307 (2004).

20. *See*, for example, UN Charter art. 2, paras. 4–7; art. 51.

21. "Case Concerning Military and Paramilitary Activities in and against Nicaragua, 1986 I.C.J. 14, para. 24.

22. Abraham D. Sofaer, *International Law and the Use of Force*, **13** Nat'l Interest 53 (1988).

23. Legal Consequences of the Construction of a Wall in the Occupied Palestinian Territory, 2004 I.C.J. 131 (July 9).

24. For additional information on Abraham Sofaer's views on the intervention in Kosovo, *see* Abraham D. Sofaer, *International Law and Kosovo*, **36** Stan. J. Int'l L. 1 (2000).

## 8. THE BUSH (41ST) ADMINISTRATION – EDWIN D. WILLIAMSON (1990–1993)

1. For additional information on the impact of the Gulf War on foreign relations law, *see generally*, David D. Caron, Lori Fisler Damrosch, Thomas M. Franck,

Michael J. Glennon, & Theodor Meron, *Agora: The Gulf Crisis in International and Foreign Relations Law*, **85** Am. J. Int'l L. 63 (1991).

2. For additional information on Abraham Sofaer's views on the War Powers Resolution, *see* Abraham D. Sofaer, *The War Powers Resolution: Fifteen Years Later*, **62** Temp. L. Rev. 317 (1989).

3. G.A. Res. 661, UN Doc. S/RES/661 (Aug. 6, 1990).

4. G.A. Res. 678, UN Doc. S/RES/678 (Nov. 29, 1990).

5. G.A. Res. 83, UN Doc. A/RES/56/83 (Dec. 12, 2001).

6. G.A. Res. 686, UN Doc. S/RES/686 (Mar. 2, 1991).

7. G.A. Res. 687, UN Doc S/RES/687 (Apr. 8, 1991).

8. G.A. Res. 688, UN Res. S/RES/688 (Apr. 5, 1991).

9. G.A. Res. 1441, UN Res. S/RES/687 (Apr. 8, 1991).

10. *Dellums v. Bush*, 59 U.S.L.W. 2401 (1990).

11. Authorization for Use of Military Force against Iraq Resolution of 2002, Pub. L. No. 107–243, 116 Stat. 1498 (2002).

12. For more information on Ed Williamson's views concerning the role of international law in the break up of the USSR and Yugoslavia, *see* Edwin D. Williamson & John E. Osborn, *A U.S. Perspective on Treaty Succession and Related Issues in the Wake of the Breakup of the USSR and Yugoslavia*, **33** Va. J. Int'l L. 261 (1993).

13. Restatement (Third) of Foreign Relations §210 cmt. f (1987).

14. UN Charter, art. 23.

15. For additional information on the UN accession process for the former Yugoslav states, *see generally*, Yehuda Blum Ove E. Bring, Vladimir-Djuro Degan, & M. Kelly Malone, *1993 Correspondents' Agora: UN Membership of the Former Yugoslavia*, **87** Am. J. Int'l L. 248 (1993).

16. *See* Paul Williams and Jennifer Harris, *State Succession to Debts and Assets: The Modern Law and Policy*, Harv. Int'l L.J. (2001); Paul Williams, *Treaty Succession: Conflicting State Practice*, **23** Denver J. Int'l L. & Pol'y 1 (1994); Paul Williams, *State Succession and the International Financial Institutions: Political Criteria or Sound Management?* **43** Int'l & Comp. L.Q. 776 (1994)

17. Case Concerning Question of Interpretation and Application of the 1971 Montreal Convention Arising from the Incident at Lockerbie (*Libyan Arab Jamahiriya v. U.S.*), 1992 I.C.J. 113 (Apr. 14).

18. *Sosa v. Alvarez-Machain*, 542 U.S. 692 (2004).

19. *See*, for example, Jules Lobel & George Loewenstein, *Emote Control: The Substitution of Symbol for Substance in Foreign Policy and International Law*, **80** Chi.-Kent L. Rev. 1045, 1071–1072 (2005).

20. G. A. Res. 748, UN Doc. S/RES/748 (Mar. 31 1992).

21. Lobel, *supra*, at 1071–1072.

22. *U.S. v. Noriega*, 117 F.3d 1206 (11th Cir. 1997).

### 9. THE BUSH (41ST) ADMINISTRATION – MICHAEL J. MATHESON

1. S.C. Res. 687 (1991), 8 April 1991, available at www.fas.org/news/un/iraq/sres/sres0687.htm.
2. For additional information on Monroe Leigh's views concerning the ICTY, *see* Monroe Leigh & Maury Shenk, *International Criminal Tribunals for the Former Yugoslavia and Rwanda*, **32** Int'l L. 509 (1997).
3. Agreement for the Prosecution and Punishment of the Major War Criminals of the European Axis, and Charter of the International Military Tribunal, London, August 8, 1945, available at www.icrc.org/IHL.NSF/FULL/350? OpenDocument; Judgment and Charter of the Military Tribunal for the Far East, available at www.ibiblio.org/hyperwar/PTO/IMTFE/index.html.
4. S.C. Res. 827 (1993), 25 May 1993), available at www.ohr.int/print/?content_id=7117.
5. Protocol II to the Convention on Prohibitions or Restrictions on the Use of Certain Conventional Weapons Which May be Deemed to be Excessively Injurious or to Have Indiscriminate Effects, October 10, 1980, available at www.un.org/millennium/law/xxvi-18-19.htm.
6. Convention on the Prohibition of the Use, Stockpiling, Production and Transfer of Anti-Personnel Mines and on their Destruction, September 18, 1997, available at www.un.org/Depts/mine/UNDocs/ban_trty.htm.

### 10. THE CLINTON ADMINISTRATION – CONRAD K. HARPER (1993–1996)

1. S.C. Res. 827, UN SCOR, 48th Sess., at 29, UN Doc. S/INF/49 (1993), reprinted *in* Virginia Morris and Michael P. SCharf, 2 An Insider's Guide to the International Criminal Tribunal for the Former Yugoslavia (Transnational Publishers, 1995), at 177.
2. For additional information on the prosecuting international crimes, *see generally, Symposium, Prosecuting International Crimes: An Inside View*, **7** Transnat'l L. & Contemp. Probs. 23 (1997).
3. For a discussion of the evolution in the NATO policy on arresting Yugoslav war criminals, *see* Paul R. Williams & Michael P. Scharf, Peace with Justice? War Crimes and Accountability in the Former Yugoslavia (Rowman & Littlefield, 2002), at 216–220.
4. For background information about the Rwanda Tribunal, *see generally*, Virginia Morris & Michael P. Scharf, The International Criminal Tribunal for Rwanda (Transnational Publishers, 1998).
5. *See The Downing of Iran Air Flight 655: Excerpts from Report of ICAO Fact-Finding Investigation Pursuant to Decision of ICAO Council of July 14, 1988*, reprinted in **83** Am. J. Int' l L. 332 (1989).

6. For additional information on the legal implications of the shoot-down, *see generally*, Marian Nash Leich, Andreas F. Lowenfeld, & Harold G. Maier, *Agora: The Downing of Iran Air Flight 655*, **83** Am. J. Int'l L. 318 (1989).

7. *See Official Document: Settlement of the Iran Hostage Crisis: Declaration of the Government of the Democratic and Popular Republic of Algeria*, **75** Am. J. Int'l L. 418 (1981).

8. *See* Marian Nash (Leigh), *Contemporary Practice of the United States Relating to International Law*, **90** Am. J. Int'l L. 278 (1996).

9. *See* The Legality of the Threat or Use of Nuclear Weapons, 1996 I.C.J. 1.

10. In 1993, the World Health Assembly of the World Health Organization petitioned the ICJ for an advisory opinion on the legality of nuclear weapons. *See* The Legality of the Threat or Use of Nuclear Weapons, 1995 I.C.J. 3–4.

11. In 1994, the UN General Assembly, in Resolution 75K, requested that the ICJ render an advisory opinion on the issue, "Is the threat or use of nuclear weapons in any circumstance permitted under international law?" G.A. Res. 75K, UN GAOR, 49th Sess., Supp. No. 49, at 71, UN Doc. A/49/699 (1994).

12. Michael J. Matheson, *The Opinions of the International Court of Justice on the Threat or Use of Nuclear Weapons*, **91** Am. J. Int'l L. 417 (1997).

13. Abraham D. Sofaer, *Iran-Contra: Ethical Conduct and Public Policy*, **40** Hous. L. Rev. 1081 (2003).

14. William Clinton, *Address at Kigali Airport, Rwanda (Mar. 25, 1998)*, reprinted *in* Jared Cohen, One-Hundred Days of Silence: America and the Rwanda Genocide, Appendix F, at 207 (2007).

## 11. THE CLINTON ADMINISTRATION – DAVID R. ANDREWS (1997–2000)

1. S.C. Res. 883, ¶17, UN Doc. S/RES/883 (Nov. 11, 1993).

2. *See*, for example, David Leppard, On The Trail Of Terror: The Inside Story Of The Lockerbie Investigation (1991); David R. Andrews, *A Thorn on the Tulip – A Scottish Trial in the Netherlands: The Story Behind the Lockerbie Trial*, **36** Case W. Res. J. Int'l L. 307, 308 (2004) (investigation included "15,000 interviews conducted in over twenty countries, 35,000 photos, and 180,000 pieces of evidence").

3. Joint United States–United Kingdom Declaration (Nov. 27, 1991): Statement Issued by the British Government, UN Doc. A/46/826–S/23307, Annex III (1991); Statement Issued by the Government of the United States, UN Doc. A/46/827–S/23308, annex (1991).

4. Agreement on Scottish Trial in the Netherlands, U.K.–Neth., Sep. 18, 1998, T.S. No. 43.

5. UN Charter art. 39–51, para.1.

6. 2 International Criminal Law 710–40 (M. Cherif Bassiouni, ed., Transnational Publishers/Brill, 3d ed. 2007).

7. S.C. Res. 883, *supra* note 1, ¶ 17.

8. For additional information on the trial of the Pan Am Flight 103 bombers, *see generally*, *Symposium, Terrorism on Trial: Lockerbie*, **36** CASE W. RES. J. INT'L L. 473 (2004).

9. Sean D. Murphy, *Contemporary Practice of the United States Relating to International Law: Legal Regulation of the Use of Force*, **93** AM. J. INT'L L. 628 (1999).

10. S.C. Res. 1244, ¶ 17, UN Doc. S/RES/1244 (June 10, 1999).

11. Steve Lee Myers, *China Rejects U.S. Actions on Bombing of Embassy*, N.Y. TIMES, April 11, 2000, at A6.

12. For a review of the case for intervention, *see* Paul Williams and Michael Scharf, *Legal Basis for NATO Military Action Taken against Serbia/Montenegro*, **5** INTERNATIONAL PEACEKEEPING (Winter 1999).

13. Julie Mertus, *Reconsidering the Legality of Humanitarian Intervention: Lessons from Kosovo*, **41** WM. & MARY L. REV. 1743 (2000).

14. North Atlantic Treaty art. 5, Apr. 4, 1949, 63 Stat. 2241, 34 U.N.T.S. 243.

## 12. THE BUSH (43RD) ADMINISTRATION -WILLIAM H. TAFT IV (2001–2005)

1. *See*, for example, Oscar Schachter, *The Lawful Use of Force by a State Against Terrorists in Another Country*, *in* TERRORISM & POLITICAL VIOLENCE: LIMITS & POSSIBILITIES OF LEGAL CONTROL 243, 250 (Henry H. Han ed., 1993) (for a discussion on the principle that a regime sufficiently implicated in terrorism, in the protection of terrorist operatives, and unrepentant about the culture of terrorism within its borders may justify an invasion of the primary "terrorist state" by a primary "victim state" of terrorism).

2. *See generally*, S.C. Res. 1368, UN Doc. S/RES/1368 (Sept. 12, 2001) (recognizing the inherent right of individual or collective to self-defense and condemning the terrorist attacks of September 11, 2001); S.C. Res. 1373, ¶ 5, UN Doc. S/RES/1373 (Sept. 28, 2001) (reaffirming "the need to combat by all means, in accordance with the Charter of the United Nations, threats to international peace and security caused by terrorist attacks"); S.C. Res. 1378, UN Doc. S/RES/1378 (Nov. 14, 2001) (condemning the Taliban, reaffirming the sovereignty of Afghanistan, and calling on Afghanistan to establish a new and transitional administration leading to the formation of a government); S.C. Res. 1386, UN Doc. S/RES/1386 (Dec. 20, 2001) (authorizing the establishment of an International Security Assistance Force).

3. *See*, for example, Declaration on the Fight Against Terrorism, NATO Parliamentary Assembly Ottawa Fall Session, ¶ 5–8 (200 http://www.nato-pa. int/Default.asp?SHORTCUT=331 1 ("we stress that Article 51 of the Charter

of the United Nations provides the right of individual or collective self-defence in case of armed attack against a member state ... we endorse our governments' declaration of 12 September that collective defence under Article 5 of the North Atlantic Treaty is an appropriate response to the acts of terrorism of 11 September ... that the attacks of 11 September were directed from abroad by the terrorist network of Al Qaida, headed by Osama bin Laden and his key lieutenants and protected by the Taliban regime").

4. *See* Authorization for Use of Military Force Against Terrorists, Pub. L. No. 107–40, 115 Stat. 294 (2001).

5. For additional information on the legal implications of the war on terror, *see generally*, Symposium, *War on Terror*, 16 Minn. J. Int'l L. 265 (2007).

6. Transcript of President George W. Bush's Address to a Joint Session of Congress and the American People, Sep. 20, 2001, *available at* www.washingtonpost.com/wp-srv/nation/specials/attacked/transcripts/bushaddress_092001.html (last visited April 9, 2009).

7. It is worth noting that in 1999 and 2000 in two separate resolutions, the Security Council demanded that Afghanistan's de facto controlling power, the Taliban regime, turn over Osama bin Laden to a country in which he was under indictment, but the Taliban regime never complied with any of these resolutions. *See* S.C. Res. 1267, UN SCOR, 54th Sess., 4051st mtg., UN Doc. S/RES/1267 (1999); *see also* S.C. Res. 1333, UN SCOR, 55th Sess., 4251st mtg., UN Doc. S/RES/1333 (2000); S.C. Res. 1363. UN SCOR, 56th Sess., 4352nd mtg., UN Doc. S/RES/1363 (2001).

8. *See*, for example, Letter from U.S. Attorney General John Ashcroft to President George W. Bush (Feb. 1, 2002) (explaining that Taliban combatants are not entitled to Geneva Convention protections because (1) Afghanistan was a "failed state" during the relevant times of combat and, as such, was not a party to the treaty, and (2) even if Afghanistan was a party to the treaty, Taliban combatants are not entitled to prisoner of war protections because they acted as unlawful enemy combatants).

9. Military Order, Detention, Treatment, and Trial of Certain Non-Citizens in the War Against Terrorism, 66 Fed. Reg. 57,833 (Nov. 16, 2001). *See also* Mike Allen & John Mintz, *Bush Grants Taliban Detainees Geneva Convention Protections*, Washington Post, Feb. 8, 2002 (noting that President Bush had determined to grant Geneva Convention protections to Taliban detainees but not to Al-Qaeda detainees).

10. Memorandum for Alberto Gonzales, Counsel to the President, from William Howard Taft IV, Department of State Office of Legal Adviser, Re: Comments on your paper on the Geneva Convention (Feb. 2, 2002), available at www.nytimes.com/packages/html/politics/20040608_DOC.pdf.

11. For additional information on international law as it pertains to detainees and the development of U.S. interrogation policy, *see generally*, Symposium, *The Rule of Law & The Global War on Terrorism: Detainees, Interrogations, and Military Commissions*, **48** Washburn L.J. 299 (2009).

12. *Hamdi v. Rumsfeld*, 542 U.S. 507 (2004) (holding that U.S. citizen-detainee, seeking to challenge his classification as enemy combatant, had due process right to notice of factual basis for his classification and to fair opportunity to rebut government's factual assertions before neutral decision maker). *See also Rasul v. Bush*, 542 U.S. 466 (2004) (holding that federal habeas statute conferred on district court jurisdiction to hear challenges of aliens who were captured abroad in connection with hostilities arising from September 11, 2001, terrorist attacks within the United States, and subject to executive detention at U.S. Naval Base at Guantanamo Bay, Cuba, to legality of their detentions).

13. For additional information on William Taft's views concerning military operations in Iraq, *see* Todd F. Buchwald & William Howard Taft IV, *Preemption, Iraq, and International Law*, 97 Am. J. Int'l L. 557 (2003).

14. William H. Taft IV & Todd F. Buchwald, *Preemption, Iraq, and International Law*, 97 Am. J. Int'l L., 557 *passim* (2003). For additional information on the legal implications of the military operations in Iraq, *see generally*, Todd F. Buchwald, Lori Fisler Damrosch, Richard A. Falk, Tom J. Farer, Thomas M. Franck, Richard N. Gardner, Bernard H. Oxman, Miriam Sapiro, Jane E. Stromseth, William H. Taft IV, Ruth Wedgwood, and John Yoo, *Agora: Future Implications of the Iraq Conflict*, **97** Am. J. Int'l L. 553 (2003); Eyal Benvenisti, Lori Fisler Damrosch, Thomas D. Grant, Bernard H. Oxman, David J. Scheffer, and Carsten Stahn, *Agora (Cont'd): Future Implications of the Iraq Conflict*, **97** Am. J. Int'l L. 803 (2003).

15. *See*, for example, S.C. Res. 660, UN Doc. S/RES/660 (Aug. 2, 1990); S.C. Res. 678, UN Doc. S/RES/678 (Nov. 29, 1990).

16. S.C. Res. 1333, UN SCOR, 57th Sess., 4644th mtg., UN Doc. S/RES/1441 (2002).

17. *See* The United States Explanation of Vote on UN Security Council Resolution 1441 (Nov. 8, 2002), available at www.staff.city.ac.uk/p.willetts/IRAQ/US081102.HTM.

18. *See* Authorization for Use of Military Force Against Iraq Resolution of 2002, Pub. L. No. 107–243, 116 Stat. 1498 (Oct. 16, 2002).

19. Lord Goldsmith, *Attorney General's Advice on the Iraq War Iraq: Resolution 1441*, 54 Int'l & Comp. L.Q., 767–778 (2005) (Lord Goldsmith stating that "having regard to the information on the negotiating history which I have been given and to the arguments of the U.S. Administration which I heard in Washington, I accept that a reasonable case can be made that resolution 1441 is capable in principle of reviving the authorisation in 678 without a further resolution").

20. S.C. Res. 1483, UN Doc. S/RES/1483 (May 22, 2003).

21. S.C. Res. 1511, UN Doc. S/RES/1511 (Oct. 16, 2003).
22. S.C. Res. 1546, UN Doc. S/RES/1546 (June 8, 2004).

## 13. BUSH (43RD) ADMINISTRATION – JOHN B. BELLINGER III (2005–2009)

1. *See* Environmental Protection Agency, An Analysis of the Kyoto Protocol 13–20 (2001), at www.epa.gov/globalwarming/publications/actions/us_position/ bush_ccpol_061101.pdf.
2. *See* communication from the United States to the Secretary-General of the United Nations (May 6, 2002), at www.state.gov/r/pa/prs/ps/2002/9968.htm.
3. *See generally*, John T. Parry, *Torture Nation, Torture Law*, **97** Geo. L.J. 1001 (2009).
4. *See* John R. Crook, *Contemporary Practice of the United States Relating to International Law: Use of Force and Arms Control: Legality of U.S.-Led Invasion of Iraq*, **99** Am. J. Int'l L. 269 (2005).
5. *See John B. Bellinger III, Legal Adviser, Testimony at Senate Foreign Relations Committee* (Apr. 15, 2008), *available at* http://foreign.senate.gov/testimony/ 2008/BellingerTestimony080415p)pdf.
6. *See* John R. Crook, *Contemporary Practice of the United States Relating to International Law: Brief Note: United States Supports Geneva Convention Protocol Authorizing New Emblem*, **100** Am. J. Int'l L. 244 (2006).
7. *See John B. Bellinger, III, Legal Adviser, Remarks at the Law of the Sea Institute: The United States and the Law of the Sea Convention* (Nov. 3, 2008), *available at* http://2001-2009.state.gov/s/l/rls/111587.htm. For background on U.S. policy toward the 1982 Law of the Sea Convention, *see* John Norton Moore, *United Nations Convention of the Law of the Sea (UNCLOS): Should conservatives Support or Oppose Ratification?* 12 Tex. Rev. L. & Pol'y 459 (2008); and John R. Stevenson & Bernard H. Oxman, *The Future of the United Nations Convention on the Law of the Sea*, **88** Am. J. Int'l L. 488 (1994).
8. Permanent Mission of India to the United Nations v. City of New York, 551 U.S. 193 (2007); John R. Crook, *Contemporary Practice of the United States Relating to International Law: State Jurisdiction and Immunities: U.S. Supreme Court Finds No Immunity in Tax Lien Case against India*, **101** Am. J. Int'l L. 642 (2007).
9. *See John B. Bellinger III, Legal Adviser, Remarks to the DePaul University College of Law: The United States and the International Criminal Court: Where We've Been and Where We're Going* (April 25, 2008), *available at* http:// 2001-2009.state.gov/s/l/rls/104053.htm. *See also* John R. Crook, *Contemporary Practice of the United States Relating to International Law: International Human Rights and Criminal Law: United States Stresses Importance of Accountability, Seeks Lessened Confrontation Over the International Criminal Court*, **100** Am. J.

INT'L L. 477 (2006); Harold K. Jacobson, Monroe Leigh, Ruth Wedgwood, *The United States and the Statute of Rome*, **95** AM. J. INT'L L. 124 (2001).

10. John R. Crook, *Contemporary Practice of the United States Relating to International law : General International and U.S. Foreign Relations Law: United States Abstains on Security Council Resolution Authorizing Referral of Darfur Atrocities to International Criminal Court*, **99** AM. J. INT'L L. 691 (2005).

11. Case Concerning Avena and Other Mexican Nationals (*Mex. v. U.S.*), 2004 I.C.J. 12.

12. Vienna Convention on Consular Relations, Apr. 24, 1963, 21 UST 77, 596 UNTS 261.

13. Case Concerning Avena and Other Mexican Nationals (*Mex. v. U.S.*), 2004 I.C.J. 12.

14. John R. Crook, *Contemporary Practice of the United States Relating to International Law: U.S. Strategy for Responding to ICJ's Avena Decision*, **99** AM. J. INT'L L. 489, 489–90 (2005)

15. For additional information on the Supreme Court's decision in *Medellin v. Texas*, *see generally*, David J. Bederman, Curtis A. Bradley & Steve Charnovitz, *Agora: Medellin*, **102** AM. J. INT'L L. 529 (2008); Symposium, *Medellin v. Texas*, **31** SUFFOLK TRANSNAT'L L. REV. 419 (2008).

16. *Medellin v. Texas*, 128 S.Ct. 1346 (2008).

17. Request for interpretation of the Judgment of 31 March 2004 in the Case Concerning Avena and other Mexican Nationals (*Mexico v. United States of America*), ICJ Slip Opinion, January 19, 2009.

18. *See* John B. Bellinger III, *Remarks on the Military Commissions Act*, **48** HARV. INT'L L.J. 1 (2007),

19. *Hamdan v. Rumsfeld*, 126 S.Ct. 2749 (June 29, 2006).

20. *Hamdan v. Rumsfeld*, 126 S.Ct. 2749 (June 29, 2006).

21. For additional information on the Military Commissions Act, *see generally*, Curtis A. Bradley, David A. Martin, & Tom J. Farer, *Agora: Military Commissions Act of 2006*, **101** AM. J. INT'L L. 322 (2007); Harold Hongju Koh, Joan Fitzpatrick, Michael J. Matheson, Daryl A. Mundis, & Ruth Wedgwood, *Agora: Military Commissions*, **96** AM. J. INT'L L. 320 (2002).

22. National Commission on Terrorist Attacks upon the United States, July 22, 2004, Chapter 12, available at www.9-11commission.gov/report/911Report_Ch12.htm.

23. http://opiniojuris.org/2007/01/11/opinio-juris-welcomes-state-department-legal-adviser-john-bellinger/.

24. Detainee Treatment Act of 2005, Pub. L. No. 109–148, 119 Stat. 2742

25. *Rasul v. Bush*, 542 U.S. 466, 124 S. Ct. 2686, 159 L. Ed. 2d 548 (2004); *Hamdi v. Rumsfeld*, 542 U.S. 507, 124 S. Ct. 2633, 159 L. Ed. 2d 578 (2004); *Hamdan v.*

*Rumsfeld*, 126 S.Ct. 2749 (June 29, 2006); *Boumediene v. Bush*, 128 S. Ct. 2229 (U.S. 2008).

## 14. DEPARTMENT OF STATE LEGAL ADVISERS' ROUNDTABLE

1. The order of the questions from the moderator and audience have been re-organized for a more logical narrative flow.
2. *See* Ruth Wedgwood, *NATO's Kosovo Intervention*, **93** AM. J. INT'L L. 824 (1999).

## 15. FOREIGN LEGAL ADVISERS' ROUNDTABLE

1. For additional information on Leonid Skotnikov's views on international security and self-defense, *see* Leonid Skotnikov, *The Right of Self-Defence and the New Security Imperatives*, **9** INTERNATIONAL AFFAIRS (2004).
2. For additional information on Hanquin Xue's views on the effects of International Law, *see* HANQUIN XUE, TRANSBOUNDARY DAMAGE IN INTERNATIONAL LAW (Cambridge University Press 2003).
3. For additional information on Seifeselassie Lemma's views concerning International Law on regulating the use of the Nile River, *see* Seifeselassie Lemma, *Cooperating on the Nile Not a Zero-Sum Game*, **38** UN CHRONICLE (2001).
4. *See* Geoffrey Marston, *Armed Intervention in the 1956 Suez Canal Crisis: The Legal Advice Tendered to the British Government*, **37** INT'L COMP. L.Q. 773 (1988).

## 16. LAWYERING THE TREATMENT OF DETAINEES IN THE WAR ON TERRORISM

1. While there were no dissenting votes to the report, only seventeen of the twenty-five Senators on the Senate Armed Services Committee voted. *See* Greg Miller and Julian E. Barnes, *Rumsfeld Blamed in Detainee Abuse Scandals*, LOS ANGE-LES TIMES, December 12, 2008, available at http://articles.latimes.com/2008/dec/12/nation/na-interrogate-abuse12?pg=1; Joby Warrick and Karen DeYoung, *Report on Detainee Abuse Blames Top Bush Officials*, N.Y. TIMES, December 12, 2008, available at http://www.washingtonpost.com/wp-dyn/content/article/2008/12/11/AR2008121101969.html. On December 19, 2008, six GOP senators released a statement criticizing some of the conclusions of the report. *Inhofe, Chambliss, Cornyn, Martinez, Sessions, Thune Statement on SASC Inquiry into Detainee Treatment*, available at http://inhofe.senate.gov/public/index.cfm?FuseAction=PressRoom.PressReleases&ContentRecord_id=5109e8c8-802a-23ad-424d-782c153b9456&Region_id=&Issue_id=.

2. *Senate Armed Services Committee Inquiry into the Treatment of Detainees in U.S. Custody*, December 11, 2008, available at http://levin.senate.gov/newsroom/supporting/2008/Detainees.121108.pdf. The full 263 page report, which was subsequently de-classified and released in May 2009, is available at http://levin.senate.gov/newsroom/supporting/2009/SASC.DetaineeReport.042209.pdf.

3. JACK GOLDSMITH, THE TERROR PRESIDENCY: LAW AND JUDGMENT INSIDE THE BUSH ADMINISTRATION (2007).

4. JOHN YOO, WAR BY OTHER MEANS: AN INSIDER'S ACCOUNT OF THE WAR ON TERROR 168 (Atlantic Monthly Press, 2006).

5. PHILIPPE SANDS, TORTURE TEAM 213 (Palgrave Macmillan, 2008).

6. JOHN YOO, WAR BY OTHER MEANS: AN INSIDER'S ACCOUNT OF THE WAR ON TERROR 33 (Atlantic Monthly Press, 2006).

7. Remarks by William Taft, Supplement to Day-Long Conference of Former Legal Advisers, at the Carnegie Endowment for International Peace, 2006, Chapter 12.

8. For the full text of the Four Conventions and the Additional Protocols, *see* Geneva Convention for the Amelioration of the Condition of the Wounded and Sick in Armed Forces in the Field, Aug. 12, 1949, 6 U.S.T. 3114, 75 U.N.T.S. 31; Geneva Convention for the Amelioration of the Condition of Wounded, Sick and Shipwrecked Members of Armed Forces at Sea, Aug. 12, 1949, 6 U.S.T. 3217, 75 U.N.T.S. 85; Geneva Convention Relative to the Treatment of Prisoners of War, Aug. 12, 1949, 6 U.S.T. 3316, 75 U.N.T.S. 135; Geneva Convention Relative to the Protection of Civilian Persons in Time of War, Aug. 12, 1949, 6 U.S.T. 3516, 75 U.N.T.S. 287; Protocol Additional to the Geneva Conventions of 12 August 1949, and Relating to the Protection of Victims of International Armed Conflicts, *opened for signature* Dec. 12, 1977, 1125 U.N.T.S. 3; Protocol Additional to the Geneva Conventions of 12 August 1949, and relating to the Protection of Victims of Non-International Armed Conflicts, *opened for signature* Dec. 12, 1977, 1125 U.N.T.S. 609.

9. The Conventions primarily govern conflicts between States, while the Additional Protocols establish further obligations for noninternational armed conflicts (civil wars). The United States has ratified the four Conventions but has not ratified the Additional Protocols.

10. Geneva Convention for the Amelioration of the Condition of the Wounded and Sick in Armed Forces in the Field art. 3, Aug. 12, 1949, 6 U.S.T. 3114, 75 U.N.T.S. 31; Geneva Convention for the Amelioration of the Condition of Wounded, Sick and Shipwrecked Members of Armed Forces at Sea art. 3, Aug. 12, 1949, 6 U.S.T. 3217, 75 U.N.T.S. 85; Geneva Convention Relative to the Treatment of Prisoners of War art. 3, Aug. 12, 1949, 6 U.S.T. 3316, 75 U.N.T.S. 135; Geneva Convention Relative to the Protection of Civilian Persons in Time of War art. 3, Aug. 12, 1949, 6 U.S.T. 3516, 75 U.N.T.S. 287.

11. JOHN YOO, WAR BY OTHER MEANS: AN INSIDER'S ACCOUNT OF THE WAR ON TERROR 47 (Atlantic Monthly Press, 2006). See also *Id*, at 22.

12. Memorandum from John Yoo to William J. Haynes, "Application of Treaties and Laws to al Qaeda and Taliban Detainees" www.gwu.edu/~nsarchiv/ NSAEBB/NSAEBB127/02.01.09.pdf.

13. Memorandum from John Yoo (signed by Jay W. Bybee) to Alberto Gonzalez and William J. Haynes, "Re: Application of Treaties and Laws to al Qaeda and Taliban Detainees" http://fl1.findlaw.com/news.findlaw.com/hdocs/ docs/doj/bybee12202mem.pdf.

14. Memorandum from John Yoo (signed by Jay W. Bybee) to Alberto Gonzalez and William J. Haynes, "Re: Application of Treaties and Laws to al Qaeda and Taliban Detainees" http://fl1.findlaw.com/news.findlaw.com/hdocs/docs/ doj/bybee12202mem.pdf.

15. Memorandum from Alberto Gonzales to President Bush, *Decision RE Application of the Geneva Convention on Prisoners of War to the Conflict with Al Qaeda and the Taliban*. www.gwu.edu/~nsarchiv/NSAEBB/NSAEBB127/02.01.25.pdf.

16. 18 U.S.C. Section 2441.

17. Memorandum from Alberto R. Gonzales, Counsel to George W. Bush, President, *Decision Re Application of the Geneva Convention on Prisoners of War to the Conflict with Al Qaeda and the Taliban* (Jan. 25, 2002), reprinted in Appendix, **37** CASE W. RES. J. INT'L L. 615 (2006).

18. Memorandum from Colin Powell, Secretary of State, to Alberto R. Gonzales, Counsel to the President, *Draft Decision Memorandum for the President on the Applicability of the Geneva Convention to the Conflict in Afghanistan* (Jan. 26, 2002), reprinted in Appendix, **37** CASE W. RES. J. INT'L L. 615 (2006).

19. The Department State subsequently concluded that the conflict with Al-Qaeda could be viewed as distinct from the conflict with the Taliban and thus the Conventions did not apply to Al-Qaeda. Remarks by William Taft, Supplement to Day-Long Conference of Former Legal Advisers, at the Carnegie Endowment for International Peace, 2006, Chapter 12.

20. *Id*.

21. Memorandum from William H. Taft, IV, The Legal Adviser, Department of State, to Alberto R. Gonzales, Counsel to the President, *Comments on Your Paper on the Geneva Convention* (February 2, 2002), reprinted in Appendix, **37** CASE W. RES. J. INT'L L. 615 (2006).

22. Memorandum from George W. Bush, President to Richard B. Cheney, Vice President et al., *Humane Treatment of al Qaeda and Taliban Detainees* (Feb. 7, 2002). www.torturingdemocracy.org/documents/20020207-2.pdf.

23. Memorandum from George W. Bush, President to Richard B. Cheney, Vice President et al., *Humane Treatment of al Qaeda and Taliban Detainees* (Feb. 7, 2002). www.torturingdemocracy.org/documents/20020207-2.pdf.

24. Memorandum from George W. Bush, President to Richard B. Cheney, Vice President et al., *Humane Treatment of al Qaeda and Taliban Detainees* (Feb. 7, 2002). www.torturingdemocracy.org/documents/20020207-2.pdf.

25. Remarks by William Taft, Supplement to Day-Long Conference of Former Legal Advisers, at the Carnegie Endowment for International Peace, 2006, Chapter 12.

26. Remarks by William Taft, Supplement to Day-Long Conference of Former Legal Advisers, at the Carnegie Endowment for International Peace, 2006, Chapter 12.

27. Remarks by William Taft, Supplement to Day-Long Conference of Former Legal Advisers, at the Carnegie Endowment for International Peace, 2006, Chapter 12.

28. Remarks by William Taft, Supplement to Day-Long Conference of Former Legal Advisers, at the Carnegie Endowment for International Peace, 2006, Chapter 12.

29. For the full text of the United Nations Convention Against Torture, *see* United Nations Convention Against Torture and Other Cruel, Inhuman or Degrading Treatment or Punishment, Jun. 26, 1987, S. Treaty Doc. No. 100–20, 1465 U.N.T.S. 112.

30. The legal reasoning of the OLC can be viewed through the lens of seeking to protect interrogators from domestic prosecution. The OLC may have been driven by a desire to create an interrogation culture where U.S. military and intelligence personnel would be free to use all necessary measures in a ticking time bomb environment.

31. Memo from Jay Bybee (written by John Yoo) to Alberto Gonzales, "Re: Standards of Conduct for Interrogation under 18 U.S.S. 2340–2340A." www.washingtonpost.com/wp-srv/politics/documents/cheney/torture_memo_ aug2002.pdf. *See also* Jack Goldsmith, the Terror Presidency: Law and Judgment Inside the Bush Administration 145 (2007). The memorandum advised that any interrogation methods that do not violate the prohibition on torture found in domestic law, 18 U.S.C. § 2340–2340A, which required intent, also do not violate obligations under the Torture Convention because of the United States' understanding attached to the Convention. The memorandum also advised that interrogators could inflict pain and suffering on detainees, up to the level caused by "organ failure" without violating the domestic and international prohibition on torture and cruel, inhumane, or degrading treatment. The OLC derived its definition of torture from a statute that authorized benefits for emergency health conditions, using the phrase "severe pain" as a possible indicator of an emergency condition that might cause serious harm if not immediately treated.

32. Memo from Jay Bybee (written by John Yoo) to Alberto Gonzales, "Re: Standards of Conduct for Interrogation Under 18 U.S.S. 2340–2340A." www.washingtonpost.com/wp-srv/politics/documents/cheney/torture_memo_aug2002.pdf

33. Memo from Jay Bybee to John Rizzo, "Interrogation of al Qaeda Operative." www.globalsecurity.org/intell/library/policy/national/olc_020801_bybee.htm.

34. Ten types of action are proposed: (1) Attention grasp, (2) Walling, (3) Facial hold, (4) Facial slap, (5) Cramped confinement, (6) Wall standing, (7) Stress positions, (8) Sleep deprivation, (9) Insects placed in a confinement box, and (10) Waterboarding. Memo from Jay Bybee to John Rizzo, "Interrogation of al Qaeda Operative." www.globalsecurity.org/intell/library/policy/national/olc_020801_bybee.htm.

35. Memo from Jay Bybee to John Rizzo, "Interrogation of Al-Qaeda Operative." www.globalsecurity.org/intell/library/policy/national/olc_020801_bybee.htm.

36. Scott Shane, *Waterboarding Used 266 Times on 2 Suspects*, N.Y. TIMES (April 19, 2009), www.nytimes.com/2009/04/20/world/20detain.html.

37. *Senate Armed Services Committee Inquiry into the Treatment of Detainees in U.S. Custody*, December 11, 2008, at xviii.

38. *Senate Armed Services Committee Inquiry into the Treatment of Detainees in U.S. Custody*, December 11, 2008, at xix.

39. *Senate Armed Services Committee Inquiry into the Treatment of Detainees in U.S. Custody*, December 11, 2008, at xxiv.

40. *Senate Armed Services Committee Inquiry into the Treatment of Detainees in U.S. Custody*, December 11, 2008, at xxiv. In his "insider's account of the war on terror," WAR BY OTHER MEANS, John Yoo dismisses the migration theory as "an exercise in hyperbole and partisan smear." JOHN YOO, WAR BY OTHER MEANS: AN INSIDER'S ACCOUNT OF THE WAR ON TERROR 168 (Atlantic Monthly Press, 2006). According to the bipartisan Senate Committee Report, however, "the abuse of detainees at Abu Ghraib in late 2003 was not simply the result of a few soldiers acting on their own. Interrogation techniques such as stripping detainees of their clothes, placing them in stress positions, and using military working dogs to intimidate them appeared in Iraq only after they had been approved for use in Afghanistan and at Guantanamo Bay." *Senate Armed Services Committee Inquiry into the Treatment of Detainees in U.S. Custody*, December 11, 2008, at xxiv.

41. *Senate Armed Services Committee Inquiry into the Treatment of Detainees in U.S. Custody*, December 11, 2008, at xxi.

42. *Senate Armed Services Committee Inquiry into the Treatment of Detainees in U.S. Custody*, December 11, 2008, at xxi.

43. Memo from John Yoo to William Haynes (DoD General Counsel), *Re: Military Interrogation of Alien Unlawful Combatants Held Outside the United States.* www.aclu.org/pdfs/safefree/yoo_army_torture_memo.pdf.

44. Memo from John Yoo to William Haynes (DoD General Counsel), *Re: Military Interrogation of Alien Unlawful Combatants Held Outside the United States.* www.aclu.org/pdfs/safefree/yoo_army_torture_memo.pdf.

45. Memo from John Yoo to William Haynes (DoD General Counsel), *Re: Military Interrogation of Alien Unlawful Combatants Held Outside the United States.* www.aclu.org/pdfs/safefree/yoo_army_torture_memo.pdf.

46. Memo from John Yoo to William Haynes (DoD General Counsel), *Re: Military Interrogation of Alien Unlawful Combatants Held Outside the United States.* www.aclu.org/pdfs/safefree/yoo_army_torture_memo.pdf.

47. Memo from John Yoo to William Haynes (DoD General Counsel), *Re: Military Interrogation of Alien Unlawful Combatants Held Outside the United States.* www.aclu.org/pdfs/safefree/yoo_army_torture_memo.pdf.

48. *Senate Armed Services Committee Inquiry into the Treatment of Detainees in U.S. Custody*, December 11, 2008, at xxii–xxiii.

49. As noted earlier, there were several GOP senators on the bipartisan panel who released a statement disagreeing with some of the conclusions drawn by the report. *Inhofe, Chambliss, Cornyn, Martinez, Sessions, Thune Statement on SASC Inquiry into Detainee Treatment*, available at http://inhofe.senate.gov/public/index.cfm?FuseAction=PressRoom.PressReleases&ContentRecord_id= 5109e8c8-802a-23ad-424d-782c153b9456&Region_id=&Issue_id=.

50. *Senate Armed Services Committee Inquiry into the Treatment of Detainees in U.S. Custody*, December 11, 2008, at xii, available at http://levin.senate.gov/newsroom/supporting/2008/Detainees.121108.pdf.

51. *Senate Armed Services Committee Inquiry into the Treatment of Detainees in U.S. Custody*, December 11, 2008, at xxviii, available at http://levin.senate.gov/newsroom/supporting/2008/Detainees.121108.pdf.

52. *Id*, at xxvii.

53. Remarks by William Taft, Supplement to Day-Long Conference of Former Legal Advisers, at the Carnegie Endowment for International Peace, 2006, Chapter 12.

54. Remarks by William Taft, Supplement to Day-Long Conference of Former Legal Advisers, at the Carnegie Endowment for International Peace, 2006, Chapter 12.

55. JACK GOLDSMITH, THE TERROR PRESIDENCY: LAW AND JUDGMENT INSIDE THE BUSH ADMINISTRATION 141–176 (2007).

56. JACK GOLDSMITH, THE TERROR PRESIDENCY: LAW AND JUDGMENT INSIDE THE BUSH ADMINISTRATION 151 (2007). According to John Yoo, notably, the 2004 OLC memo that replaced Yoo's 2002 work contained a footnote saying that "all the

interrogation methods that earlier opinions had found legal were still legal." JOHN YOO, WAR BY OTHER MEANS: AN INSIDER'S ACCOUNT OF THE WAR ON TERROR 183 (Atlantic Monthly Press, 2006).

57. JACK GOLDSMITH, THE TERROR PRESIDENCY: LAW AND JUDGMENT INSIDE THE BUSH ADMINISTRATION 148 (2007).

58. JACK GOLDSMITH, THE TERROR PRESIDENCY: LAW AND JUDGMENT INSIDE THE BUSH ADMINISTRATION 155–156 (2007).

59. JACK GOLDSMITH, THE TERROR PRESIDENCY: LAW AND JUDGMENT INSIDE THE BUSH ADMINISTRATION 144 (2007). In explaining why he did not rescind the August 1, 2002 Yoo/Bybee memorandum to the CIA, Goldsmith writes: "And in contrast to my sense of the Defense Department techniques [which Goldsmith believed would be legally justified under proper legal analysis], I wasn't as confident that the CIA techniques [including waterboarding] could be approved under a proper legal analysis. I didn't affirmatively believe they were illegal either, or else I would have stopped them. I just didn't know yet. And I wouldn't know until we had figured out the proper interpretation of the torture statute, and whether the CIA techniques were consistent with that proper legal analysis." Id.

60. Yoo has asserted that Goldsmith's withdrawal of Yoo's 2002 opinion was merely "for appearances' sake" to divert public criticism in the immediate aftermath of the Abu Ghraib controversy. "In the real world of interrogation policy nothing had changed." JOHN YOO, WAR BY OTHER MEANS: AN INSIDER'S ACCOUNT OF THE WAR ON TERROR 182–183 (Atlantic Monthly Press, 2006).

61. This approach has been described as a "roadmap to the outsourcing of torture and other forms of abuse" to Egypt, Jordan, Morocco, Saudi Arabia, Yemen, & Syria. Jose E. Alvarez, *Torturing the Law*, **37** CASE W. RES. J. INT'L L. 175, 210–211, 213 (2006).

62. Pub. L. 109–148. 119 Stat. 2680, 2739–44 (2005), available at http://thomas. loc.gov/cgi-bin/cpquery/T?&report=hr359&dbname=109&. To avoid the President's threatened veto, the Detainee Treatment legislation was revised before enactment to exempt the CIA from its requirements and to stipulate that detainees do not have a right to challenge their detention in U.S. court.

63. Remarks by John Bellinger, Supplement to Day-Long Conference of Former Legal Advisers, at the Carnegie Endowment for International Peace, March 7, 2009, Chapter 13.

64. Remarks by John Bellinger, Supplement to Day-Long Conference of Former Legal Advisers, at the Carnegie Endowment for International Peace, March 7, 2009, Chapter 13.

65. For a review of the views relating to the legality of the Guantanamo detentions and the treatment of detainees by the UN Secretary-General, the UN Special Rapporteurs on Torture and Arbitrary Detention, the United

Kingdom House of Commons, the International Committee of the Red Cross, and the Inter-American Commission on Human Rights, *see* UN Econ. & Soc. Council [ECOSOC], Comm. On Human Rights, Situation of Detainees at Guantanamo Bay, UN Doc. E/CN.4/2006/120 (Feb. 15, 2006); Foreign Affairs Committee, Human Rights Annual Report 2005, 2004–05, H.C. 574, available at http://www.publications.parliament.uk/pa/cm200506/cmselect/cmfaff/574/57402.htm; Neil Lewis, *Red Cross Finds detainee Abuse in Guantanamo*, N.Y. Times, November 30, 2004, at A1; Inter-American Commission on Human Rights, Detainees at Guantanamo Bay, Cuba (March 12, 2002), available at http://www.photius.com/rogue_nations/guantanamo.html.

66. Remarks by John Bellinger, Supplement to Day-Long Conference of Former Legal Advisers, at the Carnegie Endowment for International Peace, March 7, 2009, Chapter 13.

67. Remarks by John Bellinger, Supplement to Day-Long Conference of Former Legal Advisers, at the Carnegie Endowment for International Peace, March 7, 2009, reproduced in Chapter 10.

68. *Rasul v. Bush*, 542 U.S. 466 (2004).

69. Order Establishing Combatant Status Review Tribunal, 7 July 2004, available at www.defenselink.mil/news/Jul2004/d20040707review.pdf.

70. *Hamdan v. Rumsfeld*, 548 U.S. 557 (2006).

71. For additional information on Abraham Sofaer's views on Military Tribunals, *see* Abraham D. Sofaer & Paul R. Williams, *Doing Justice during Wartime: Why Military Tribunals Make Sense*, Pol'y Rev., Feb. 1, 2002.

72. Pub. L. 109-366, Oct. 17, 2006, available at www.loc.gov/rr/frd/Military_Law/pdf/PL-109-366.

73. *Boumediene v. Bush*, 553 U.S. (2008). For additional information on Harold Koh's views concerning military commissions, *see* Harold Hongju Koh, *The Case Against Military Commissions*, **96** Am. J. Int'l L. 337 (2002).

74. Bob Woodward, *Detainee Tortured, Says U.S. Official*, Washington Post, Jan. 14, 2009, at A1.

75. *See* Audio Transcript, Presidential Foreign Policy Advisers' Panel, American Society of International Law Annual Conference, April 10, 2008.

76. *See* Audio Transcript, Presidential Foreign Policy Advisers' Panel, American Society of International Law Annual Conference, April 10, 2008.

77. Executive Order of January 22, 2009, Review and Disposition of Individuals Detained at the Guantanamo Bay Naval Base and Closure of Detention Facilities, Section 2, available at www.whitehouse.gov/the_press_office/ClosureOfGuantanamoDetentionFacilities/.

78. Executive Order of January 22, 2009, Ensuring Lawful Interrogations, available at www.whitehouse.gov/the_press_office/EnsuringLawfulInterrogations/.

79. Charlie Savage, *To Critics, New Policy on Terror Looks Old*, N.Y. TIMES, July 2, 2009.

80. Mark Mazzetti, *Panetta Open to Tougher Methods in Some C.I.A. Interrogation*, N.Y. TIMES (February 5, 2009).

81. Remarks by John Bellinger, III, Supplement to Day-Long Conference of Former Legal Advisers, at the Carnegie Endowment for International Peace, March 7, 2009, reproduced in Chapter 10.

82. Remarks by Davis Robinson, Day-Long Conference of Former Legal Advisers, at the Carnegie Endowment for International Peace, April 1, 2004, Chapter 6. (describing L as "the moral conscience of American foreign policy.")

83. PHILIPPE SANDS, TORTURE TEAM 33 (Palgrave Macmillan, 2008). *See also* MARK OSIEL, THE END OF RECIPROCITY: TERROR, TORTURE, AND THE LAW OF WAR 330–333 (2009).

84. Barbara Slavin, *Abuse of Detainees Undercuts U.S. Authority, 9/11 Panel Says*, USA TODAY, Nov. 15, 2005, at 8A.

85. *Senate Armed Services Committee Inquiry into the Treatment of Detainees in U.S. Custody*, December 11, 2008, at xxv.

86. *Text, Obama's Speech to the United Nations General Assembly*, N.Y. TIMES, September 23, 2009, available at www.nytimes.com/2009/09/24/us/politics/24prexy.text.html?pagewanted=all.

87. Announcement, The Norwegian Nobel Committee, The Nobel Peace Prize for 2009, October 9, 2009, available at http://nobelpeaceprize.org/en_GB/home/announce-2009/.

## 17. CONCLUSION

1. John R. Bolton, *Is There Really "Law" in International Affairs*, **10** TRANSNAT'L L. & CONTEMP. PROBS.1, 48 (2000).

2. Memorandum from Colin Powell, Secretary of State, to Alberto R. Gonzales, Counsel to the President, *Draft Decision Memorandum for the President on the Applicability of the Geneva Convention to the Conflict in Afghanistan* (Jan. 26, 2002), reprinted in Appendix, **37** CASE. W. RES. J. INT'L L. 615 (2006).

3. Gerald Fitzmaurice, *Legal Advisers and Foreign Affairs*, **59** AM. J. INT'L L.72, 73 (1965).

4. John O. McGinnis, *Principle versus Politics: The Solicitor General's Office in Constitutional and Bureaucratic Theory*, **44** STAN. L. REV. 799 (1992)

5. As Mike Matheson explains in Chapter 14, The Legal Adviser "has a duty to give honest legal advice and not to change it based on what the client may expect or desire."

6. As Conrad Harper recalls in Chapter 14, "[w]hen I had to go and advise the Secretary of State, the fact that I was the person who knew the law was not the

reason I was there. I was there to offer my best judgment." *See also* the comment of Abe Sofaer in Chapter 14, "[O]f course it is important for the Legal Adviser to tell the clients – and I'm sure every one of us has done it–'Don't do this; this is NOT a good idea.' And in fact, when they don't ask us it's almost always a disaster."

7. Stephen M. Schwebel, *Remarks on the Role of the Legal Adviser of the U.S. State Department*, 2 Eur. J. Int'l L. 132, 133 (1991).

8. For background, *see* Geoffrey Marston, *Armed Intervention in the 1956 Suez Canal Crisis: The Legal Advice Tendered to the British Government*, 37 Int'l & Comp. L.Q. 773 (1988).

9. For background about Wilmshurst's resignation, *see* Paul Eastham, *Iraq: Is This the Smoking Gun?* Daily Mail (London), March 25, 2005, at 7.

10. Louis Henkin, How Nations Behave 337 (2d ed. 1979).

11. Aaron Gichteblerg, Law at the Vanishing Point 146 (Ashgate Publishing Ltd., 2008).

# Annex: Legal Advisers of the U.S. Department of State

| Adviser | Years in Office | Administration |
|---|---|---|
| Green Hackworth | 1931–1946 | Franklin D. Roosevelt and Harry S. Truman |
| Charles H. Fahy | 1946–1947 | Harry S. Truman |
| Ernest A. Gross | 1947–1949 | Harry S. Truman |
| Adrian S. Fisher | 1949–1953 | Harry S. Truman |
| Herman Phleger | 1953–1957 | Dwight D. Eisenhower |
| Loftus Becker | 1957–1959 | Dwight D. Eisenhower |
| Eric H. Hager | 1959–1961 | Dwight D. Eisenhower |
| Abram Chayes | 1961–1964 | John F. Kennedy |
| Leonard C. Meeker | 1965–1969 | Lyndon B. Johnson |
| John R. Stevenson | 1969–1973 | Richard M. Nixon |
| Carlyle E. Maw | 1973–1974 | Richard M. Nixon |
| Monroe Leigh | 1975–1977 | Gerald R. Ford |
| Herbert J. Hansell | 1977–1979 | James E. Carter |
| Roberts Bishop Owen | 1979–1981 | James E. Carter |
| Davis Rowland Robinson | 1981–1985 | Ronald W. Reagan |
| Abraham D. Sofaer | 1985–1990 | Ronald W. Reagan and George H. W. Bush |
| Edwin D. Williamson | 1990–1993 | George H. W. Bush |
| Conrad Kenneth Harper | 1993–1996 | William J. Clinton |
| David Andrews | 1997–2000 | William J. Clinton |
| William Howard Taft IV | 2001–2005 | George W. Bush |
| John Bellinger III | 2005–2009 | George W. Bush |
| Harold Hongju Koh | 2009– | Barack H. Obama |

# Select Bibliography of Legal Scholarship by Department of State Legal Advisers

**Gene Hackworth – served under Franklin D. Roosevelt and Harry S. Truman (1931–1946).**

Gene Hackworth, *Book Review*, **42** YALE L.J. 153 (reviewing CHIRAKAIKARAN JOSEPH CHACKO, THE INTERNATIONAL JOINT COMMISSION BETWEEN THE UNITED STATES AND CANADA [1932]).

**Charles H. Fahy – served under Harry S. Truman (1946–1947).**

Charles H Fahy, *Book Review*, **73** HARV. L. REV. 811 (reviewing LOUIS HENKIN, ARMS CONTROL AND INSPECTION IN AMERICAN LAW [1960]).

Charles H. Fahy, *Book Review*, **65** YALE L.J. 1232 (reviewing EDMOND CAHN, THE MORAL DECISION. RIGHT AND WRONG IN THE LIGHT OF AMERICAN LAW [1956]).

Charles H. Fahy, *The Judicial Philosophy of Mr. Justice Murphy*, **60** YALE L.J. 812 (1951).

**Adrian S. Fisher – served under Harry S. Truman (1949–1953).**

Adrian S. Fisher, *Book Review*, **76** AM. J. INT'L L. 870 (reviewing ROGER FISHER, IMPROVING COMPLIANCE WITH INTERNATIONAL LAW [1982]).

Adrian S. Fisher, *Book Review*, **67** YALE L.J. 1148 (reviewing ALEXANDER M. BICKEL, THE UNPUBLISHED OPINIONS OF JUSTICE BRANDEIS [1958]).

**Abram Chayes – served under John F. Kennedy (1961–1964).**

ABRAM CHAYES & ANTONIA HANDLER CHAYES, PLANNING FOR INTERVENTION, INTERNATIONAL COOPERATION IN CONFLICT (Kluwer Law International 1999).

ABRAM CHAYES, MANAGING CONFLICT IN THE FORMER SOVIET UNION – RUSSIAN AND AMERICAN PERSPECTIVES (MIT Press 1997).

ABRAM CHAYES & ANTONIA HANDLER CHAYES, THE NEW SOVEREIGNTY: COMPLIANCE WITH INTERNATIONAL REGULATORY AGREEMENTS (Harvard University Press 1996).

ABRAM CHAYES & ANTONIA HANDLER CHAYES, PREVENTING CONFLICT IN THE POST-COMMUNIST WORLD: MOBILIZING INTERNATIONAL AND REGIONAL ORGANIZATIONS (Brookings Institution Press 1996).

Abram Chayes et al., *Foreign Policy, Law and Administrations in Transition*, **83** AM. SOC'Y INT'L L. PROC. 295 (1989).

Abram Chayes & Antonia Handler Chayes, *Testing and Development of 'Exotic' Systems under the ABM Treaty: The Great Reinterpretation Caper*, **99** HARV. L. REV. 1956 (1986).

Abram Chayes, *Nicaragua, the United States, and the World Court*, **85** COLUM. L. REV. 1445 (1985).

Abram Chayes, *The United States and the World Court*, **85** COLUM. L. REV. 1445 (1985).

Abram Chayes et al., *International Lawlessness in Grenada*, **78** AM. J. INT'L L. 172 (1984).

Abram Chayes, *Public Law Litigation and the Burger Court*, **96** HARV. L. REV. 4 (1982).

Abram Chayes, *The Role of the Judge in Public Law Litigation*, **89** HARV. L. REV. 1281 (1976).

ABRAM CHAYES, THE CUBAN MISSILE CRISIS: INTERNATIONAL CRISIS AND THE ROLE OF LAW (Oxford University Press 1974).

ABRAM CHAYES & G. W. RATHJEN, NUCLEAR ARMS AGREEMENTS PROGRESS AND IMPACT (Carnegie Endowment for International Peace 1974).

Abram Chayes, *An Inquiry Into the Workings of Arms Control Agreements*, **85** HARV. L. REV. 905 (1972).

ABRAM CHAYES & JEROME B. WIESNER, ABM: AN EVALUATION OF THE DECISION TO DEPLOY AN ANTIBALLISTIC MISSILE SYSTEM (Harper & Row 1969).

ABRAM CHAYES, THE INTERNATIONAL LEGAL PROCESS (Little Brown & Co. 1968).

Abram Chayes, *A Common Lawyer Looks at International Law*, **78** HARV. L. REV. 1396 (1965).

**John R. Stevenson – served under Richard Nixon (1969–1973).**

John R. Stevenson & Bernard H. Oxman, *The Future of the United Nations Convention on the Law of the Sea*, **88** AM. J. INT'L L. 488 (1994).

John R Stevenson, *Book Review*, **60** COLUM. L. REV. 894 (reviewing PHILIP C. JESSUP, THE USE OF INTERNATIONAL LAW [1960]).

John R. Stevenson, *The Relationship of Private International Law to Public International Law*, **52** Colum. L. Rev. 561 (1952).

John R. Stevenson, *Effect of Recognition on the Application of Private International Law Norms*, **51** Colum. L. Rev. 710 (1951).

**Carlyle E. Maw – served under Richard Nixon (1973–1974).**

Carlyle E. Maw et al., *The Use of the Federal Injunction in Constitutional Litigation*, **43** Harv. L. Rev. 426 (1930).

**Monroe Leigh – served under Gerald Ford (1975–1977).**

Harold K. Jacobson, Monroe Leigh, & Ruth Wedgwood, *The United States and the Statute of Rome*, **95** Am. J. Int'l L. 124 (2001).

Cristian DeFrania & Monroe Leigh, *International Law Societies and the Development of International Law*, **41** Va. J. Int'l L. 941 (2001).

Monroe Leigh & Maury Shenk, *International Criminal Tribunals for the Former Yugoslavia and Rwanda*, **32** Int'l Law. 509 (1997).

Monroe Leigh, *1996 Amendments to the Foreign Sovereign Immunities Act with Respect to Terrorist Activities*, **91** Am. J. Int'l L. 187 (1997).

Monroe Leigh, *The Yugoslav Tribunal: Use of Unnamed Witnesses Against Accused*, **90** Am. J. Int'l L. 235 (1996).

Monroe Leigh, *The Political Consequences of Economic Embargoes*, **89** Am. J. Int'l L. 74 (1995).

Monroe Leigh, *Evaluating Present Options for an International Criminal Court*, **149** Mil. L. Rev. 113, (1995).

Monroe Leigh, *Is the President Above Customary International Law?* **86** Am. J. Int'l L. 757 (1992).

**Herbert J. Hansell – served under Jimmy Carter (1977–1979).**

Herbert J. Hansell, *Robert Hellawell – A Remembrance*, **102** Colum. L. Rev. 539 (2002).

**Roberts B. Owen – Served under Jimmy Carter (1979–1981).**

Roberts B. Owen, *The Final Negotiation and Release in Algiers*, *in* American Hostages in Iran 297–324 (Yale University Press 1985).

**Davis R. Robinson – served under Ronald Reagan (1981–1985).**

David A. Colson, Bruce C. Rashkow, & Davis Rowland Robinson, *Some Perspective on Adjudicating Before the World Court: The Gulf of Maine Case*, **79** Am. J. Int'l L. 578 (1985).

**Abraham D. Sofaer – served under Ronald Reagan and George H. W. Bush (1985–1990).**

Abraham D. Sofaer, *International Security and the Use of Force*, *in* Russell A. Miller & Rebecca M. Bratspies, eds., Progress in International Law (2008).

Abraham D. Sofaer, *Presidential Power and National Security*, **37** PRESIDEN-TIAL STUD. Q. 101 (2007).

Abraham D. Sofaer, *A Legacy of Reykjavik: Negotiating with Enemies*, in SIDNEY D. DRELL & GEORGE P. SHULTZ, IMPLICATIONS OF THE REYKJAVIK SUMMIT ON ITS TWENTIETH ANNIVERSARY **127** (2007).

Abraham D. Sofaer, *On the Necessity of Preemption*, **2003** EUR. J. INT'L L. 209 (2003**).

Abraham D. Sofaer, *Iran-Contra: Ethical Conduct and Public Policy*, **40** HOUS. L. REV. 1081 (2003).

Abraham D. Sofaer & Paul R. Williams, *Doing Justice during Wartime: Why Military Tribunals Make Sense*, POL'Y REV. (2002).

Abraham D. Sofaer, *International Law and Kosovo*, **36** STAN. J. INT'L L. 1 (2000).

Abraham D. Sofaer, *The Legality of the United States Action in Panama*, **29** COLUM. J. TRANSNAT'L L. 281 (1991).

Abraham D. Sofaer, *Terrorism, the Law, and the National Defense*, **126** MIL. L. REV. 89 (1989).

Abraham D. Sofaer, *Treaty Interpretation: A Comment*, **137** U. PA. L. REV. 1437 (1989).

Abraham D. Sofaer, *The War Powers Resolution: Fifteen Years Later*, **62** TEMP. L. REV. 317 (1989).

Abraham D. Sofaer, *The U.S. Decisions Not to Ratify Protocol I to the Geneva Conventions on the Protection of War Victims (Cont'd): The Rationale for the United States Decision*, **82** AM. J. INT'L L. 784 (1988).

Abraham D. Sofaer, *The ABM Treaty and the Strategic Defense Initiative*, **99** HARV. L. REV. 1972 (1986).

Abraham D. Sofaer, *Executive Privilege: An Historic Note*, **75** COLUM. L. REV. 1318 (1975).

**Edwin D. Williamson – served under George H. W. Bush (1990–1993).**

Edwin D. Williamson, *US–EU Understanding on Helms–Burton: A Missed Opportunity to Fix International Law on Property Rights*, **48** CATH. U. L. REV. 293 (1999).

Edwin D. Williamson & John E. Osborn, *A U.S. Perspective on Treaty Succession and Related Issues in the Wake of the Breakup of the USSR and Yugoslavia*, **33** VA. J. INT'L L. 261 (1993).

**Conrad K. Harper – served under Bill Clinton (1993–1996).**

Conrad K. Harper, *The State Department at Work, Arbitration and U.S. Foreign Relations*, **49** DISP. RESOL. J. 8 (1994).

Conrad K. Harper, *Friedman Award Address*, **35** COLUM. J. TRANSNAT'L L. 265 (1997).

**David R. Andrews – served under Bill Clinton (1997–2000).**

David Andrews, *A Thorn on the Tulip – A Scottish Trial in the Netherlands: The Story Behind the Lockerbie Trial*, **36** CASE W. RES. J. INT'L L. 307 (2004).

**William Howard Taft IV – served under George W. Bush (2001–2005).**

Todd F. Buchwald & William Howard Taft IV, *Preemption, Iraq, and International Law*, **97** AM. J. INT'L L. 557 (2003).

**John B. Bellinger III – served under George W. Bush (2005–2009).**

John B. Bellinger III, *Enforcing Human Rights in U.S. Courts and Abroad, The Alien Tort Statute and Other Approaches*, **42** VAND. J. TRANSNAT'L L. 1 (2009)

John B. Bellinger III, *Legal Issues in the War on Terrorism – A Reply to Siljan N. U. Voneky*, **8** GERMAN L.J. 871 (2007).

John B. Bellinger III, *Remarks on the Military Commissions Act*, **48** HARV. INT'L L.J. 1 (2007).

John B. Bellinger III, *Reflections on Transatlantic Approaches to International Law*, **17** DUKE J. COMP. & INT'L L. 2 (2007).

**Harold Hongju Koh – currently serves under Barack Obama (2009–).**

Harold Hongju Koh, *Restoring America's Human Rights Reputation*, **40** CORNELL INT'L L.J. 635 (2007).

Harold Hongju Koh, *The Future of Lou Henkin's Human Rights Movement*, **38** COLUM. HUM. RTS. L. REV. 487 (2007).

Harold Hongju Koh, *The Value of Process*, **11** INT'L LEGAL THEORY 27 (2005).

Harold Hongju Koh, *A World Without Torture*, **43** COLUM. J. TRANSNAT'L L. 641 (2005).

Oona Anne Hathaway & Harold Hongju Koh, FOUNDATIONS OF INTERNATIONAL LAW AND POLITICS 2004 (Foundations Press 2004).

Harold Hongju Koh, *International Law as Part of Our Law*, **98** AM. J. INT'L L. 43 (2004).

Harold Hongju Koh, *Difference but Equal: The Human Rights of Persons with Intellectual Disabilities*, **63** MD. L. REV. 1 (2004).

Harold Hongju Koh, *Why American Should Ratify the Women's Rights Treaty (CEDAW)*, **34** CASE W. RES. J. INT'L L. 263 (2002).

Harold Hongju Koh, *The Case Against Military Commissions*, **96** AM. J. INT'L L. 337 (2002).

Harold Hongju Koh, *Legal Response to Terror: The Spirit of the Laws*, **43** HARV. INT'L L.J. 23 (2002).

Harold Hongju Koh, *The Globalization of Freedom*, **26** YALE J. INT'L L. 305 (2001).

Harold Hongju Koh, *Is International Law Really State Law?* **111** HARV. L. REV. 1824 (1998).

Harold Hongju Koh, *Transnational Legal Process*, **75** NEB. L. REV. 181 (1996).

Harold Hongju Koh, *The Haitian Refugee Litigation: A Case Study in Transnational Public Law Litigation* **18** MD. J. INT'L L. & TRADE 1 (1994).

Harold Hongju Koh, *Protecting the Office of Legal Counsel from Itself*, **15** CARDOZO L. REV. 513 (1993).

Harold Hongju Koh & John Choon Yoo, *Dollar Diplomacy(Dollar Defense: The Fabric of Economics and National Security Law*, **26** INT'L LAW. 715 (1992).

Harold Hongju Koh, *The President Versus the Senate in Treaty Interpretation: What's All the Fuss About?* **15** YALE J. INT'L L. 331 (1990).

Harold Hongju Koh, *Why the President (Almost) Always Wins in Foreign Affairs: Lessons of the Iran-Contra Affair*, **97** YALE L.J. 1255 (1988).

Harold Hongju Koh, *The Legal Markets of International Trade: A Perspective on the Proposed United States–Canada Free Trade Agreement*, **12** YALE J. INT'L L. 193 (1987).

# About the Authors

## Michael P. Scharf

Michael P. Scharf is the John Deaver Drinko–Baker & Hostetler Professor of Law and Director of the Frederick K. Cox International Law Center at Case Western Reserve University School of Law. In February 2005, Scharf and the Public International Law and Policy Group (PILPG), a nongovernmental organization (NGO) he cofounded with Paul Williams, were nominated for the Nobel Peace Prize by six governments and the prosecutor of an international criminal tribunal for the work they have done to help in peace negotiations and the prosecution of major war criminals, such as Slobodan Milosevic, Charles Taylor, and Saddam Hussein.

During the elder Bush and Clinton Administrations, Scharf served in the Office of the Legal Adviser of the U.S. Department of State, where he held the positions of Attorney-Adviser for Law Enforcement and Intelligence, Attorney-Adviser for United Nations Affairs, and delegate to the United Nations Human Rights Commission. In 1993, he was awarded the State Department's Meritorious Honor Award "in recognition of superb performance and exemplary leadership" in relation to his role in the establishment of the International Criminal Tribunal for the former Yugoslavia.

A graduate of Duke University School of Law (Order of the Coif and High Honors), and judicial clerk to Judge Gerald Bard Tjoflat of the Eleventh Circuit Federal Court of Appeals, Scharf is the author of more than seventy scholarly articles and twelve other books, including *Balkan Justice*, which was nominated for the Pulitzer Prize in 1998, *The International Criminal Tribunal for Rwanda*, which was awarded the American Society of International Law's Certificate of Merit for the Outstanding book in International Law in 1999, *Peace with Justice* (with Paul Williams), which received the International Association of Penal Law Book of the Year Award for 2003, and *Enemy of the State* (with Michael Newton), which received the International Association of Penal Law Book of the Year Award for 2009.

Scharf has testified before the U.S. Senate Foreign Relations Committee and the House Armed Services Committee; his op-eds have been published by the *Washington Post, Los Angeles Times, Boston Globe, Christian Science Monitor*, and *International Herald Tribune*; and he has appeared on *ABC World News Tonight*, the *NBC Today Show, Nightline, The O'Reilly Factor, The NewsHour with Jim Lehrer*, the *Charlie Rose Show*, the BBC, CNN, and NPR. Recipient of the Case School of Law Alumni Association's 2005 "Distinguished Teacher Award" and *Ohio Magazine*'s 2007 "Excellence in Education Award," Scharf teaches international law, international criminal law, the law of international organizations, and a war crimes research lab. In 2002, Scharf established the War Crimes Research Office at Case Western Reserve University School of Law, which provides research assistance to the prosecutors of the International Criminal Tribunal for Rwanda, the Special Court for Sierra Leone, the International Criminal Court, the Cambodia Genocide Tribunal, and the Iraqi High Tribunal on issues pending before those international tribunals. During a sabbatical in the fall of 2008, Scharf served as Special Assistant to the Prosecutor of the Cambodia Genocide Tribunal in Phnom Penh.

## Paul R. Williams

Dr. Paul R. Williams holds the Rebecca Grazier Professorship in Law and International Relations at American University where he teaches in the School of International Service and the Washington College of Law. He is also the cofounder and Executive Director of PILPG. Since 1995, PILPG has provided pro bono legal assistance to states and governments involved in peace negotiations, drafting postconflict constitutions, and prosecuting war criminals.

Dr. Williams is regarded as a social entrepreneur for his practical and innovative approach to providing pro bono legal assistance to states and governments. During the course of his legal practice, Dr. Williams has assisted more than a dozen states and governments in major international peace negotiations, including serving as a delegation member in the Dayton negotiations (Bosnia-Herzegovina), Rambouillet/Paris negotiations (Kosovo), Lake Ohrid negotiations (Macedonia), and Podgorica/Belgrade negotiations (Serbia/Montenegro). He also advised parties to the Key West negotiations (Nagorno-Karabakh), the Oslo/Geneva negotiations (Sri Lanka), the Georgia/Abkhaz negotiations, and the Somalia peace talks.

He has advised fifteen governments across Europe, Africa, and Asia on matters of public international law. Dr. Williams has advised the Governments of Afghanistan, Bosnia, Iraq, Kosovo, Montenegro, and Nagorno-Karabakh on the drafting and implementation of postconflict constitutions. He is also experienced in advising governments on issues of state recognition, self-determination, and state succession, including advising the president of Macedonia and the foreign minister of Montenegro. On issues relating to border and sea demarcations and negotiations, Dr. Williams has advised the President of Estonia and the foreign minister of East Timor.

Dr. Williams has testified before the U.S. Congress and provided expert commentary in the British House of Commons on matters of public international law and peace negotiations.

Previously, Dr. Williams served in the Department of State's Office of the Legal Adviser for European and Canadian Affairs, as a Senior Associate with the Carnegie Endowment for International Peace, and as a Fulbright Research Scholar at the University of Cambridge. He is a

Member of the American Society of International Law and serves on the Board of Directors of several nonprofit organizations.

Dr. Williams is a leading scholar on peace negotiations and postconflict constitutions. He has authored four books on topics of international human rights, international environmental law, and international norms of justice, and more than two dozen articles on a wide variety of public international law topics. Dr. Williams is also a sought-after international law and policy analyst, and has been interviewed more than 250 times by major print and broadcast media and has published numerous op-eds.

# Other Books by the Authors

ENEMY OF THE STATE: THE TRIAL AND EXECUTION OF SADDAM HUSSEIN (Michael Scharf and Michael Newton) (St. Martin's Press 2009) (Winner of the International Association of Penal Law's 2009 Book of the Year Award).

CRIMINAL JURISDICTION: 100 YEARS AFTER THE 1907 HAGUE PEACE CONFERENCE (Michael Scharf and Willem van Genugten) (Asser Institute, Cambridge University Press 2009).

THE THEORY AND PRACTICE OF INTERNATIONAL CRIMINAL LAW (Michael Scharf and Leila Nadya Sadat) (Martinus Nijhoff Publishers 2008).

SADDAM ON TRIAL: UNDERSTANDING AND DEBATING THE IRAQI HIGH TRIBUNAL (Michael Scharf and Greg McNeal) (Carolina Academic Press 2006).

PEACE WITH JUSTICE? WAR CRIMES AND ACCOUNTABILITY IN THE FORMER YUGOSLAVIA (Paul Williams and Michael Scharf) (Rowman & Littlefield 2002) (Winner of the International Association of Penal Law's 2003 Book of the Year Award for Scholarly and Theoretical Contribution to the Field).

SLOBODAN MILOSEVIC ON TRIAL: A COMPANION (Michael Scharf and William Schabas) (Continuum Press 2002).

THE LAW OF INTERNATIONAL ORGANIZATIONS: PROBLEMS AND MATERIALS (Michael Scharf) (Carolina Academic Press 2001; 2nd ed. 2007).

INTERNATIONAL CRIMINAL LAW: CASES AND MATERIALS (Michael Scharf and Jordan Paust et al.) (Carolina Academic Press 1996; 2nd ed. 2000; 3rd ed. 2007).

INDICTMENT AT THE HAGUE: THE MILOSEVIC REGIME AND CRIMES OF THE BALKAN WARS (Paul Williams and Norman Cigar) (NYU Press 2002).

THE INTERNATIONAL CRIMINAL TRIBUNAL FOR RWANDA (Michael Scharf and Virginia Morris) (Transnational Publishers 1998) (2 vols.) (Winner of the 1999 American Society of International Law Certificate of Merit for the Outstanding Book in International Law).

MAKING JUSTICE WORK (Paul Williams, Michael Scharf, and Diane Orentlicher) (Century Foundation Press 1998).

BALKAN JUSTICE: THE STORY BEHIND THE FIRST INTERNATIONAL WAR CRIMES TRIAL SINCE NUREMBERG (Michael Scharf) (Carolina Academic Press 1997) (Nominated for a Pulitzer Prize in Letters).

INTERNATIONAL LAW AND THE RESOLUTION OF CENTRAL AND EAST EUROPEAN TRANS-BOUNDARY ENVIRONMENTAL DISPUTES (Paul Williams) (Palgrave Macmillan 2000).

AN INSIDER'S GUIDE TO THE INTERNATIONAL CRIMINAL TRIBUNAL FOR THE FORMER YUGOSLAVIA (Michael Scharf and Virginia Morris) (Transnational Publishers 1995) (2 vols.).

TREATMENT OF DETAINEES: ISSUES OF DETENTION AS EXAMINED BY THE UNITED NATIONS HUMAN RIGHTS COMMITTEE (Paul Williams) (Henry Dunant Institute 1990).

# Index